EXPLORATIONS INTO
HIGHLAND NEW GUINEA,
1930–1935

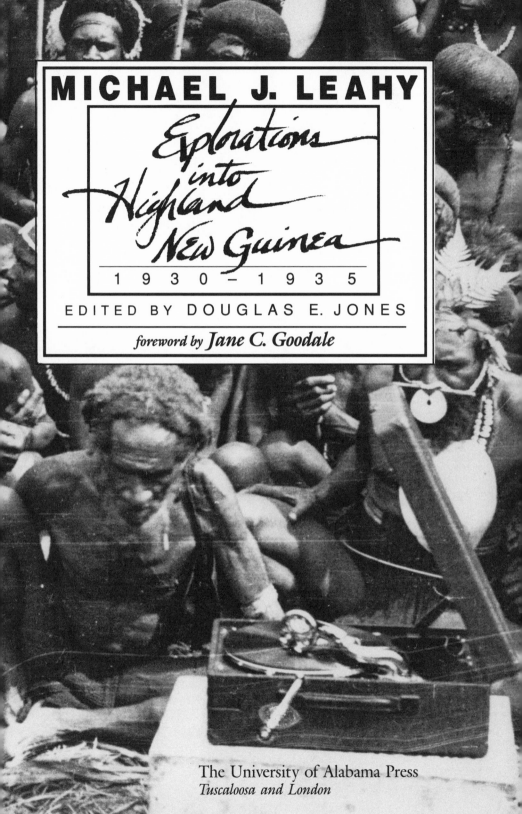

MICHAEL J. LEAHY

Explorations into Highland New Guinea

1930–1935

EDITED BY DOUGLAS E. JONES

foreword by **Jane C. Goodale**

The University of Alabama Press
Tuscaloosa and London

Copyright © 1991 by
The University of Alabama Press
Tuscaloosa, Alabama 35487–0380
All rights reserved
Manufactured in the United States of America

designed by zig zeigler

∞

The paper on which this book is printed meets the minimum
requirements of American National Standard for Information
Science-Permanence of Paper for Printed Library Materials,
ANSI Z39.48-1984.

Library of Congress Cataloging-in-Publication Data

Leahy, Michael J., 1901–1979.
    Explorations into highland New Guinea, 1930–1935 / Michael J.
Leahy ; edited by Douglas E. Jones and with a foreword by Jane C.
Goodale.
        p.   cm.
    Includes index.
    ISBN 0-8173-0446-0
    1. Ethnology—Papua New Guinea.   2. First contact of aboriginal
peoples with Westerners—Papua New Guinea.   3. Leahy, Michael J.,
1901–1979.   4. Papua New Guinea—Description and travel.   5. Papua
New Guinea—Social life and customs.   I.   Jones, Douglas E.
II.   Title.
GN671.N5L43   1991
305.8'009953—dc20   91-9027

British Library Cataloguing-in-Publication Data available

*Photographs in this volume are reproduced
with permission of the Michael J. Leahy Collection
of the National Library of Australia
and of Mrs. Jeanette Leahy.*

CONTENTS

Foreword by Jane C. Goodale / vii

Editor's Preface / xi

Introduction / 1

The Year 1930 / 6

The Year 1931 / 23

The Year 1932 / 49

The Year 1933 / 79

The Year 1934 / 143

The Year 1935 / 236

Conclusions / 243

Editor's Afterword / 245

Index / 251

FOREWORD

Leahy's account of his probes into the interior of Papua New Guinea in the 1930s is an extraordinary document because of the exceptional quality of the man. In some ways he set the pattern for others who, after him, would venture into the unknown for a variety of personal reasons. All would be young and independent, courageous and ambitious, self-confident, and above all intelligent. These character traits, held in high value by the Western world, also manifested themselves, as the reader will see, in individual highlanders whom Leahy came to know and respect and who joined his expeditions into the unknown. Additional qualities that Leahy possessed—the ability both to see and to describe, verbally and with the camera, his own personal experiences—give the reader a vivid sense of the man, the land, and the people.

The character of a first contact has rarely been described in such detail. After all, such an encounter lasts only for a fleeting moment. The explorers, anthropologists, and missionaries who have written of such events often focus on their own emotions when meeting the "other" for first time. Rarely do they possess Leahy's sensitivity to the perceptions of the primitive peoples contacted.

Leahy was remarkably objective in his descriptions of the appearance and demeanor of the natives whom he met in his travels through the heretofore unknown highland region of Papua New Guinea. But he also reflected his own cultural milieu and time. His openness of mind was sometimes tempered by his Western cultural beliefs concerning the origins of culture and society and the evolutionary development of the races of mankind.

The local people regarded Leahy as a "spirit ancestor" coming back, perhaps to haunt them. For his part he saw them as "primitives" who were in some external respects distinct from his own people. So defined, they fell into a category which according to his worldview was associated with emotions, values, and a mentality in contrast to those of Western cultures. He regarded the natives, for example, as exhibiting a limited range of reactions, as exhibiting (even after contact) a very thin veneer of civilization, and as having not yet developed the brain to cope with conditions that Westerners find commonplace.

The concept of the "noble savage" of the Western age of "Enlightenment" seldom appears in Western writings today. Rather the so called primitive is seen to be somewhat retarded in his technological mastering of the physical environment. The industrial revolution and the concomitant development of the "work ethic" fundamentally altered Western society, leading it to consider itself superior to those who were not technologically "advanced." Unfortunately, many Westerners still often believe that technological development is the response of superior minds to challenging physical environments. As Leahy wrote (in 1962), the Papua New Guineans' "environment limited their thinking to a technology and culture foreign to ours. . . . Their people will have to . . . work or starve." "We, [the exploring party] survived," he wrote, "by virtue of the magic with which they [the primitives] had endowed us, our superior mentality, and our firearms in that order." For Leahy, the highland Papua New Guinean was "a congenital thief, murderer, cannibal . . . , bent on the obliteration of anyone and anything his . . . armament and animal cunning" could conquer.

From the native's standpoint, Leahy and his party enjoyed "magic" power, but Leahy was keen enough to recognize that these primitives would (and they soon did) learn the limits of that power and would discover the strangers to be fundamentally human, like themselves. The reader will find that at times Leahy speaks as a member of a Western "civilized" culture and at other times as one who grew to know and respect the intelligence of these particular "others," the people with whom he came into contact. Some of them became trusted boss boys (foremen) in his line of carriers and were fellow explorers of heretofore unknown regions of highland Papua New Guinea.

Therefore, to focus on ways in which Leahy contrasted himself and his culture with the local people and their culture is to lay undue emphasis on what was and still is a very commonly held erroneous Western view of non-Western others. Anthropologists have recently come to appreciate the extent to which their descriptions and evaluations of others are filtered through their own culture. What results from anthropological description and analysis of another person's culture, then, is never completely objective. It may best be described as "one culture's interpretation of another."

What is remarkable in this work is not that Leahy shows cultural bias in his interpretation but that he rarely does so. In fact, as the reader will see, Leahy made it his policy to select "natives of superior intelligence" to travel with him. He thereby gave them the opportunity to journey beyond their known world so that they might inform their fellow tribesmen of the world from which the strangers in their midst had come. He frequently praises specific individuals for their intelligence and ability to learn new ways.

Far from considering the local population of the country through which he was traveling an obstacle to progress or an enemy to be overcome by force, Leahy reserved his strongest words of reproach and anger for "armchair administrators" and other "so-called experts." He held them indirectly responsible (through their ignorance of reality and for not always honorable political motives) for the few "murders" of European invaders by local people during the time period of which he writes.

Western readers may wince at the frequent use of the word "boy" to refer to a Papua New Guinean of any age, but Papua New Guinean readers will readily recognize it as a Pidgin English word, "boi." Pidgin English is one of two national languages of Papua New Guinea today. It had its origins in the early contact of Westerners along the coastal regions of Papua New Guinea and became the lingua franca among the laborers in the plantations and other multicultural settings established by Europeans in the nineteenth century. Leahy's original manuscript anglicized the spelling of phrases spoken in "tok pisin" [Pidgin English]. These phrases have been rendered in this book in the now standardized written "tok pisin" so that they would more intelligible to the modern audience. For those unfamiliar with this language, text translations have been provided.

I hope that all readers of this book will appreciate Leahy's descriptive skill. This is an important story, a meeting of histories, to be taken not as a "true history" but as an interpretation of history by a remarkable Westerner whose "nem" [name] will long be remembered. I hope that this account will stimulate some of the Papua New Guinean others who remember the first contact with these "spirits from another world" to write their own history of the encounter. For those readers who are fortunate to have access to it, there is a film, *First Contact*, in which both Leahy and those he contacted compare notes. Perhaps there will also be an account written from the viewpoint of Papua New Guineans. In the meantime, they as well as Westerners will appreciate the extraordinary detail and candor present in this written and pictorial record of a moment in time. Readers of both cultures will find here a small piece of their shared history, at once rich and vivid, written by one who had no small part in the making of that history.

Jane C. Goodale
Bryn Mawr

EDITOR'S PREFACE

This book is an edited version of a manuscript prepared by the Australian expatriate Michael J. Leahy in the early 1960s from daily fieldnotes he kept during five years of gold prospecting and exploring in New Guinea between 1930 and 1935. In conjunction with the editor's father, whom he met in Australia during World War II and with whom he shared a fascination with New Guinea, Leahy hoped to have this particular story told during their respective lifetimes. Neither lived to see the work completed; consequently, the editor's personal commitment has been to complete this book as a memorial to these two men.

The original manuscript was given standard copyediting to regularize spellings of places and tribal names, rearrange some material for ease of reading, clarify words and minimize repetition of incidents. Throughout this editing process, careful attention was given to preserving the author's tone and viewpoint on the Stone Age culture with which he came into contact.

The explorations recounted here probably represent the last of their kind in this century. The discovery of gold in New Guinea in 1926 lured Mick Leahy (and a short time later his brothers Pat, Jim, and Dan) into an adventure that resulted in important geologic, geographic, and ethnographic observations of Stone Age people in a region unknown to the rest of the world at that time.

Mick Leahy's travels provided the world with the first glimpse of a region of cloud-covered mountains and valleys occupied by tens of thousands of people whose very existence had been unknown before 1930, in spite of nearly 300 years of colonial interests by half a dozen nations. Leahy's chronicles report on terrain, geology, flora and fauna, and, most imoprtant, the customs and circumstances of these primitive people. Over five thousand 35-mm still photographs and several hours of 16-mm movie film were taken by Mick Leahy and frequently developed in the field under the most adverse conditions (he had taken correspondence courses in photography and journalism). His explorations had a lasting impact on the development of New Guinea and earned him recognition by the Royal Geographic Society in 1936 and the U.S. Explorers' Club in 1971.

Between 1930 and 1935, Leahy and his companions made ten prospecting and exploring trips throughout much of what is known today as the Central Highlands of New Guinea. Their grueling travel through some of the most rugged terrain in the world and dangerous encounters with the natives did not lead Mick Leahy and his partners to realize fortunes. At only one prospect, Kuta in the Western Highlands, did they find significant amounts of gold. Their financial gain from the New Guinea gold rush was derived primarily from prospecting for mining companies and providing construction and labor services for the industry.

On the first expedition in April of 1930, Leahy and his partner, Michael Dwyer, were grubstaked to prospect for gold on the headwaters of the Ramu River. Along one of these tributary streams, the Dunantina, they were the first white men to look on the Goroka Valley, which sparkled at night with the cooking fires of thousands of people. They discovered the Wahgi River, where bloated corpses gave further evidence of a dense population farther up in the Highlands. They also made the first crossing of the Bismarck Range, the central mountain chain of New Guinea. The band, including fourteen native carriers, ended up at Port Romilly on the Gulf of Papua, having discovered, among other things, the headwaters of the Purari River. They traveled by steamer to Port Moresby and hiked 150 miles in thirteen days across the upper end of the Owen Stanley mountain range to Morobe on the Huon Gulf, arriving at their base in Salamaua in September. This first journey lasted six months and covered more than 800 miles, most of it traveled on foot.

Some of the routes covered previously traveled terrain, including places visited by German traders in prior years, but most trails brought Mick and his party into areas never before seen by white men. Beginning in the fall of 1932, the last five of the journeys were in the Mt. Hagen region, the most distant from the permanent Leahy base at Salamaua. From this point Leahy hoped to prospect and explore the Sepik River, which flows into the Bismarck Sea 150 miles to the north, but this goal was not realized.

The Mt. Hagen area held a special attraction for Mick Leahy for the rest of his days. His hope ultimately to acquire fertile agricultural lands there never materialized. He lived to see Papua New Guinea's independence from Australia, an event which he saw as ending white domination and causing ultimate disaster for the Highland peoples themselves.

D.E.J.

EXPLORATIONS INTO HIGHLAND NEW GUINEA, 1930–1935

INTRO-
DUCTION

Toowoomba in Queensland, Australia, where I was born in the year 1901, is today a city of more than 50,000 people. Perched on the crest of the Great Dividing Range, it is 2,000 feet above sea level, and some eighty miles from Brisbane, and the state capital.

The blue haze of distance over the scrub-covered ranges toward the coast always fascinated me. With barefooted friends and a few dogs, we hunted wallabies and hares and trapped the small, beautifully marked finches which abounded in the ranges. I walked the up-and-down terrain, through thick scrub and grassy open forest ranges and camped under the stars or in a crudely built bush shelter when rain came. The experience fueled my enthusiasm and my urge to see what was on the other side of the haze-shrouded ranges.

The years of my youth that I spent hunting, trapping, and traveling were an admirable introduction and training for the life of a gold prospector and explorer in the then unknown inland of Papua

New Guinea, whose mountains made their counterparts in Australia's Great Dividing Range seem no more than molehills. Its rivers, which rush to the sea, tearing down the country and carrying it away in their cascading waters, stand in vivid and striking contrast to Australia's aged streams, which flow serenely along their meandering beds and peacefully inundate the adjacent countryside after flood rains.

My walks led me from thick scrub country into the open forests of scattered gum trees and blazing sunshine. Sometimes I stalked ducks on the billabongs, the stagnant pools in the truncated bends of old riverbeds. Sometimes I fished the quiet reaches in the deep, isolated chain of waterholes in the dry seasons of the year. I never forgot such pleasures.

After leaving school, I worked first as a clerk with the Queensland Railways. This job restricted my hunting but did give me a free pass on the railway system, which enabled me to travel to see the towns and hamlets that pioneer settlers were making from the virgin bush or black soil plains. I transferred to Cairns in the far north of the state, in those days accessible only by boat from Townsville, the northern terminus of the railway. After a few months I resigned from the railways and exchanged pen and paper for a three-and-a-half pound Kelly axe, a broadaxe, and a seven-inch adze (New Guinea natives call it "brother belong tomahawk"). Over the next few years, in between tramping and hunting the eastern slopes of the coast range from Cairns to Ingham, I cut timber, broadaxed bridge girders out of the blue gums, bloodwoods, and stringy bark hardwoods, split fenceposts, and adzed the rail beds out of hundreds of sleepers (crossties) for the railroad being constructed to link Cairns with Townsville and Brisbane.

In 1926, when I was cutting wood blocks and hauling them in a Model T Ford truck to a railside sawmill to be cut into sleepers, news of the fabulous gold strike at Edie Creek in New Guinea reached me. I left my truck by the side of the road in Townsville, teamed up with a group of men who, like myself, knew nothing about gold mining or about the country into which we were so impulsively heading, and caught the first steamer to New Guinea. One of our party had brought along his wife, who did not at first seem the outdoor type, but who roughed it, coped with roadside camps, and tramped the ranges better than some of the men. We optimistically took with us four mules to pack in stores. Arriving in Rabaul, the port of entry for the Australian Mandated Territory of New Guinea, as it was then called, we encountered our first obstacle. Administering authorities would refuse us a permit to land at Salamaua, the goldfields port, unless we could produce the fare back to Australia plus enough to prevent us from becoming a charge on the country and having to be shipped out at Administration expense. None of us could produce the necessary sum of money, but by pooling our meager resources we managed to build up quite a presentable roll of notes which we passed from one person to another as we were interrogated by a very sympathetic official. We were all granted landing permits.

We landed at Salamaua in August 1926. A few days later we shouldered our packs, headed out along the beach to the mouth of the Buang River, and turned inland to cross the coastal range into the goldfields. The mules with light packs negotiated the 6,000- to 7,000-foot climb over the mountains, but steep rock faces on the inland side forced us to abandon the mules on the grassy slopes of the range. They lived well, looked after by then still primitive natives, and became showpieces for the surrounding district. Months later they were brought into Wau and carried many tons of cargo up the mountainside from Wau to Edie Creek, 3,000 feet above.

On the inland side of the coast range, we met a miner trekking out with his line of native carriers to bring in stores from the coast. He pointed out the dome-shaped mountain, called Kaindi, where miners with teams of boys were winning up to 200 ounces of gold a day in some of the fabulously rich tributaries running into Edie Creek. He also informed us that there was to be a ballot for a number of 100-by-200-foot claims on the Merrie Creek, a rich tributary of the Edie, on the following Sunday morning. We had a day and a half to get there. My mate, Jack Logan, and I were elected to take the names of all of the party and reach Edie Creek in time for the ballot.

We traveled light, walked until it was too dark to see the track, and spent a miserable night in drizzling rain, waiting for the dawn and enough light to travel again. In the semidarkness of early morning we heard sounds of a party approaching, and having visions of cannibals on a foraging raid, we hid in the grass at the side of the track until they passed. The marauders we had feared proved to be merely a line of carriers in the charge of native police. After a tremendous effort we reached Edie Creek utterly exhausted but in time for the ballot, only to find that we could not have the rest of our party included in the ballot. Logan and I both drew claims but, lacking food, were unable to work them. I spent a week in a leaf-thatched lean-to, recovering from malaria, which I had caught on the coast.

In those days every ounce of food and equipment was packed in from Salamaua on the backs of natives. The trip was a grueling eight- to ten-day walk over precipitous ranges. Having no boys and only what food we could carry in, I returned to the coast as soon as I was fit enough to make the trip. I needed to recruit native labor and pack in stores to work the claim won on the headwaters of the Merrie. Halfway back to the coast, in a mountain village of the Buang people, I met Helmuth Baum, who handed me the keys to his storehouse at Salamaua and afterward supplied labor for another trek back to the goldfields. After a four-day journey in from the coast, the new carriers dumped their packs and deserted. Baum once again came to the rescue and supplied more boys. Eventually I won my first alluvial gold from a claim on Edie Creek. Four months later an appendix operation obliged me to return to Australia. In July 1927 I again landed in Salamaua and became a bartender in a tin shed known as the Salamaua Hotel. The nail ends from the corrugated iron roofing were all crowned with champagne corks, and miners in their cups won more gold than they ever did in actual fact on Edie Creek.

My next job took me to the Waria River to peg (stake) alluvial gold and platinum leases on old German finds. I then went overland to Edie Creek and overland from Lae to Madang and back with a line of laborers for roadbuilding from Wau to Edie Creek. By 1930 Edie Creek miners had begun to think about fresh territory and bigger and better goldfields. I was asked to outfit and lead the expedition to try to find them. The logical place to look was the huge area marked "unexplored" across the face of the New Guinea maps of the early 1930s (see map).

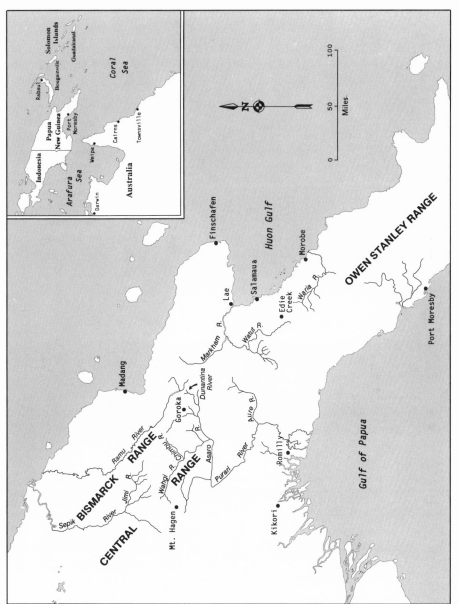

Eastern New Guinea prior to the Leahy Explorations.

1930 Photo taken on headwaters of Purari River near Ramu-Karmarmentina Divide. *L-R*, Back row: Tarec, Aitaipe, Gerepo, Suva, Mick Dwyer, M. J. Leahy. Middle row: Jotam, Guna, Gesupo, Ewunga, Sakai, Tautu. Front row: Tarpi, Gevarbi, Menekai, Yumunga, Pulici.

THE YEAR 1930

Until the early 1930s, the interior of New Guinea was considered to be a jumbled mass of unpopulated, timber-covered mountain ranges. Some of the mountains on the Bismarck Range were visible from the north coast around Madang. Their peaks were estimated to stand just over 15,000 feet above sea level. Snow was occasionally visible on the top of Mt. Wilhelm.

In 1930 I had been living in New Guinea for four years, having arrived with the 1926 gold rush to Edie Creek, which was an eight-day walk inland from the port of Salamaua. Although good gold was being won in that area, I thought it unlikely that Edie Creek was the only goldfield in this unexplored country. When the miners on Edie Creek asked me to go ahead and find "another Edie Creek," I asked a friend, Mick Dwyer, to accompany me. Natives were selected from our gold mining operations—some Warias, the best fighters in New Guinea; Markhams for crossing or rafting down fast-flowing rivers; and some coastal natives who knew all about canoes. All of them were good strong young men, good walkers and carriers.

A prospector named Ned Rowland had reported finding gold in the headwaters of the Ramu River, which heads on the south fall of the Bismarcks, runs southeast, and then turns and drops into the Markham-Ramu-Sepik rift and reaches the sea north of Madang. I figured on crossing the Bismarcks and dropping down into the headwater tributaries of the Ramu, where I hoped to find another Edie Creek at the source of Rowland's gold. Each of the boys packed thirty pounds of gear. We walked from Lae on the coast up the heat-scorched Markham Valley to Kaigulen village on the Ramu, a distance of 120 miles.

We left Kaigulen village on May 24, 1930, and, after crossing the fast-running, armpit-deep Ramu River, climbed about 3,000 feet up grass ridges to the small village of Lehuna, where we camped to check our supplies and gear. Leaving some of our stores there, we started off on May 26 to cross the Bismarck Range. We experienced great difficulty in finding a guide who would show us the track. All of the natives appeared terrified of the mountain and the people beyond. They pantomimed sudden death for us all from arrows and clubs!

We tried to follow the overgrown track, but communication over the range had evidently ceased many months before, and we concluded that there might be trouble for anyone approaching from our direction. We wandered about for an hour or so without making much headway, until an old native dashed forward and indicated that he would show us the track. He was probably a member of some of the many earlier parties heading over the range on a feuding raid. He took us to the top of the range. There, from a small clearing, we gazed into a vast area of steep, timber-topped, grass-covered ranges and high mountain peaks. Fenced gardens in straight rows and smoke curling up from barricaded villages gave promise of food and direction and—and, almost inevitably, trouble!

We made camp late in the bed of the small stream down which we had paddled, starting from the source on the mountainside. We spent a rather restless night concealed by a thick fog. In the morning our campfires attracted attention, and a heavily armed party came to investigate. We made contact without incident. Once the natives had identified us as the strange people of whom they had presumably heard on excursions over the ranges, they became quite friendly. When there was a lull in their almost constant tribal fighting, they brought along plenty of native foods—sweet potatoes, sugarcane, bananas, and even pigs—establishing the importance of the meeting and giving promise of food and direction farther on.

We pushed on downstream from our creek camp, passing near the villages of Tinofy, Hofrona, and Karuna, and camped near a large village called Badanofera, where a tall, fine-looking old native was evidently in charge. In response to signs from our tired and hungry boys, he spoke with authority, and food arrived in great abundance. We found that the first contact with whites was always quite a shock to the natives. They gave no thought to food until they saw us picking up pieces of sugarcane and sweet potato skins, when they seem to have realized that, although we were spirits of some of their dead relatives, we were also very hungry spirits!

The men were naked except for a narrow fringe of bark string or butterfly-shaped wooden shields that protected their pubic parts and which were suspended from a very greasy, and probably (to judge from the scratching) louse-inhabited string belt. A few leaves were tucked under the belt at the back and often nothing at all. A heavy string bag suspended from the neck was all that covered their rear. This heavy string bag was thrown over one arm when its owner was fighting, so that it served as a foil to deaden the speed of an enemy arrow. There was no chewing of betel nuts and rarely any smoking. We concluded that there was no contact between these people and the slightly more sophisticated natives over the mountains.

The men had their noses pierced in up to five places to hold pieces of pig tusk, bone, and quartz. The weight suspended from the septum caused a continual snuffling. They wore head ornaments consisting of strings of tambu shell, a small seashell, cowrie shells, and green iridescent beetles, arranged in wide bands. Skins of opossums' tails and bits of fur, cane, or bamboo were suspended from their ears. All wore bark string wrist gauntlets to protect their skin from the cutting backlash of the bow strings. All carried bows and bundles of spare arrows in bamboo quivers on their backs, and they fed arrows to their bows with incredible speed. Their stone axes were mostly poor things and nothing like the greenstone working axes we later found farther west.

The women, like the men, were short and squat, but all were very active and agile; their lives depended on their agility in their continual intertribal wars. They wore a wide bark-string covering in the front and rear that was suspended from a string belt. The girls wore the shell ornaments until marriage. All carried sharp garden sticks and the usual string bags suspended from the head. These bags held native foods, babies, pigs, and often the skull and bone or two of a dead relative. Both men and women had fingers cut off, and some had all of one hand missing. We found such amputations to be a mourning custom, and we learned that the funnybone at the elbow was deadened by a blow before the finger was chopped off.

The natives' gardens were very well laid out in long straight rows, whereas a straight line is practically unknown in lower parts of New Guinea. The gardens were fenced with swamp canes, which were tied together with a vine resembling kudzu. The villages were barricaded with thick walls of swamp canes, with bays to protect the walls from their blunt stone axes.

For days we followed the stream down which we had paddled, which the local natives called the Dunantina, never going less than 5,000 feet above sea level. It ran through steep grass-covered ranges and past a prominent rock outcrop on the end of a low range which the natives called Sunubia. The country gradually opened out into wide grass-covered valleys populated by thousands of Stone Age natives living in barricaded villages with compact garden areas nearby. We passed on from group to group. Our appearance often caused such consternation that we were able to bring warring tribes together and so to find guides and food for the next day.

To the west we could see the large, flat, grass-covered valley known today as the Goroka Valley. Although we were tempted, we kept to the main river. We expected it to turn south and east and take us to Rowland's gold find. We had stocked supplies for a limited trip only. After more than two weeks of travel downstream, we found that the river had grown to a large, wildly rushing torrent thundering through an almost endless gorge. We realized then that it was not the Ramu and that we had discovered a totally new country. This land was populated by tens of thousands of Stone Age natives, whose village fires at night extended in the distance as far as the eye could see across the grass valleys and ranges. Thus far we had escaped unpleasant incidents with the natives because of their initial astonishment at seeing whites for the first time. The natives endowed us with supernatural powers and associations. We had no illusions about the probable nature of their reactions once they recovered from the first shock and understood the value of the shell and other treasures we carried. Furthermore, as far as they could see, we were defenseless; guns and rifles meant nothing whatever to them.

To retrace our steps was out of the question. Our weapons consisted of two .12-gauge shotguns, two .22-caliber rifles, two .45-caliber revolvers, and two .32-caliber rifles, with a relatively small amount of ammunition for any of them. Should any trouble start, we would face almost certain death, and the natives would regard our murder as just incidental to the looting of our gear. We decided to continue down the river, prospecting the streams coming in on the eastern side. The river was now too fast and wide for us to cross and test streams entering from the west. We consoled ourselves with the thought that water must run downhill and that it must sometime, somewhere, run into the sea. We managed to arrange for guides from one village to the next. The people were rather skeptical of us and anxious to see us leave their particular village. Still, we were always able to find an adventurous soul who would take us to within shouting distance of the next village. After exchanging what appeared to be the local greeting or peace words, we were handed over, and the guide quietly disappeared into the bush.

From a village named Knoo we looked down into a large river coming in from the west, which the natives called the Marki but which we now know was a distortion of the word "Wahgi." This river affords the main drainage from as far west as Mt. Hagen and runs through the most thickly populated part of the New Guinea Highlands. The grass ranges gave way to heavily timbered ranges from the junction of the Marki. The population thinned considerably, and the river racing through its narrow gorge became at times impossible to follow. We always left the river with some misgivings, as we depended on it to take us ultimately to the sea somewhere on the south coast of New Guinea. Our detours around the precipitous gorges always brought us back within sight of the river again. From some of our camps and in small clearings that overlooked the gorge, we imagined we could see the sea, a blue sky in the distance beneath the clouds that always surround New Guinea's mountains. Our belief led us on, and we continued downriver toward the blue sky. My boss boy, a Waria named Ewunga, was less sure than we about our chances of getting out. When I asked him his opinion, he made the gloomy prediction in Pidgin English, "Bye-m-bye, bone belong you-me stink along bush!"

Below the Marki junction our track sometimes ran right alongside the comparatively slow-running reaches of the main river, now called the Tua. At such times we saw the bloated bodies of natives floating aimlessly by in the current. In some bends of the river, where it had thrown up an acre or so of sand together with the river's flotsam and jetsam, giant iguanas could be seen picking the bones of numerous bodies thrown up on the beaches. From the innumerable skulls and bones littering the sands, we concluded that there must be an even larger valley or valleys drained by the Marki we saw coming in from the west and that the native population must be huge. We were now reaching the leech country. Our shoes, which were almost worn out, gave us a bad time and slowed the party down. Bluey, the dog, picked up a leech on the tip of his nose and amused us in his efforts to blow or rub it off.

We managed to persuade two or three men from each camping place to show us the track leading in the general direction in which the Tua was running. Each evening we camped near a small group of natives living in bush clearings. From them we were able to buy sweet potatoes, sugarcane, and sometimes a small pig. Sacsac, native sage, began to appear as we descended to about 2,000 feet above sea level. We shot down large blue pigeons and numerous smaller pigeons with a .22-caliber rifle, to the astonishment of any local natives who happened to be with us. Those birds augmented our scanty food supply.

Our guides eventually escorted us to a large, fast-running river which could not be forded. Thereafter we were on our own. This was the Pio, coming in from the east and running fast and deep; a few hundred yards below, it cascaded over rocky outcrops through a gorge. Our Markhams could cross by swimming across the current and getting swept downstream a couple of hundred yards, but the only way to get the boys and cargo across was to make a canoe. It took us a few days to hack out a dugout canoe. We used plane blades, which we carried as trade, and tomahawks. We erected an outrigger on the canoe and used a piece of bark in a cleft stick as a paddle. In this way all our gear and boys were ferried across. As a precaution a long length of lawyer cane was fastened to both ends of the canoe so that it could not be carried down the rapids. We pulled our boat well up above the water level and hid it under bushes, just in case we had to retrace our steps upriver—a dreadful thought to us at this stage!

We picked up a pad (path) through the thick undergrowth and towering trees. After following the bent-over branches of small shrubs, which exposed the contrasting underside of the leaves, we eventually walked onto a well-worn pad. In a small clearing we found a large double-story native house about thirty feet wide and ninety feet long, built onto tall straight trees from which the tops had been lopped about forty feet off the ground. The approach to the top floor was a long ladder of springy saplings with crosspieces notched and attached by lawyer cane at intervals of about every foot. It was an ideal defense position against attack! The top story was divided into stalls, and a passage four to five feet wide ran through the whole length of the house to a sheer drop at the other end. The ashes were still warm in the fireplaces. We posted a boy at the top of the steps to give the alarm when the owners returned. We were very anxious to contact them and resume our travels from village to village. In the house we also found a piece of bottle glass and a coconut shell which must have been traded in from the coast; but how far away that coast might be we could only guess.

Here there was somewhat more security than we had had for a long time, and the chance to rest came as a relief. Dwyer and I selected the stall nearest the door. We took off our heavy revolvers and put our rifles down to enjoy a cup of tea. Suddenly Dwyer, who was facing the door, stopped talking and began to stare in the direction of the door. There was a very surprised expression on his face. Looking around, I was horrified to see one, two, three, four young warriors, complete with bows and arrows and decorations, bound off the springy ladder into the room. Pandemonium broke loose! Our boys tried to grab for the natives, but they were well greased and were much more surprised and terrified than we were. Three of them broke loose, rushed the full length of the house, jumped onto a tree trunk, and slid down to the ground to disappear into the bush. Grabbing my revolver, I took a hasty look out the door. Finding no more warriors charging up the ladder, I tried to quiet the captive, whom the boys were holding down. "Aboo" was the last peace word we had heard, so we abooed the fellow but to no avail. He was terrified. We gave him a few beads, a piece of red laplap (cloth), a handful of food, and his bows and arrows, which he had lost in the struggle. Then we escorted him to the top of the ladder. We were sorry to see him go in such haste, but were afraid that, if we tried to hold him, his friends might stage a rescue. In retrospect I think that the four must have been very hungry hunters. Seeing the smoke coming from the house they had bounded out of the bush and up the ladder, expecting to find their supper ready and their people at home.

We moved on to the river next morning and followed it down through loose stone gorges. We had to shoot one of our dogs after it was almost cut in half when a loosened rock rolled down in a landslide. The country began to flatten out. The river was now running wide and deep and almost slow enough for us to risk rafting. As soon as we found enough sago palms to supply a week's food, we decided we would build a raft and go wherever the river took us. We felt like our boots, clothes, and boys—worn out; badly in need of a rest from the blood-sucking leeches, lawyer vines, and stinging trees; and weary from restless nights in improvised shelters that let rain in through all the cracks. We had reached the canoe country. The natives, traveling mostly in dugout canoes, had a system of tracks not parallel with the river but only at right angles to it. Consequently we had to cut a track through the thick tropical jungle alongside the river.

A steady roar during the night from downriver direction changed our raft-building plans, and we decided to cut our way downstream for another day or so to find the cause. After only a few hours' walk we saw that the river narrowed to less than half its usual width between sheer walls of limestone, where it dropped some 50 or 100 feet in towering waves of white water through an S-shaped gorge. We could find no sign of any track through this gorge and retraced our steps upriver. We camped above the gorge alongside a wide, slow-running reach of the river, cutting down a sago palm for food. The next day natives abooed us from the opposite side of the river. We abooed back and made signs for them to come over and show us the way out of the gorge downriver. It took quite some abooing and sign language to persuade two to cross in a dugout canoe. They stayed just offshore and I feel sure studied our camp, in particular the stock of sago we had just pulped out of one of their cultivated palms. We were not yet in the low country, where great acreages of swamp sago palms grow wild. They indicated that they would come over the next morning and show us the track over a range bypassing the gorge, thus sending us out of their area and saving their sago supply.

The next morning two natives, after an exchange of aboo-aboos, paddled over and led us upriver about a mile, then over a range track which in places climbed trees and steps cut in steep sides of creek beds. Eventually we reached a small clearing in the bush. There our guides pointed out the river far below us, running flat and slow through level tropical jungle as far as we could see. Here we could raft. Our guide then indicated, by doubling up a wide leaf, that they wanted a drink of water. We were puzzled, because they were standing in a clear stream running off the range. Nevertheless they quietly disappeared into the bush, and we made our way, following a bent-twig track, down to the river where we camped. The next day, laboriously cutting our way along the river, we were discovered by a canoe filled with natives. In sign language they made it clear that we would encounter only impassable sago swamps, with their needle-sharp thorn-studded fronds, hordes of mosquitoes, and crocodiles. A canoe was pushed over to us and we were directed downstream—the sooner the better!

Dwyer had developed a tropical ulcer on his leg which was gradually getting bigger and more painful. Some of the other boys had bad sores too. We decided to camp and put an outrigger on the dugout; amateurs cannot balance a dugout canoe without many spills and much practice. The next morning Dwyer and a few boys with all the cargo except our weapons floated downstream while the rest of the boys and I cut a track through the scrub alongside. Before long there was an uproar ahead of us and we heard what sounded like a stampede through the scrub near us. We pushed on. Dwyer from the river warned us of a village just ahead of us. It was so deserted when we arrived that we suspected the inhabitants of having left in a hurry. Seeing Dwyer canoeing downstream and hearing my party noisily cutting through the scrub, they might well have decided we were trying to surround them. They never waited to find out!

It was now evident that we needed river transport to reach the coast. We commandeered two more dugout canoes at the village, tied two together, and had an outrigger fitted on the other before daylight. We left the last of our trade axes, knives, plane blades, and laplap in a prominent place in the village in payment for the canoes. Then we set sail downstream as fast as the current and our paddlers could take us, keeping well out in the middle of the wide river in case a few arrows were shot at us.

It was wonderful to rest, drift down with the current, and observe the animal and bird life in the trees on both sides of the river. On bends where the river current increased, we had visions of more gorges, but apart from the vicious-looking whirlpools which could consume a swimmer, we found no more drops in the river. From the pigeons, flying fox (fruit bat) camps, and crocodiles which slid into the river off almost every sandbank, we concluded that we were on a coastal flat somewhere around sea level. For three days we drifted downriver, camping on shore each night, and were devoured by mosquitoes and the millions of wogs (flies) bred in coastal tropical swamps. We found sago palm lean-tos that the river natives had built as temporary shelters when working the sago palm, and here and there were pieces of glass and empty meat tins, which suggested to us that we were not too far from the coast.

The river appeared to become shallow, and trees growing out of the water puzzled us until we realized that we had reached a delta formation. We hoped we had drifted down the right channel. One morning we found the tied-up canoes almost swamped and straining on the cane tie ropes. We then knew that we were in tidal waters. The boys put new vigor into their rowing. We eventually came upon some natives whose Motuan language was a sign that we were in Papua and that we had crossed New Guinea from north to south. We did not know we were on the Purari, the second largest river in Papua, until we were taken into Charlie McKinnon's sawmill at Port Romilly. From our story he concluded that we had paddled down the Purari right from its source in the Bismarck Range. At Port Romilly we boarded the *Papuan Chief*, a round-bottomed coastal steamer, for Port Moresby. By the time we arrived we felt ready to walk our boys back across New Guinea from Port Moresby over the Kokoda Trail of World War II fame and back to Salamaua, our starting point.

Having missed Rowland's gold strike on the Ramu River, whose source we had set out to find in May 1930, and having twice walked across New Guinea looking for it, Mick Dwyer and I were still determined to have a look at the area. We decided that we should perhaps follow the Ramu River up to its headwaters rather than again try to find its source and follow it down from its headwaters in the moss forests of the Bismarck Range. We left Lae on October 3, 1930, and headed up the Markham Valley once more. By this time Rowland had reported his find. We heard that he had taken the mining warden from Wau back with him to look over the find and register his claim.

An Administration patrol is usually well equipped with supplies. After again walking up the Markham River to the turnoff over the range into the Ramu Valley country about 100 miles from Lae, we discovered that the warden's party had included a rice pack which leaked a few grains, so that we could follow the tracks quite easily. We found no bonanza in the headwaters of the Ramu, but from the top of Munafinka, a prominent rock outcrop, we looked northwest into the open valley down which we had tramped a few months earlier. Sunubia, the rock outcrop on the Dunantina River, was a conspicuous landmark for us. A day's walk from where we stood would have taken us to our 1930 track alongside Sunubia, but our supplies were low. We had to retrace our steps two days back to Kaigulen village on the Ramu River and up to our base at Lehuna on the slopes of the Bismarck Range to pick up stores we had left there on our first trip. We found some of our stores rather motheaten, but there was enough to feed us while we spent a month or so prospecting in the big valley running northwest from Sunubia. After again crossing the Bismarcks, we found ourselves well received by the people we had contacted earlier, but the demand for shells and other goods in exchange for food was a little more definite, and the people were much less overawed by our gear and the strangeness of our appearance. I brought in a gold-lipped shell for the benign looking old patriarch I had met before; he had obviously coveted one on our earlier meeting. This one he took, I thought, rather grudgingly. He returned later with a small emaciated pig and demanded a tomahawk for it. I parted with one, but refused any further demands, which were the usual trading tactics by which a primitive established values.

We followed the Dunantina down for a few miles and crossed the divide into Karmarmentina River. The headwaters of this stream flattened out and snaked through a very rich though limited valley that supported hundreds of Stone Age people living in barricaded villages of cane grass bound together with vines. They approached in full war regalia, complete with plume-decorated shields, bows and arrows, and stone axes. We calmed them down and reinstituted our system of introductions from one village group to the next. The vociferous yells and yodeled messages from every lookout in the first village, however, must have alerted every village within miles of our route.

We crossed a grass-covered range from the Karmarmentina into the Garfatina, its river flats supporting the large and very alert villages of Komperere. Their extensive gardens, laid out with mathematical precision and fenced with cane grass to keep the village pigs out, were bursting with sweet potatoes, sugarcane, yams, beans, and other crops. Pigs were numerous, and our boys feasted well. They crowded in around our camp, and I began to consider what chances we would have if they with their stone axes made a sudden and determined attack on us and our sixteen native carriers.

I picked a small bird off the top of a high tree with a .22 rifle to impress them with our arms and created a diversion sufficient to clear the camp. We then fenced off our camping area with a length of fishline and allowed no one inside. In this way we kept them out of stone axe and club range in case the desire to loot our packs became too great a temptation. We knew now that killing was merely incidental to looting, and we did not want to take too many chances.

Escorted by literally hundreds of loudly chattering natives in full war gear, we passed from village to village down the Garfatina to its junction with the Karmarmentina, where a few colors of gold in a dish induced us to stop and have a good look at the area. We dug a hole in a beach on a bend in the slow-running stream, but although we did not strike bottom, the prospects were much too lean to warrant further intensive prospecting in the locality. We camped on a grassy terrace well away from a barricaded village on the junction. We succeeded in clearing the camp area before dark and regarded with suspicion any movements around the camp after dark.

An old chap with a four-inch length of white calcium through his nose became our friend, philosopher, and next-day guide. We called him "Sniffler" because the weight of his nose stone kept him continually sniffling. Next morning he and his rowdy villagers escorted us along the road and duly handed us over to the next group at the foot of the Sunubia, the Gavitula people living on the Dunantina River. We camped alongside a large, isolated patch of magnificent hoop pine trees, which appeared to be the roosting place for thousands of hawks, and put up our fishline fence around the camp. Our Waria boys, who as the sons of some of New Guinea's most renowned warriors had been taught many tricks of primitive man's cunning and treachery by their experienced forebears, suggested that we release the bowstring of the villagers' bows as a gesture of peace and so that we would be alerted to impending hostility if they began pulling the strings back over the bow ends again.

Every male from toddlers up wore gauntlets on his wrists to protect against the cutting bowstring. The men carried a strong black palm bow about five feet long and had a handful of arrows ready to use. The ordinary fighting arrow was a shaft of reed tipped with eight to ten inches of needle-pointed black palm. Neatly bound into the reed were fine strips of cane. All carried a few murderous-looking barbed arrows, the palm barbs having been cut out of arrow tips with sharp pieces of stone and bone and smoothed off with a rough, sandpapery surface leaf found there. Between the barbs the shaft was bound with fine strips of colored cane which came from high-altitude orchids growing in the moss forests of the ranges and which the grass-country tribes obtained in trade. The barbed arrows we found were "finishing off" arrows, shot into crippled enemies by all and sundry to claim some part of the kill. Their owners were people whom we had contacted on our downriver trip a few months earlier.

After crossing the Bena Bena River, we were again in new country and traveled up the north side of the Asaro River, which we thought the natives were calling the "Garfuku" River. We know now that the Garfuku is a small tributary of the Asaro. We found a few colors in some of the streams but not enough to warrant following them into the ranges. The slates, granites, and oxidized gravel in the streams all the way up the valley gave promise of gold but never fulfilled that promise. The valley was very thickly populated. The villages in the open grass country, because of intertribal wars, were denied access to the timber and firewood on the sides of the surrounding ranges. They had evolved a reforestation system using principally a semihardwood casuarina, a fast-growing tree that splits easily, makes good firewood, and is a very valuable village asset. The victors in intertribal wars not only destroyed any life, human or animal, demolished gardens, and burned houses, but also ringbarked all the cultivated trees—quite a chore with stone axes and an indication of the ferocity of primitive man's wars.

In many places we found villages destroyed and arrow-filled bodies left for the pigs to tear apart. These people were cannibals. Inside the barricade any casualty was just so much meat. Relatives of the dead person would refrain from eating any of the flesh but were quite happy to see it being divided among the villages. The bones were later gathered and buried with the usual grief and sorrow.

I heard of one case where a native whose brother was killed in an ambush propped up the body and would not allow it to be removed until his anger, as he watched the process of decay and gradual disintegration, reached the point where he, beside himself with grief, was killed trying to "back" (avenge) his brother's death. Our roped-off camping area represented the greatest show ever to visit the valley. We insisted on maintaining a clear space inside the fishline fence, and judging by the waiting multitude, a truce must have been declared over a large part of the valley. Even the ringbarked trees around the camp became grandstands for those who could not push through the closely packed sightseers around our fence.

Every item of gear provoked vociferous discussion and speculation. I feel sure that Europeans' initial contact with Stone Age people creates so much interest and superstitious speculation, that the primitive people give no thought to challenging the invaders' ability to defend their gear or lives. The natives were fascinated by steel axes which could cut a tree almost straight through, knives which cut off a stick with one clean blow, houses made of the finest and best woven bark they had ever seen, and bright camping gear and clothing. Firearms meant nothing to them. In some places the natives broke off sticks the same length as our firearms and shouldered them to be on equal terms with us. Bows and arrows, spears, and stone clubs or axes were the only weapons they associated with defense. They imagined that we must have some very powerful sorcery that would allow us to travel through such awful people as their enemies and show no fear of those we wanted to contact the next day. Such is the first contact. The second arouses some doubt of the defense magic. On the third visit, look out for trouble!

We prospected every stream and the main river to the northwestern end of the valley. We passed through villages of conical grass-roofed houses behind barricade fences of cane grass, some with bays off the main wall to prevent shield-protected attackers from cutting the fence down with stone axes; over grass-covered flats; and up and down gullies cut through the old lake bed of the valley. This prolific and colorful country more than 5,000 feet above sea level with an eternal spring climate is today the center of a rich coffee-growing area and encompasses Administration and missionary activities. The airstrip at Goroka, laid out during the war by an American army engineer, is one of the busiest in this country. So rapid has been its postwar development that roads from Lae are not as yet operational for heavy traffic all year round. American army engineer Colonel L. J. Sverdrup located and pegged out this strip at Goroka and arranged for its construction during the war.

A low gap in the Bismarck Range suggested that there was more new country to prospect that must drain into the lower Ramu. We climbed up and along a track on top of a grass-covered ridge accompanied by the usual escort of dozens of chattering natives, some of whom appeared concerned that we were heading out of their valley or that we were going into unusually hostile enemy country. Our escort gradually disappeared until we had only a few well-armed men, who also left us where the grass track ran into the moss forest range country. The devastated remains of a village in a clearing a little farther on accounted for their rather abrupt departure. They had evidently destroyed the village and had chased the survivors farther into the ranges not long ago; there might still be a few very hostile survivors waiting around the ruins of their homes. We knew that our approach from enemy country would prompt the bush people, as usual, to shoot first and talk afterward. Sooner or later we would meet the vanquished refugees rebuilding their villages and gardens somewhere in the bush-covered ranges ahead of us. Everyone was alerted to watch for signs of natives along the almost obliterated track through the bush. We were heard first, and the frantic call to arms was bellowed through the ranges.

We answered the call to let the natives know that our party was not an ambush attempt. There was a roar from above us, and we could hear someone coming through the scrub. A very agitated warrior appeared on the track behind us, ready to do battle with his enemies from over the range. Instead, he stopped in his tracks when he saw us and gave us time to wave the peace signs of a few leaves at him and induce him to calm down. He then called to his cobbers. They led us down the range, and we camped on the bank of a fast-running creek heading towards the Ramu River.

We spent a hungry night, as our new contacts had not reached the stage where they had food to spare. A few came along, duly showed us the track, and bellowed an introduction to the villages perched on the opposite side of the stream. We climbed to about 6,000 feet and camped among enough villages to provide food for the boys. We tried to use sign language to make our way down into the Ramu River, which we could now see running flat through the wide, bush-covered valley far below us. Once we had made contact with the natives, they appeared to think we were a road show and conspired to lead us from one group to another like a traveling circus. The villages were perched on opposite sides of deep gorges, so that we had always to go a few thousand feet down and up the other side. Moreover, this was heavily timbered country alive with leeches. We therefore decided to take the most direct route down the range to the Ramu River, which we could see every now and then as we looked down the steeply falling gorges we were crossing. Eventually after four days we ignored our guides and picked our way down a spur of the range along an almost overgrown track into the heat and the sparsely populated Ramu River. As we meandered through its wide, flat, heavily timbered valley, a great variety of pigeons, pigs, and fish in the drying billabongs of old riverbeds kept us and our boys well fed. We were resigned to the heat and humidity of inland New Guinea at low altitude.

We headed back upriver along well-defined tracks through the bush country, pausing to shoot pigeons, which noisily flapped up from feeding grounds into the trees, where they sat waiting to be shot. We reached the wide grass stretches of the valley near wartime Dumpu airstrip and Shaggy Ridge, crossed over the barely perceptible divide, merely a continuation of the rift valley which runs through New Guinea and here divides the Ramu and Markham River falls, and made our way back down the Markham Valley to Lae. We reached Lae on Thursday, November 27, 1930.

Kukakukas in
native dress.

THE
YEAR
1931

Early in 1931 I was employed by New Guinea
Goldfields Limited, which had established mining headquarters in Wau to work gold leases in
the area. I was asked to prospect the country in
the headwaters of the gold-bearing Watut River, which headed on
the northern slopes of the Owen Stanley Range and joined the rich
Bulolo to form the main Watut River. After roaring through mountain gorges, it in turn joined the fast-running Markham River,
which runs out at the eastern end of the vast 1,000-mile-long rift valley, extending through New Guinea from Lae to the Memberambo
River in West Irian.

For the first time in this country, I used a small plane to recon-
noiter the area and judge the country into which we were going to
walk. I also wanted to assess the population, to gauge distances
between villages—the source of our food both for ourselves and for
our boys—and to look for areas of flat, grassy country that could
serve as future airstrips to replenish our supplies. We found no flat

area, only timber-covered ranges and the scarred, precipitous sides of the mountains once over the divide or border between Papua and New Guinea, which in these parts was merely a line on a map. Limestone country dominates the rock structures of the Papuan side, and massive limestone formations are not good indicators of gold in this part of the world.

The flight started at a small airstrip on a terrace of the upper reaches of the Watut River before it gorged and was joined by the Bulolo River lower down. A single-seater Gipsy Moth piloted by Les Trist took me over the head of Roaring Creek, a gold-bearing tributary of the Watut, and then over the unknown country beyond. We had a rough ride and were continually buffeted and bounced by air currents shaped by the deep ravines and timber-covered ranges. We flew southwest over the Papua–New Guinea divide to what appeared to be the limestone barrier and then turned back east of our route out, coming back over country which had already been prospected by Helmuth Baum, who had lived in German New Guinea before World War I. Baum was working al-luvial gold on Surprise Creek, a tributary of the Watut, and he was then preparing to go on what he termed his last trip to find his Golconda. He thought the area over the Owen Stanley Range from the Bulolo and Watut fall was worth a last try. When he returned, he said, he would go back to Germany to live.

Mick Dwyer, my brother Pat, and I started off from the Watut base on March 24, 1931, and followed Roaring Creek to its head, crossing the map-marked Papua-New Guinea divide through the low Djambi Pass, 6,500 feet above sea level. After leaving the grass ridges of the Watut, we followed native tracks through heavily timbered, sparsely populated ranges, prospected the numerous streams we crossed, and stayed on the lookout for villages. We did not want to walk unexpectedly into groups of unfamiliar natives and thus precipitate a brawl before we could introduce ourselves.

The country on the Papuan side fell away rather sharply. We made slow progress over the sodden bush track, traversing the spurs and tops of ridges and moving up and down over the fast-running streams in the bottom of the ravines. This was poor mineral country, and the going was rough. The natives, seeing Europeans for the first time, were very suspicious of any strangers but

Kukakuka in
native dress.

were so curious and hungry for the steel knives and axes which our
boys carried that we generally managed to contact some of them
and traded shell and small knives and tomahawks for native foods
and pigs.

The natives of this area, Kukakukas, have established a reputa-
tion for being the most treacherous cannibals in New Guinea and
are said to stalk the ingredients of their meals with the same impersonal single-mindedness that a cat shows in pursuit of a mouse.
Being mountain people they are usually short and blocky, although
some are as tall as five feet ten inches and solidly built. Their dress,
ornaments, and personal getup are distinctive and peculiar to the
tribe. The men wear a sporranlike covering of dried rushes found in

the high, swampy patches of the ranges. A bark cape is suspended on a length of native string from a patch of hair left on the tops of their heads. The cape covers the back and sides and reaches below the knees.

The Kukakukas weave the canelike runners of the mountain orchid, a plant which flourishes in the perpetual dampness of parasite-loaded treetops on New Guinea's mountain ranges, into long lengths and various widths which are draped in multiple strands across the shoulders and around the waist, arms, and legs. Bands of the same material are used extensively by both men and women. Their noses are pierced, and pieces of bone or cane or shaped stones are worn through the septum. We never saw the men without a bow and arrow. They carry extra arrows in a string bag, or bilum, slung from the shoulders. Extra bow canes, neatly knotted and ready to replace a broken one, are tied in a coil to one of the numerous bits and pieces dangling from their bodies. We sometimes saw various lizards, rodents, grubs, and even large grasshoppers suspended from strands of the sporran. These animals were killed with a special knob-tipped arrow, always part of native artillery equipment. Their bows were the usual black palm, and their fighting arrows plain palm-tipped reeds, the tapered needle-sharp tips neatly bound to the reed shaft with the same orchid cane that was wound over their shoulders and waist.

In this section, which lay between the areas of Baum's earlier probes into the Kuka country, the natives had never seen a white party before, although they must have heard tales of white miners and prospectors, repeated with the usual native exaggerations, on their trading trips between tribal areas. The lack of steel tools or weapons reflected their isolation from white contacts. A small quantity of trade steel had reached these people from the Papuan coast. We saw half an axe head which had been cut in two to make two tomahawks. Months and months of patient rubbing with slivers of hard cutting stone must have been required to cut through the steel axe head. We saw pieces of shovels, probably stolen from miners working isolated patches of alluvial gold and traded in, cut into sections by the same method and mounted in the traditional Stone Age way—bound to a bent L-shaped piece of branched sapling. Their round, conical-shaped, grass-roofed houses located in patches of secondary growth and reeds were hard to see or locate, and gardens were the clue that a village lay nearby. A heavily used track, together with the increasing evidence of pig droppings, always forewarned us that we were approaching a small village. In some cases the final approach was made through deep mud and pig dung in tunnels of high cane grass. This easily defended approach, one which no strangers would attempt without a villager's guidance, allowed the inhabitants to monitor their visitors. The surrounding thick cane grass afforded almost impregnable protection unless it was assaulted by waves of warriors.

The Kukas do not wage a war of direct assault; they are experts in treachery. They are bush people and, I think, the remnants of some of New Guinea's earliest inhabitants. The stone pestle and mortar people, food grinders, relics of whose culture are still found, were probably the first. The Kukas, who inhabit New Guinea's main backbone, have been driven back garden by garden into the most inhospitable part of the ranges, to places almost above a food-producing altitude, where sweet potatoes, the inland natives' staff of life, grow slowly and produce little. Down through the centuries the Kukas were driven back by the encroachment and superior fighting technology of waves of immigrant outrigger canoe people. Living in fog-shrouded ranges, immune to the cold and dampness of their moss and lichen stamping grounds, they hunt their food and stalk their enemies like wraiths, soundlessly and stealthily maneuvering through the bush. Unlike grass-country natives whose visiting card is a smoky grass fire for all to see, who come in peace and whose custom is to talk first and shoot after, the treacherous Kuka, almost indistinguishable from his surroundings, pops out from behind trees or bushes, shoots first, and talks later.

We traveled east across the southern fall of the country at about the 3,000-foot level. The streams were fast running, some of them too turbulent to cross and too wide to be spanned by a tree. We had to cut a track upstream through boulder-littered terrain, overgrown by heavy tropical growth, to where the stream forked and we could cross two smaller and much less hazardous streams. The country near enough to the main mountain range and on the opposite fall to the Edie Creek-Bulolo gold shed on the northern side was mostly slates and granites and showed some mineralization but lacked the extensive oxidation of the heavily mineralized gravels in the Edie and Bulolo. We raised a color or two and found bottom, which was never deep in these fast-running torrents. We drew a blank as far as payable gold was concerned. There are hundreds of streams in New Guinea, particularly on the northern fall of the main central range, where a color of gold and even traces of platinum and osmiridium shed from belts of serpentine country can be dished. There is too much New Guinea mixed up with it to make separation a paying proposition, however, despite unlimited hydraulic power and natural tailraces that roar through gorges cut deep in the solid rock.

On April 10 we camped at 3,500 feet above sea level near a recent campsite used by my friend, Helmuth Baum. Baum's camps were distinctive. Baum himself was unique in his ability to travel around this country with no more equipment than a couple of extra pairs of shorts and shirts. He wore no boots or hat. A couple of natives could easily carry all his food and personal gear and a few more would transport native trade. Yet despite Baum's spartan habits, I had never seen him very travel-stained or dirty. His head was shaved to the scalp, and his cold country complexion was clean and fresh looking as it probably ever was in his pre-World War I job of managing a German trading post in Madang or Rabaul.

Baum's camps seemed, even to us, austere in the extreme and were easily recognizable. A light, open-ended tent fly was pitched sharply to let the rain run off rather than dripping down inside, as it would have on a flatter-rigged shelter. His bunk was a few thin, pliable green sticks, vine tied to top and bottom crosspieces, resting in forked sticks driven into the ground. In grass country it is sometimes possible to sleep on dry ground, but in the wet, mossy, root-covered ranges, even the ground was hidden under a foot or so of matted, wet tree roots. All his gear was carried in a native bilum, or string bag, slung from the shoulder on a stick. He took a small iron pot which could be used to boil or bake his bit of local pig or pigeon and sweet potato. His main standby on the track was a taro—a lily root—roasted on the coals, which he nibbled as he walked along. Water was his drink, and in this country there was never any danger of running out of clear, cold mountain water.

From pantomimed inquiries we decided that Baum had slept at this camp two nights, had bought native foods and a pig with beads and a tomahawk, had dug shallow holes in the creek, and had washed dishes of gravel, which meant he had eliminated this stream from consideration and would be prospecting the country to the southeast, which appeared to be the way he was heading. From his camp sticks we thought he might not be too far away. We decided to contact him before we turned back for the base. The natives became very concerned when it became obvious that we were following Baum's route. At each stream crossing they gesticulated excitedly and attempted to bar our progress. They bent over the cold water and splashed water over their necks, which we interpreted to mean there was an impassable waterfall just ahead of us and we should return along Baum's track. We were ready to head back; Baum would prospect the country, and we would see him on the Watut when he came back.

We climbed back up the range from 3,500 feet above sea level to the top of the range and camped at 8,700 feet. Soaked by the wet moss which covered everything and the rain which drenched the gear before we could rig our tent, we spent a bad night in a sodden camp. Our boys had food enough; we had insisted that they carry a supply from the last village for a two- to three-day mountain crossing, as there was little chance that we would find native gardens once we left the lower country. Starting a campfire at a frost altitude in New Guinea's cold, wet, moss forest-covered ranges is always a difficult job. Bossboy Ewunga organized a search on the underside of decaying roots and the accumulated debris of centuries of growth and decay and found dry moss and wood splinters, which produced enough heat to fire the semidecayed deadwood and make a fire with lots of acrid, eye-watering smoke. Smoke does not rise in the wet, fog-shrouded ranges; it just flattens out about eye and nose level and stays there. As long as a native has a few smoldering stick ends pushed together, he appears to be quite happy sitting over it, "winding" the smoking, semidecayed fuel and wiping the smoke tears from his eyes. Given a fire, any sort of a fire, to sleep or doze beside with a belly full of half-roasted kaukau or yam, he can forget his hard day's toil up and down ranges and will not give tomorrow's probably much more arduous trail a second thought. Following Baum's route back to the Watut camp, apart from the usual up and down route from the top of the divide, we arrived back at our Watut base at 4:25 P.M., on Saturday, April 4, 1931. Baum had not returned to his base on Surprise Creek—if indeed Baum had any "base" other than a native village to trade him his few traveling essentials.

We were glad to have an undisturbed and comfortable rest at our base on the small upper Watut strip. Guinea Airway's single-engine Junker plane and a small Gipsy Moth brought in mail and stores for the small group of men then developing the gold in the gravels of the Watut and its tributaries—Surprise, Roaring, and Irowat creeks. There was gold all the way down the main Watut, right from its source on the opposite fall of the range that had shed such phenomenal gold into Edie Creek, a headwater tributary of the Bulolo River. I was sure there must be another such rich shed into some of the rivers and streams coming off a continuation of the main mountain range which divides the Northwest from the southeast fall of Papua New Guinea.

That Sunday evening we had one of this country's thunderstorms with accompanying torrential downpours, and the Watut descended in a wall of dirty water and debris, with an occasional small animal and lizard bobbing along, paddling desperately for the side—any side. Shortly after the storm blew over, we saw a young chap named Woods, who was working with a surveyor, coming down the opposite side of the now very swollen river. As we thought he would cross the river on the swing bridge which spanned a narrow part of the stream in front of the camp, we walked across the airstrip to greet him. By the time we reached the river, he had disappeared. His dog, wet and battered looking, was found downriver a few hundred yards from the bridge, but no trace was ever found of Woods's body. We could only assume he preferred the roaring river to the rather tricky swing bridge which gave the illusion of racing upstream as fast as the current below. A person making a first crossing who did not know the strength of New Guinea's streams could step into the river, as Woods had done, to be immediately engulfed and swept away.

By this time we had crossed and recrossed New Guinea and Papua with two shotguns, two Winchester .32-caliber rifles, a couple of .45-caliber revolvers, a .22-caliber rifle, and sixteen natives who had been schooled by their fathers to fight for survival and who had eaten their share of vanquished foes before they passed their teens. We had also penetrated and prospected part of the strongholds of the most bloodthirsty and treacherous natives in the island, the Kukakukas. In the wake of these experiences we were sure the stories of attacks and treacherous murders must have resulted from some indiscretions or untimely actions on the part of the prospecting parties or administrative patrols. We quite believed Sir Hubert Murray's declaration of some years before that Papua was patrolled to the border and that nothing more lethal than a walking stick was needed to prospect or patrol the Papuan Inland.

We felt there must be more than one Edie Creek-Bulolo El Dorado in this world's second largest island. We thought we had mastered the art of contacting, pacifying, and traveling among these so-called treacherous murderers and cannibals. Being young, strong, optimistic, and sure that over the next range we would look down into a valley with a slow-running river meandering through it—giving promise of another bonanza with the feeder streams going five to ten ounces of gold to a dish—we set out determined to find a better strike than Edie Creek.

The grass houses of the natives were grouped closely together in barricaded villages. The smoke of numerous small cooking fires drifted over the peaceful valleys. These villages held no threats for us. We were reassured by our civilized background, being, as we thought, experienced officers who had already explored and brought under control large areas of primitive country in both Papua and New Guinea. We had few needs—tea, sugar, salt, a twenty-five-pound tin of flour, a luxury in comparison to the meager fare we would accept later on, depending on how far we went from our base and what our prospecting indicated.

Outfitted again and still hoping to find our fortunes this time to the northwest of the area covered in our last trip, Pat and I with fourteen boys, most of them by now veterans but nevertheless completely dependent on our superior intelligence and weapons, were ready to set out. Following almost hereditary instincts developed in years of campfire conversations with their experienced relatives, they warned us that we, in our brash, theoretical inexperience, would encounter trouble in the moss-forested ranges around the headwaters of the gold-bearing Langemar, Tauri, and Vialalla rivers, whose headwaters were deep in the Papua-New Guinea dividing range. We left our upper Watut base camp on Thursday, April 23, 1931, following Big Slate Creek, which headed in the divide northwest of our last trip. The lower reaches of some of the streams flowing into the Watut off the northern fall of the dividing range had already been prospected by miners who were working alluvial gold from the headwaters of the Bulolo. We proposed to cut all these streams well up in the ranges and to follow any promising gold prospects. We knew from miners who had dish prospected the lower reaches of the fast-running Langemar and Banir rivers that gold was coming down these streams into the Watut. I pictured high, grass-covered valleys and ranges similar to the upper Waria Valley, which I had prospected in 1927. I could never understand why there should not be many more such valleys and people throughout New Guinea.

The first couple of days out are always hard going. We had to accustom ourselves to base camp conditions and to the up-and-down terrain through moss forests of slippery roots and rocks. We discovered an abandoned native garden which held promise of future guidance and food if we could contact the Kukas who, we were quite sure, were watching and following us through their stamping grounds. We followed native pads running in the general direction in which we were going until they petered out into hunting tracks indistinguishable from the surroundings. Then we cut our way across the fall of the country until we found, usually on the tops of the ridges, better-looking native pads. We contacted no natives on the first day and used some of the small store of rice carried by each boy in addition to his thirty- to thirty-five-pound pack. It was a cold and wet camp at 5,000 feet above sea level, with the usual eye-watering smoky fires, but after a first day's sweat-producing walk, any place to rest was welcome. Bossboy Ewunga arranged for a two-hour watch for the line and was emphatic about the need to stay awake and move around without going near a fire and thus becoming a good target for an arrow.

Pat and I gratefully climbed into our canvas sleeves on sapling bunks and dropped off to sleep. We were rather amused at Ewunga for his timidity, quite sure that the expert theorists had all the answers and would not consciously expose unsuspecting parties of natives and whites to what I now know was a constant threat from our shadowy trailers. We were glad to move on from Camp 1 and to warm up, following a track over the serrated mountain, prospecting the fast-running mountain streams as we worked our way northwest to 6,700 feet and down to 4,500 feet, covering all the gullies in between. We contacted a few hunting Kukas, but they were very shy and melted into the surrounding bush after looking us over. We camped at 6,400 feet near a Kuka hunting hut. A few angled saplings with leaves had been stacked over it to keep out the rain and cold. Unfortunately we found no native foods, and our supply was dwindling. We moved off early, following the hunting track, but it petered out after we had followed it to 1,500-feet. We decided we were too far down and angled slowly back up again across the range through open scrub country, where the boys found young bush palm trees, the firm hearts of which were edible and filled some empty spaces. I do not think the food value was very high, but palm hearts were something to chew and were not unpleasant to the taste.

We sent a boy up a tall tree on top of a ridge where the country flattened out a little. He spied a native garden, which promised food and perhaps contact with a guide to the next people. We found a still hot fire and dug some kaukau, leaving in payment beads and a small knife tied to a stick in front of the grass hut. Although we were quite sure we were being watched from not far away, we could not induce the natives to come near. This again was new country never previously visited by outsiders. Still, we knew the local natives would have heard of white men and their peculiar habit of washing dishes of stones from creek beds. We were in soft, schisty country but could not get a color in any of the streams. On Sunday, April 26, we headed towards a few houses we had seen from a ridge and found a few native houses and garden patches. The natives had left before we arrived. We decided to camp early and try to contact some natives who could introduce and guide us to the next village. The country was now a thick forest rather than scrub and was flattening out. Ahead there might be tableland areas, and any gold shed into streams would have a better chance of still being there than it would in the torrents running down the mountainside.

We dropped into a large, fast-running creek and tried to follow it up, but passed through a steep-sided gorge, so we climbed out again and returned to our previous camp. We picked up some more food and cut our way about northwest through the bush across the ridges. We camped at 4,000 feet and could see the top of a high kunai (type of grass) ridge in the distance. We pushed on until the bush-covered ranges began to give way to grass ridges. After seeing smoke, we managed to contact a man whom we calmed down by presenting him with some trade. We used sign language to promise him an axe if he showed us the track to the next village. He settled down quite happily but slipped away during the night. Millions of dog fleas made this camp a most uncomfortable one, and we were glad to leave the place at daylight. Following native tracks, we passed a corpse sitting up in his little eyrie on the top of long poles under a flat kunai roof. Arrows pushed through his limbs kept him in a squatting position. His bits and pieces of sporran, bilum, bow, and arrows were all draped around his little shelter.

We were now on a large, grass-covered area and could look down into the Watut and Markham rivers, the wide, flat, grass-covered rift valley through which the Markham flows to the sea and the barely perceptible divide where the Ramu was running out to the sea more than seventy miles north of Madang. This country drained into the Watut, so we figured we were now in the head of the Langemar River. We were on the watch for a native contact—a Kuka—as we believed ourselves still in Kuka country. We contacted no natives, and the weather turned out wet. Thick clouds cut our visibility to a few hundred yards. We did not want to appear suddenly out of the fog and surprise the bowstring-happy Kukas, and so we camped another night in the hope of better visibility next day.

From a nearby hill and a break in the clouds we spotted a village about a day away and headed toward it, cutting a track through high sawgrass and bracken fern up and down the numerous gullies. Here and there we came upon a little-used, barely defined native pad. The relative absence of paths hinted at a state of war between these villages and a hazard for anyone approaching from that direction. We kept a sharp watch for lookout sentries, but we had left the dark, heavily timbered country with its cold, damp, sodden, moss-covered roots and rocks and its lichen and aereal-vine-festooned trees dripping water and depression over the muddy or damp, deadened humus from centuries of forest decay. We could see above the coarse grasses and stunted shrubs and covered our gulley crossing by waiting on one side until part of the line had crossed and climbed to the top of the other side of the gulley and could cover the rest of the line.

The watercourses showed no mineral prospects. We saw no native pads, or even signs of them, and slowly cut our own path through the tangled grasses and bracken fern across the fall of the country, hoping to find a track or a stray native to guide us to friendly contact with his cobbers. We never found the Kukakukas—they found us first—as we took a chance and were making our way up the bed of a narrow creek cut through deep terraces.

Without any introductions, arrows began to fall among our widely separated, single-file line of boys, and all ducked for whatever cover the creek banks could afford against the bowmen on top. After a snap shot from the kunai cover at a prancing, shield-carrying warrior and a few more to speed them on their way, we hurriedly climbed out of the creek bed in order to negotiate any further contacts on more open country. We walked into the village that afternoon. After arranging a camp in an open space on top of a cleared hill, we managed to contact some of the very wary warriors and used sign language to persuade them to bring us sweet potatoes and sugarcane. Before long even the women and children were peering at our camp from a safe distance, and by nightfall we were on good terms with the village. We remained there the next day, putting a hole down in a big river flat. We got a few colors in a dish but not sufficient to warrant further prospecting up the river, which we decided was the headwaters of the Langemar, a tributary of the Watut. The next morning the villagers gave us a friendly sendoff. They could not be persuaded to show us the track to the next village, preferring to fight between themselves for any camp flotsam left. On our own, then, we climbed a long, grass-covered ridge and crossed the divide into a southern-flowing creek at the 6,100-foot level. We were again in heavily timbered, moss-covered country, but the wide native pad cut through the bush was easy to follow, and we made good time in a westerly direction.

From a small clearing on the top of a bush-covered ridge, we could see smoke from village fires on the top of the range across the stream. Water roared down its bush-covered course below us. We could not hope to reach the village and make contact before dark, and so we decided to go down and camp alongside the creek. We would climb up to the village next morning; we would have plenty of daylight hours to contact the people and make friends, buy food, or resolve any difficulties before dark. We slipped and clambered down the muddy, slippery root track, grabbing small saplings beside the track to brake ourselves. Natives can bound down steep, wet tracks by using both hands and almost swinging from one sapling to the next, their feet just sliding down the wet ground and roots. We camped at 4,600 feet on a small creek flat in semiopen scrub and cleared a small camp area near the fast-running, boulder-covered stream. It was the usual rather miserable camp improvised with tomahawks and knives in the wet-timbered ranges. The boys started their smoky fires in front of the leaf-covered lean-tos and set their lumps of kaukau with pieces of cold pork to heating in the fires. Just at dusk there was a yell and a grab for arms. Tupia said three Kukas who had just bound out of the bush had fired an arrow at one of the boys. The Kukas raced up the track to their village above, howling like dogs as they went. No one had been hit, and no shots were fired.

In retrospect, Pat and I should have read the sign and taken appropriate precautions, but we did not. Conditioned by the literature and lies, which newcomers to countries such as New Guinea so avidly read and completely accept as unbiased, we paid for our trust! Our fly-covered tent was rigged beside the stream near a log bridge that we used when rain made a crossing more hazardous than usual. Our canvas sleeve beds had two poles through the sleeve and crossed saplings hammered into the ground. They were kept taut top and bottom by a short sapling with a V nicked into each end. In this case they were rigged across the tent rather than the erected parallel with the ridgepole as usual to allow passage between bunks in cramped quarters. My bunk was just inside the back of the tent, which was rigged high enough for me to use the back of the tent, rather the front, to come and go. The dip in the canvas sleeve made a good warm bed, preventing the blankets from sliding off during the night. Our rifles were placed beside the head, and an army brass band hung from the sapling. Our heavy .45 revolvers, which we wore on a bullet-studded belt during the day, hung in their holsters, one end of the belt being tucked under the eiderdown mattress far enough down the bed to be reached quickly if the camp was attacked during the night. We had a supply of matches, and the only light came from a few torches, or "shoot lamps," as they are known to the natives. Mine was within reach, with the rest of the gear. We slept in a clean change of shorts and wool shirts, each morning enduring the ordeal of putting on our sweat-dampened, moisture-specked shorts and shirts of the day before. We got the okay from Ewunga that all the boys were as comfortable as they could make themselves. We settled down to sleep when it became too dark to read. Rifle and ammunition were at the head of the bed. I had a revolver under my hand, and Junker, the dog, in whom we put some trust as camp watcher, lay asleep under the bunk.

We were shocked into wakefulness just before daylight by the screams and yells of our boys. "Masta, Masta, kanaka killim me fella!" I grabbed the revolver. Still not quite awake, holding my pants up with one hand and the revolver in the other, I ducked under the back of the tent and stood up beside a figure whom I took to be one of our own boys who had raced to our tent for protection. His back was to me, and he was looking along the side of the tent where the clash of tomahawks against the bows, the twang of bowstrings and some shooting marked the center of a struggle. Our boys were in its midst, as was Pat, who had dashed out the front of our tent with his rifle. Half asleep, I peered into the still dark bush surroundings. I said to the man beside me, "Where are the bastards?" At the same time, in the dim morning light filtering down the narrow open space above the streambed, I saw a figure with a bow and arrow. The bark cape hanging from his topknot identified him as a Kukakuka. He was halfway across the log bridge about thirty feet away when I turned and fired at him, but I do not know even now whether or not I hit him.

I remember nothing of what happened over the next few minutes. Minutes later I found myself on the creek side of our tent, near the front, partially blinded by blood streaming down from my head over my eyes. Still holding the revolver, I dimly heard Pat demanding more rifle cartridges. Then he cried, "My God, they have brained you!" I remember saying, "Here take my .45, I can't see," but Tupia handed him some .32's. He jammed them into his rifle and rushed back, firing point blank at the now retreating Kukas. I fell into Pat's bunk as my head began to clear. The noise of primitive man's war screams mixed with gunfire urged me outside again, but although I could stand upright and wag the revolver about, I could not focus on anything long enough to shoot. Tupia handed my rifle to me and pointed to the Kukakukas now beating a retreat. I took a leaning shot from a tree nearby at a figure who had stopped to fire an arrow at the camp, but I cannot say that I scored a hit. The fight stopped almost as suddenly as it had commenced. The raiders, howling, bounded up the bush-covered track. We took stock of our casualties. Pat had taken two arrows, one through his left arm and one high upon the right-hand side of his chest. I was afraid that the second one might have gone down into his lung, but he was still full of fight and appeared rather sorry that it was all over.

As my head cleared and I cleaned up in the cold mountain water, I found I had received a crack on the right side of the head from the figure whom I had mistaken for one of our boys outside our tent. My spoken words had evidently caused him to whirl around just as I fired at the Kuka coming over the log bridge. The flash of fire and the report from my revolver somewhat broke the force and direction of the blow from his stone pineapple club. Before he had time to finish me off with a second blow, one of our boys from Maralinin on the lower Watut skewered him with an arrow, undoubtedly saving my life. I received a narrow gash across the cheekbone from an arrow or from falling into a cut twig. I will never know which. Afterward, in Lae at Henry Eekhoff's Trade Store, I told the boy I would give him anything he wanted for having saved my life. He rather disconcerted me by asking for five shillings' worth of tobacco.

As Ewunga described the fight, a fairly strong force had silently surrounded the camp and with bows and arrows and stone clubs had attempted to murder us before we could use our weapons. Fortunately, the watchboys had withstood the initial assault and had roused the camp. There ensued a stone club, bow-and-arrow melee. Some of the boys I had armed with bows and arrows to give them some means of defense if and when their lives were endangered. Tupia, who was one of them, was assailed by a club-swinging, howling Kuka. Ewunga, his "one talk," (speaks same language) who was armed with one of our single-barrel shotguns, poked the barrel over Tupia's shoulder and almost blew his would-be assassin in half. Guna, a Waria boy, panicked and ran back the way we had come but returned to the camp when the shooting stopped. Minower, another Waria, had an arrow in his right side and was rather sorry for himself after I pulled it out but was so anxious to leave the place that he did not delay our departure.

It took a pair of pliers to pull out the arrow embedded in Tanta's knee. I doubted that he could walk back to Lae, but he and Guna both realized that they just had to stagger along somehow. We found six Kukakukas dead in the camp area, and I think we must have wounded others who reached their village on the top of the ridge above us. Pat was the hero of the fight, according to the boys. They were very impressed by his nonchalance in pulling arrows out of his own arm and chest and by his ability with the rifle. "Masta Paddy man belong fight true." I decided to get Pat, the boys, and myself back to Lae for medical help as soon as I could in case any of the wounds turned septic. I was very concerned about Pat's chest wound, thinking he might develop blood poisoning from the dirty arrow. I knew our trip back to the coast at Lae would be slow and rather painful for all of us. Junker, the dog, had slept through it all!

We boiled the billy (tea), and some of the boys cooked some kaukau while others pulled down the camp and packed up. A very close watch was kept in all directions by a few scouts a short distance away. Evidently our attackers had no stomach for further fight. Months later, after contact had been made with them, we heard that they had evacuated their village, fearing a follow-up attack from us. By this time Pat had cooled down, and the reaction had set in. I was not feeling well myself, but it was up to me to get us all safely away. We dumped some of our stores and heavy prospecting tools, rigged Pat's canvas bedsleeve between the two poles, and broke camp, carrying Pat in relays back up the slippery, timbered mountainside down which we had come the day before. Pat was no lightweight even in those days; honed down with weeks of walking over these ranges, he still tipped the scales at about 200 pounds. Yet there was no scarcity of willing recruits to carry him. Everyone was anxious to put as much distance between us and that camp as the daylight hours allowed. Minower could carry a couple of cooking tins, his axe, and his bow and arrows. The boys had retrieved spent arrows and some of the stone clubs. These would be souvenirs of the fray and, if necessary, additional weapons should we again be attacked by any of the hundreds of Kukas through whose villages and gardens we had to travel to reach the Watut and Markham rivers.

Tanta's knee must have been very painful, but he never allowed it to stiffen. If I could prevent the wounds from becoming septic, I could see he would manage to stay with us. Each morning it was an ordeal for him to start walking, but he nevertheless kept up. Our pace carrying Pat was very slow. If Tanta cracked under the strain, we would have to camp until all were fit to travel, which meant further attacks if the Kukas thought we were weakened. I cleaned and sterilized all the arrow holes as we reached the grass country and then set hot antiflogistine plasters on them to keep them clean and sterile. We pushed on over another range and camped at 2,600 feet in the open kunai, far enough away from a village to get food and to guard against surprise raids. We slept little, but the night's rest helped, and we moved off again as soon as we could see the track down to the Watut River, which we intended to follow as closely as the terrain and native tracks would permit. The going was tough; the river was dropping rapidly and the narrow, steep-sided gorges were impossible to cross. We had to climb up and out and detour along the range until it flattened out again for a mile or so. Pat was now very gingerly struggling along on his feet; it was impossible to carry him in such country. He had to walk or we would have to camp where we were until he recovered sufficiently to carry on. Tanta was battling along manfully, his one-talks helping him over the rough going. Minower was as good as ever. Evidently the arrows had not penetrated Pat's lung or Minower's vital parts. My head was giving me hell, but my eyes were settling down. Except for a chronic ache and the shock when I accidentally bumped my head on a rock overhead, I had the situation well in hand. We just had to keep moving. Our food supply was what we could barter from the Kukas, and their villages were some distance off the river. Abandoned gardens near our track gave us enough secondary growth, small kaukau, and sugarcane for survival, and I advised the line to carry as much as they could in case our food supply became insufficient to allow us to reach the semicivilized villages of the Langemar and Watut rivers.

We camped at dusk beside the river, which was now too big to cross and at about 1,500 feet was still a whitewater torrent roaring over great boulders. We had no fear of an attack from that side of the river; the rock cover around the camp gave our firearms an advantage in case we were surprised during the night. The whole camp now had no illusions about the Kukas' raiding instincts. Any time of night even a whispered "Watch" would bring a quick and alert reply from the sentries. Pat was now making good progress, and the boys were also improving. The initial early morning warm-up was something of an ordeal, but we believed that we were not far from the Watut. Navatack told me he had recognized some features of the country not far from his home village of Maralinin (or Sillit Sillit—a U.S. advanced air base, as it was known during the war).

After another scrambled detour up the side of the gorge to the top at 3,000 feet, we looked into a patchwork of flat grass- and bush-covered country through which the Watut meandered in slow-running reaches and bows before it joined the Markham away in the distance. The Langemar gave promise of better going, with no more ranges to negotiate. We felt much safer from surprise raids in this no-man's-land between the populated lowlands debilitated by warfare, disease, and tropical heat and the highlands that were home to the agile, alert, aggressive Kukakukas. Tensions eased as we began to follow well-defined hunting tracks downriver along bush-covered reaches of the river. Our Watut boys, who were now in their own stamping ground, assured us that Sankaf could be reached before dark. It was a treat to find ourselves with a good supply of native food and fruit and to sleep without the tension of interpreting the night bush noises as signals between marauding Kukas. Our injuries showed no signs of turning septic, and we were in much better spirits. Despite my chronic headache, I urged the line along a well-trodden bush track downstream. We came upon the junction of the Watut and Langemar about lunchtime and, after crossing a couple of rather big streams, reached the village of Sodens at 4:30 P.M. Now only 500 feet above sea level, we had eighty to ninety miles of raftable river between us and the coast at Lae. A patrol officer named Sanson happened to be in the next village, and he came up to us after dark with his medical kit and reported that all was well with the wounded; rest and time would mend them.

We stayed one day at Sodens. Patrol officer Sanson took details of the fracas and did not anticipate that any charges would be brought against us; the evidence of arrows and clubs was too obvious. It was plain that the arrows had actually taken effect in our bodies before we took action to defend our boys and ourselves. The importance of establishing that we had not taken the initiative shocked and amazed us. It became the chief topic of conversation and the subject of concern as we considered future prospecting expeditions into new country populated by natives who had never seen or even heard of white-skinned human beings.

We were also shocked to hear from Sanson that my good friend Helmuth Baum had been murdered by the Kukakukas and most of his boys butchered with him. We then realized that the Kukakukas who had become so agitated, bending over and splashing the cold mountain water on their necks, had really been pantomiming Baum's lifeblood flowing away from his severed head and were not, as we had thought, describing an impassable waterfall. Kukakukas are evidently the same wherever they are found.

The cold-blooded murder of Baum, the cannibalistic devouring of his decapitated body, and the callous and determined hunting down and hacking to death of most of his unarmed and very timid Buang carriers shocked me into the realization that perhaps the so-called experts regarding primitive man's reactions were suffering from too much purely academic knowledge. Some of these experts had apparently never encountered a primitive savage in his natural element and did not know that he would suspect any strange two-legged human of being an enemy just waiting to murder a native and his people. Sometimes, too, as is the case in underdeveloped countries, administering authorities, hungry for capital to keep their treasury afloat, distort reality, a fact that would come as a shock to the world's do-gooders, who are often the keepers of the purse. Such "armchair administrators" can be found in any of the world's cities, sitting in their easy chairs, with a policeman on every other corner guarding their lives and property. These ill-advised officials are just as surely responsible for the murders of people like Baum as the Kukakukas and other club-wielding savages.

Baum was an idealist about the natives. He carried a couple of shotguns with which to shoot game for his boys and himself but never allowed his boys to keep a gun in their leaf-covered lean-tos when they camped. He was quite sure that the noble savage would never attack him without provocation. He scrupulously paid for all foodstuffs or services in trade or steel, and in these isolated areas any trade was many times the value of food for a few boys, if indeed there was such a notion of relative values for such unrelated barter articles in New Guinea's remote ranges.

According to the natives, Baum's party had been visited by a few Kukas late in the evening when they were building their camps beside a fast-running mountain stream in the bush-covered ranges. The natives had stayed on until near dark. After telling Baum in sign language that they would bring him some native foodstuffs the next day, they faded into the bush along a faint pad recognizable from the bent-over bushes.

Baum's sleeping arrangement under his eight-by-ten-foot fly was a narrow bed of thin sticks rigged onto the forked saplings holding up the ridgepole of his tent. A piece of canvas for a mattress and his single blanket were all the bed he ever carried. His boys built their open-sided lean-tos from moss-covered saplings. A fine spray of raindrops dribbled through the hurriedly arranged leaf roof. A smoky fire, kept alive only by frequent mouth winding, supplied some warmth and served for cooking facilities. Mountain people, experienced hunters in the ranges above their villages, appeared to be immune to the cold and wet of these bush camps. Baum stowed all his trade, steel knives, and tomahawks, together with his shotguns and cartridges, under his sapling bed before he went to sleep. His confidence in the natives' integrity and goodwill was beyond question. Just at daylight he awoke to find a few Kukas holding small bilums (net carrying bags) of sweet potatoes and waiting at the foot of his bed to barter for beads. These Kukas at the foot of his bed distracted his attention long enough to enable another Kuka, waiting at the other end of his bed, to bring his stone pineapple club down on Baum's head before he could rise. The killer then picked up one of Baum's long trade knives and hacked off his head. In the meantime, the ambushers had closed in on the carriers and clubbed or shot arrows into the now panicked and fleeing Buang boys. A few escaped into the surrounding bush. Had it not been for the irresistible attraction of looting Baum's camp, not one of them would ever have reached a police post in Bulolo to report the incident.

District officer Eric Feldt and patrol officer Nick Penglase spent three weeks tracking down and bringing in the murderers. Their effort involved travel, hardship, and tenacity of purpose equal to any recorded for law enforcement in any part of the world. The murderers were not hanged. They served a term of imprisonment—the first stage in primitive man's introduction to law and order. Baum's body was never found. Only recently (early 1960s) I talked to an old Buang native whose claim to have been in Baum's party may have reflected his anticipation of remuneration for his hearsay account. He was emphatic that Baum had been eaten. The body, according to this informant, had been cut up into small pieces and cooked in short lengths of bamboo which were carried back to the villages for the women and children. Some parts had just been thrown onto hot coals and eaten on the spot half raw.

We knew from our earlier expeditions across New Guinea down the Purari that there must be thousands of still primitive people in the grass-covered ranges and valleys which we hoped to prospect and explore in the not too distant future, finances permitting. The most difficult part of our expeditions was arranging for funding. We could expect no financial assistance from the Administration. The Morobe Goldfields were producing so much gold and so many problems that prospecting was almost a dirty word to the authorities on this side of the island. On the Papuan side, Governor Murray had a soft spot for the "old gully rakers" who had survived the treachery, the ambushes, and the ever-present fear of the silent arrows and murderous spears launched by primitive man. He and his single-file line of foreign natives had to follow in the throes of gold fever. Very often, before the discovery of quinine gave relief and some immunity from malaria fever, he became a semiconscious automaton driven on by an acute combination of both afflictions.

Governor Murray's outposts were under orders to assist prospectors in any way possible by sending carriers for cargo and storing packs on stations to be safe from the ever-present native pilferers while the surrounding country was prospected for gold and other minerals. But on this side of the island prospectors who penetrated into new country did so at their own expense and at their own risk. The Administration insisted on ten firearms and a reasonably well equipped outfit plus some confidence in the white personnel in charge of the venture. New Guinea Goldfields Company of Wau shared my conviction about another Edie Creek-Bulolo River gold show in the still unexplored interior and backed us financially to go and find it.

I had no intention of allowing the present pain in my head or my concern that the still sore, tired, and frightened members of our party should have the nearest medical help in Lae, still a few days' rafting away, to divert me from having a look at the area then labeled "unexplored" on the maps. We were learning in the hard school of experience despite the unfamiliarity of contact with primitives who were seeing whites for the first time. The world has conveniently forgotten that, after the initial shock, primitive people with a history of intertribal war and cannibalism revert to their age-old savagery. They kill if they can or they are killed. The white man's plainly superior possessions are the main incentive; murder is of incidental importance compared with the acquisition of these goods and chattels.

First contact usually elicits undisguised awe and terror, in the absence of a friendly voice speaking the native tongue, followed by stunned silence and tears, dances of what appeared to be joy, and loud, windy speeches by stone-axe-wielding old men who eventually give all and sundry their visions of the encounter. The first contact and pause for a night among new people usually produced a plentiful supply of sweet potatoes, sugarcane, some yams, bananas, and pigs by the dozen. They bartered for almost any article of trade—discarded tins, bottles, or even the colored labels around meat tins; old razor blades or empty cartridge or bullet shells; or a thin strip of colored cloth. The natives considered anything associated with our party to be impregnated with the spirits and magic that apparently protected us as we traveled among their neighbors and hereditary enemies.

From Sodens, a couple of hours' walk through river flats, we reached the now slow-running Watut River, where Mr. Sanson had arranged to have rafts waiting for us. We took the gear and the wounded boys, who were now in good shape. The rest of the party set out on the track to walk to Lae, five days away. Once I was on the raft with my worries past, my reaction set in. My first day was one long headache. Drifting along on the slow current through heavily timbered scrub country, however, I soon recovered and started to enjoy the trip. Ducks, pigeons, parrots, and crocodiles offered plenty of diversion. We camped that night beside the river. We were too tired to worry about the mosquitoes or marauding crocodiles. We caught up on our sleep. We used lawyer cane to lash a log to each side of our raft for more bouyancy and drifted with the slow current. The raft-wise Maralinin boys, wielding their improvised paddles trimmed from bush saplings, fended us off and around the snags waiting to trap us. On the advice of the local natives, we had securely lashed our movable gear to the raft for such emergencies. There was little chance of drowning in this river, but lots of camp gear had been lost on snags, and rafts wrecked in the snag-studded rivers. The torrential downpours and swollen rivers meandering through heavily timbered flats continually undermine banks and trees, which flop into the water to become octopus-armed snags.

We disappointed our river boys by failing to stop with a .32 bullet a large crocodile fifteen to twenty feet long which was sunning itself on a sandbank. Soon thereafter we swept into the Markham River, which runs almost straight in braided streams to the coast. We were now moving much faster than on the Watut, but every so often we picked the wrong stream and found ourselves in ankle-deep channels too shallow for our rafts. We pulled in and camped near Nadzab, the American army air base in World War II, as night fell. The snags made night navigation an impossibility. We had spent more than thirteen hours on the rafts and were glad for a chance to stretch our legs. Before dark a corpse drifted by, whirled along on the fast-running dirty water. We hoped it was not one of our boys. We camped on a high bank in open grass country free of mosquitoes. We left at daylight and pulled into a patch of bush below Nadzab, where the coastal bush country meets the grassy plains, to shoot for our boys a meal of flying foxes, which hung in festoons from trees beside the river. We reached the mouth of the Markham at about noon and left the rafts there. Then we walked into Lae, arriving there at 2:00 P.M. on Thursday, May 14, 1931.

Vic Horsley, the "liklik" doctor (medical aide) who had a hoarse voice and was known by the natives as "Neck-e-fast," looked at the arrow wounds. My rough first aid and natural good health and resistance had almost healed the arrow holes. Although some soreness and stiffness remained, time, the great healer, had repaired Pat's damaged tissues. He immediately began to celebrate on his arrival in Lae and fought the good fight all over again to the accompaniment of war cries as he so ably defended our camp.

In Lae we were greeted by Dan, Pat's and my younger brother, then eighteen years old, who had made his way to New Guinea to help us find El Dorado. However, some months passed before we had enough capital to start out and see what the open grass ranges and wide open valleys held for us. This was the area we had conjured up in our imaginations on the strength of sunlight and blue skies over the ranges beyond Goroka-Bena Bena valleys and the numbers of bodies sailing down the "Marki."

We left for Salamaua, then the main goldfields port, which was a pinnace trip from Lae of about two hours. Salamaua had a doctor and a hospital. None of us required hospitalization, and the only permanent damage any of us suffered involved my hearing in my left ear. Deafness in one ear has its compensations, I discovered; down through the years I have found it a convenient means of escape from bores and borrowers. I have yet to find a hearing aid for my particular disability.

My other brother, Jim, who had been keeping the home fires burning, was at this time on the Bulolo River constructing a water race to supply the hydroelectric power needed to dredge the river flats. We flew into Bulolo from Salamaua with the intention of resting a while with him, but there we learned that our pilot friend Les Trist was missing in a single-engine Junker plane. He had been bringing in a load of cargo from Lae to Wau. His load had included our guns, cameras, and camping gear. Although all available planes and a search party scanned the tree-covered ranges and grass country on the short flight from Lae to Wau, the wreck was never sighted from the air. Weeks later a local native hunting possums and cassowaries in the heavily timbered ranges about halfway between Lae and Bulolo found Les's head. It had been picked clean by bush rodents and was identifiable only by dental fillings. His completely wrecked plane was well hidden from the air by the dense tropical growth, into which he had plunged head-on.

The low, grass-covered Zenag divide, which is 4,000 feet above sea level and separates the inland flowing Snake River from the Wampit, is still the main aerial highway from Lae to Bulolo and Wau. The hot, moisture-laden coastal air blowing up over the divide and meeting the comparatively dry, cool air over the grass country forms a thick fog which blots out the low divide. Les Trist had evidently flown up the wrong gorge. His heavily loaded plane had been unable to rise above the ranges on each side of the now narrowed route. Trist had shared our enthusiasm and perennial urge to have a look over the next hill. In 1930 he flew Mick Dwyer on the first flight from Wau to the Waria River, where I was waiting on a newly cleared landing strip on a grassy terrace near Garaina village. Weaving his way over the range from Wau, Trist had discovered the lake which today bears his name. There were few pioneer pilots intrepid enough to fly the bush-covered ranges at a time when flying itself was a hazard. Les Trist gave us something more than a tangled mass of wrecked plane, rotting away in the fog-shrouded isolation of New Guinea's ranges, by which to remember him.

Bena Bena-Asaro
fighting men
on the prowl.

THE YEAR 1932

The early 1930s were years of active development in the Morobe Goldfields. Bulolo Gold Dredging had pioneered air freighting of heavy machinery from Lae to airstrips hacked out of the jungle along the Bulolo River. New Guinea Goldfields Limited at Edie Creek was developing the hard-rock mines above the fabulously rich streams where miners with primitive box and dish methods were getting 100 to 200 ounces of gold a day. Hydroelectric power was being wired on from Bulolo about twenty miles down the Bulolo River. I took a job with the lineman, Ted Allison, cutting power line posts and hauling them with teams of boys and lawyer cane vines downhill to the places on the line where they were to be erected. Of necessity, we cut them out of timber above their line holes. It would have been impossible to pull them uphill; the power line ran almost straight up over the range.

Wau, the airport for the Edie Creek and Wau area gold workings, was the depot for all cargo flown in from Lae, which was then carried on boys' backs or by mule to Edie Creek eight miles away up a long, steep track that wound around the side of the range. The last couple of miles before the terrain changed to a more gradual grade into Edie Creek, 6,400 feet above sea level, the track degenerated into a series of zigzags up the heavily timbered mountainside. We contracted to deliver to Edie Creek the heavy machinery air freighted to Wau. A narrow two-wheeled cart just wide enough for the heavy compressors and the narrow track was built for the purpose. With more than forty natives and two long ropes we made one trip each day, maneuvering the cart up and around the sharp and narrow zigzags with drops of a few hundred feet alongside.

In October 1932, New Guinea Goldfields Limited decided it might be worthwhile to send its geologist, Kingsbury, out into the newly discovered Highlands to assess its mineral worth. By this time a small airstrip had been cleared on top of a flat, grassy ridge. Not far away Ned Rowland was working a patch of alluvial gold on the headwaters of the Ramu River near present-day Kainantu and was pursuing promising leads of reef formation. Lapumpa was a small plane strip. The aircraft flying in from Lae could carry no more than 350 to 400 pounds of cargo, but they did eliminate the long, hot walk with heavily laden boys from Lae through the jungle-shaded coastal belt, then out along narrow tracks, walled in by high cane grass, into the blazing heat of the open flatlands. Night travel with a hurricane lamp lead as a precaution in case of the sluggish and lethal death adders was always a hazard, but we preferred that risk to the heat of daylight travel.

The fast-running Erap, Ramu, and Leron rivers that braided out across the country were always fordable. The fast-running Umi, concentrated in one boulder-studded channel, was less easy to cross. Even today, trucks loaded for the Highlands are sometimes swept downstream, their cargo destroyed and the vehicles themselves hardly worth salvaging. The climb to the top of the range from the village of Onga, up and down and around narrow native tracks, skirting precipitous gorges, was steep and exhausting. Down below, a highland river thundered along to the low country and over the range to the Highlands. Plentiful supplies of native food, new and interesting natives, and country always made the ascent into the Highlands from the heat and sweat of the low country a pleasure.

With a plane to carry in our supplies, Dan and I left Lae on October 26, 1932, to walk to Lapumpa on the Ramu headwaters. Traveling light and at a leisurely pace, we reached Lapumpa strip on Friday, November 4, and camped alongside the strip to wait for supplies and for geologist Kingsbury and officer Bob White. By November 9 we were ready to start off again along our 1930 track and down into the Purari fall. We prospected the main streams—the Garfatina, Karmarmentina, Dunantina, Bena Bena, and Asaro rivers. The Bena Bena showed promise of being a possible gold dredging area, and plans were made to peg it and fly in drilling gear to test it at depth for gold values. We could get up to half a grain of good-looking gold to a dish in Goretufa Creek, a tributary of the Bena Bena which lay between two rock-walled gorges cut deep in the prehistoric lake bed deposits of the valley. Its yellowness suggested little base metal in its makeup. Some pieces up to a grain and a half, washed from gravel backwashed by flood currents into rock-strewn protected corners, were well worn by the water and had apparently traveled a long way from the source in the parent rocks. My prospector's optimism conjured up another Edie Creek somewhere in the Bismarck Range that walled in the valley on two sides. Some of the feeder streams, still bringing down reworked gravels from a hard-rock-barred plateau high in the bush-covered ranges would lead us to the bonanza of our dreams. All we had to do was to prospect every creek above the old gravel levels of the lake bed. To be sure, we were testing gravels representative of the material eroded and washed down by the drainage channels of that area. To do so we had to cut each stream around the valley, moving up and down over the grass-covered ridges just below the treeline. The barrier was between the invariably hostile camps of the grass-country people and their enemies, who had been driven into the wet and cold timber-covered ranges and were waiting to ambush firewood and building material parties from the warm, open grass country below.

We would finish our present survey and come back after we had put Kingsbury and White safely on the plane at Lapumpa. At

Korofagu village on the Bena Bena, we foolishly camped in a thick clump of trees and high cane grass (pitpit) near the river which we were prospecting. The natives seemed friendly enough but were looking for an opportunity to steal any gear left unguarded. An unguarded axe was too much of a temptation to one of the hundreds clustered around our fishline-fenced camp—a quick grab and he made off with it at a great pace. Immediately the natives rushed away from our camp; this was the usual ending to barter meetings when some avaricious native tried to acquire other people's property at no cost to himself. With a few boys armed with shotguns and rifles, I used sign language to tell the now rather frightened-looking old men who were lurking half hidden just beyond bow-and-arrow range that they should bring back the stolen property. Across the open stretches of the fast-running, shallow river I could see bow-and-arrow-armed reinforcements high-stepping across the river to minimize the splashes of cold water as they forded the stream. Our camp was indefensible in its present position; it was almost walled in with low bush and cane grass. Arrows could rain down on us from three sides and from the high embankment above. I decided to shift the camp onto the high open grass terraces above the river and to move farther downstream to a more easily defended position where our firearms would have the advantage in the open grass country. Any show of retreat is always a bad move in a new country among primitive natives, however. In their eyes, we evidently had no magic or sorcery with which to overwhelm them; we were pulling down our camp and running away from their evidently superior fighting ability.

The camp came down in quick time and was carried onto the high open terrace, but before we could tie up and shoulder our gear, the arrows started to fly. The natives were well out of range of a shotgun but were well within rifle range. Gunfire created a diversion of some consternation, and a bullet wound sent them rushing back to the high grass and bush cover to figure out the mystery of such damage from so far away. Perhaps we really did have a secret weapon which could outrange their best bows. We moved off to put as much distance as we could between Korofagu and our night camp. At dusk we camped above the junction of the Bena Bena and the Asaro (the Garfuku of our 1930 expedition), a much larger river

Bena Bena boy, hair in grease ringlets, gum shell around neck, Jobs lairs, jews harp, wrist gauntlet, plaited cane around waist.

draining the southern side of the valley. A village, Kartu, lay across the river, but a flood-swollen Asaro would discourage any night crossing should the Korofagu people try to enlist the villagers' help to wipe us out and share the loot.

The Korofagu natives did not follow us far downstream, and we saw no sign of them next morning. We crossed the Bena Bena and headed back in a wide circle south of our outward route toward the Ramu. The country here, where all the main streams come together to form the primary headwaters of the Purari River and down which Mick Dwyer and I crossed New Guinea in 1930, is mostly grass-covered ranges. The hot sun made midday traveling rather uncomfortable, and we camped early near the village of Seerupu. Thus far in this new country we had depended on objects and pantomime when we wanted to locate tracks and to learn names of villages, rivers, and mountains. Once we had learned the name of a village by pointing to it and calling the name, we managed to learn the name of the village we were in and any others to which we pointed in the surrounding ranges. We found out the local names of mountains and rivers in the same way, although we found that different people had different names for things.

We camped at Seerupu village, which appeared to be the center of a very big group of natives, all well armed, their skins well coated with pig grease, and smelling as only a stale mixture of human sweat, pig grease, and the influence of the hot sun could smell. We were glad to have our fishline fence around the camp to keep them at a little distance. Dan and I now decided that we would return to this valley. A few local natives who would soon learn enough Pidgin English to become "turnim talks," or interpreters, would make our contact with the different villages much less hazardous and more understandable. We managed by pantomime and sign language to interest two young men in coming with us in the morning on our way back to Lapumpa. Only one of them, Narmu, showed up in the morning. Although he was very definitely nervous about his adventure into the unknown and certainly not encouraged by many wailing relatives, he took his place in the line under the charge of Ewunga, who put a laplap over his native dress and gave him a small pack to put on his back and a billycan to carry, making him "one of the boys."

Narmu's nervousness increased alarmingly once we moved out of his stamping grounds. The Mainhaline people who attempted to take him from us had to be repulsed by rifle fire. I felt sure that he would have bolted back home but for Ewunga's watchfulness. Our boys were also very interested in attracting a line of camp followers and interpreters to carry their packs and help with the camp chores. We camped again at Epunka, now Henganofi Police Post. Narmu was immediately recognized as an enemy and therefore as fair prey. Narmu was terrified and so were we. If anything had happened to him now to prevent us from delivering him safely back to his people, nothing would convince them that we had not killed and eaten him. Rather than inspiring confidence, we would become objects of suspicion. Any future prospecting or exploration of the country farther on would probably become much more difficult, if not impossible, with our small force and arms. Accordingly, we placed Narmu under double guard all night and tied his hand to Ewunga in the morning to prevent him from bolting in panic once we reached the no-man's-land area between villages. We then saw another trait of primitive natives. The next villagers, seeing Ñarmu being led along tied to Ewunga and probably very frightened, made efforts to rescue him as we passed through the villages on route to the Ramu. It was a long, eleven-hour walk from Epunka to Lapumpa, but we still had Narmu with us when we camped on the strip at dusk.

We strapped Narmu into Bob Burgey's small Gipsy Moth plane, head bowed, resigned to his fate. Bob Gurney told us later he perked up and started to look over the side of the open cockpit until the slipstream hit him; after that he kept away from the slipstream. I had sent a note to my old trade store friend, Henry Eekhoff in Lae, Guinea Airway's base, asking him to give Narmu any trade or gear he wanted. Gurney looked after him and with much difficulty he was induced to approach the sea. He was apparently scared by small scuttling crabs and beach life. He even paddled in the salt water, beating a hasty retreat from the small waves breaking on the beach. A taste of the salt water transformed Narmu's fear into intense interest. Here was an unlimited supply of salt, real salt, not the insipid, dirt-colored stuff that his people laboriously manufactured from reeds growing in the swamps. He filled many beer bottles with the precious water and would, if he could, have filled a huge pile of empties as well. To him the sea represented an endless supply of probably the scarcest and most valuable commodity the inland natives know. The coastal people before the coming of the white man always exacted a price from inland traders who came to fill their gourds with sea water. Murders and wars and changes of ownership often occur near inland mineral springs. Even pigs and women take second place to a salt-flavored spring, however poor.

A horse which galloped up with a European in the saddle was a startling event. Narmu could not understand why he was pulled away from the horse's rear end and shown how to stroke his head. He refused to put his hand anywhere near the ferocious-looking mouthful of teeth. He asked for a few hairs out of its tail to take home to show his one-talks how big the white man's pigs grew.

Henry Eekhoff gave him bright red laplaps, white cotton singlets, knives, a tomahawk, a bright empty flour tin in which he packed beads, shells picked up from the beach and a couple of metal jews' harps, which were far superior to the natives' own bamboo harps. Bob Gurney's wild man created a furor among the natives in Lae. His hair remained rather smelly from rancid pig grease and a bit of fur-covered opossum tail still dangled from his ear lobes. He had discovered that wooden matches made quite good plugs for the holes around his nose tip, the still live red tops forming a semicircle around his nose. His rather tattered wrist band, frayed from the impact of his fighting bowstring, testified to his warrior status and to service in numerous intertribal wars. The natives of Lae imagined Narmu a ferocious man-killing cannibal who might even now be looking over their stamping grounds with an eye to future forays. They were intensely interested but left him severely alone. Narmu had no qualms next morning about climbing into the plane. He saw his gear safely stowed away, and he fumbled with his safety belt, trying to fasten it around him. He did not understand its purpose, but knew that the white man wanted it fastened. So far he had rather liked the white man's sometimes incomprehensible foibles. He was disappointed at being able to bring with him only two bottles of salt water; he would have stacked them on the wings had he been allowed!

Narmu's return trip with us back to his place was a triumph all the way, and he played it for all it was worth. He had seen things and done things no tribal warrior had ever done, and he had the evidence to prove it. We could follow his lectures to his now enraptured and fascinated enemies. A straw dipped into one of his precious bottles was passed around for tasting, but some of the older men evidently suspected this of being an artfully contrived plot to poison them and refused to taste.

Stone Age man becomes overwhelmed by the European's seemingly endless and startlingly complex appurtenances—bits of sticks that spurt fire when scratched on a box, food that tastes awful to them, hard sticks with holes in them that can put holes in ten of even their best wooden shields held farther away than any bow can shoot an arrow. Salt they understood, being salt hungry as only inland natives can be. Sugar was of no interest; they had it in its original form. The horse's tail hairs were fingered and smelled and discussed for hours. Although Narmu in his white singlet and red laplap, with his large bright flour tin holding his collection of trade, his new steel axe, and his long shiny bush knife held the crowd's interest, we never allowed him to go too far away from our camp during the day and saw that he was well guarded on the camps back to his own place. We still had to deliver him safely back to his village and people, complete with his treasures.

En route we passed through the village area of the Mainhaline people, who met us waving leafy shrubs as a peace sign and claimed that some of Narmu's people had called on them to rescue Narmu from us. We watched one bright young warrior who had a graze across the ribs from a rifle bullet. Narmu's adventure became again the main topic of conversation and he the center of interest. We had to chase them home at dusk to guard against any treachery to Narmu's person or to his possessions. Next morning practically the whole male population of the village wanted to come with us to carry packs or work, anything for the laplaps that would make them members of the party. We selected a couple of young men who would quickly pick up our Pidgin English and who by traveling with us would see for themselves the innocuous purpose of our excursions into their country.

Narmu was accorded a vociferous reception from his people, in which we also shared. They became very affectionate and demonstrated their feelings by mauling us all over. It took lots of warm water and soap to get rid of the aftereffects. We resisted a shoulder-high parade around the camp area, much to the relief of some of our Waria boys, whose faith in the trustworthiness of primitive people did not permit them to feel comfortable when they were surrounded by excited natives and cut off from our firearms, although our heavy .45 revolvers would have been most effective at close quarters.

The next morning was a repetition of the day before; dozens of natives wanted to come with us. Narmu decided to rest on his fame and enjoy the interest and attention which his account of the trip to Lae would command for many days and the pig feasts which would be held in his honor. We selected a couple of his friends, and after traveling to what we considered to be their boundary, we shooed all the relatives, friends, and very eager adventurers back home. From high ground or a ridge, a few watched our progress toward the next village from high ground or a ridge, started a smoky grass fire, and then yodeled news of our progress toward their own village. This custom proved to be a great help in contacting chronically suspicious villagers and made our approaches entirely free from the consequences of a surprise appearance in their country. We cut the headwaters of the streams coming in off the southern fall of the Bismarcks well above the old lake bed gravels, automatically increasing our camp followers by one or two of the most obviously intelligent and adventurous young warriors and now and again a redskinned fight leader who could with safety go only a couple of villages away from his own current allies.

We noticed quite a number of redskinned natives, not albinos, and many men with plenty of authority who were nervous and abrupt in their talk and movements. They were the ones we propitiated. The natives responded with shocked amazement when we entered their barricaded villages without fear. Firearms meant nothing to them: we appeared to have no weapons. They therefore suspected us of possessing unknown and fearful magic and we did nothing to disabuse them of the idea. We never approached waving a handful of leaves in peace but casually slipped the bowstring off the ever-present bows. This gesture, together with the grass-fire smoke and vociferous sendoff and shouted instructions from the last mob, saw us safely through the next village area. The scene repeated itself from one village to the next. Villagers who brought food to our campsites stayed to sightsee, packed rows deep around our fishline fence. They carried on an animated and general conversation with their one-talks from neighboring villages, who huddled together in their mutual fear of now common enemies.

Judging by the volunteers who wanted to join us when we moved off, we were getting a good press from our local camp followers. We made slow progress along the south side of the Bismarcks, negotiating the numerous creeks from the Bena Bena River up and down from 9,000 to 5,000 feet above sea level, across the steep gashes cut by centuries of swollen drainage channels fed by torrential downpours of rain in the bush-covered ranges above. It was hard going, even with numerous stops to dish prospect every stream. We could get fine colors of gold, but colors could be found in almost any of the streams from the islands east of Samarai in Papua to the Dutch border and meant little in the small creeks where the bottom was exposed in places as the water raced down to the river. We put a deep hole on a river flat near the village of Mahometofe. Familiarity began to breed the contempt that primitive people have for seemingly unarmed and defenseless members of any community outside their own village relatives and allies of the moment. The idea that we wielded magic began to take second place to avarice and acquisitiveness intensified by the uniqueness and evident utilitarian and decorative value of our camp gear. The theft of a knife along a straight stretch of the river gave us a good opportunity to demonstrate the power of the rifle to the gathered hundreds who had scattered from around the camp and were watching to see the outcome of this daring effort to plunder our property.

I started to drop high-powered bullets into the water beside the track and the fleeing thief, who in no time dropped the knife and dived into the pitpit. The knife, tied to the end of a long stick and flashing in the sun, was brought back by a gray-haired old man who was or appeared to be full of apologies. The watching hundreds closed in again to discuss this latest development in a hubbub, each shouting his own version to the countryside. They respectfully patted the rifle of the guard when he was close enough to the fence. They seemed duly impressed.

We cut every stream between 5,000 feet, the floor of the valley, and 7,800 feet, up and down through grass- and bush-covered gorges cut deep by the runoff from tropical rainstorms. There was a fine color from holes where the stream slowed down and flattened out for a hew hundred yards, but there was nothing to encourage intensive prospecting. Goretufa Creek joining the Bena Bena above Korofagu was still the best bet. We cut all its headstreams and followed it down to the wide, comparatively flat hogback ridge, where we would put in an airstrip and establish a base for further probes into the ranges west and southwest.

Firewood and building timber are very scarce on the valley floor, and new growth takes time to reach the harvesting stage if it survives the chronic intertribal wars of death and devastation. Food was abundant on this extremely fertile soil and could be bought for a few shells or bright-colored beads, a pinch of salt, or anything, including bright labels off tins of food. Empty tins or bottles were in short supply and in great demand. Nothing from our camp was valueless, and our boys exploited the fact shamelessly. They got a small pig for a box of matches and eventually the attentions of women. Premarital promiscuity was evidently the custom among these highland people, as the key boys quickly learned.

Although our semisettled camp on the drome area was demarcated by sharpened pickets and long pitpit rails, we had no effective barrier in the event of a massed rush on the camp. The pitpit girls and their relatives began to undermine the exclusiveness of our camp enclosure. Concerned about an eventual threat to the camp, we prohibited all affairs within the camp enclosure and kept a strict watch on the boys' houses, which were pitpit and grass lashed together with a vine similar to kudzu. We prohibited all bows and arrows except in the parking area and insisted that all bowstrings be loosened. Many natives from adjacent hostile villages were arriving, probably under a temporary truce, and the weapons park emphasized our wish for peace. It did not, however, altogether prevent a few skirmishes and ambushes when the time came for natives to return to their villages. Men, women, and children, using sharp digging sticks in relays, soon had the old garden rows and small drains leveled off. Being on a ridge with good drainage, the surface was seasonably hard and was almost ready to receive a light plane near the end of December.

Patrol officer Jim Taylor and some police boys walked in from Kainantu Police Post and back to Kainantu the next day. Jim was one of the very few Administration officials who spoke our language and shared our views about the country over the ranges northwest from the Bena Bena. The densely populated, wide, grass-covered valleys and ridges topped by heavily timbered ranges up to 12,500 feet above sea level must, we were sure, occur again farther on. Sometimes when the morning sun had burned off the cloud cover shrouding the tops of the barrier to the promised land, bright sunlight in a cloudless sky helped us envision our great valley populated by relatives of the numerous bodies Mick Dwyer and I had seen floating down the Wahgi in 1930. Our conjectures contrasted with the jumbled mass of uninhabited ranges thought to be New Guinea's interior. Through a gap in the ranges on a bright clear morning we could see the scarred, rocky tips of a very high mountain from our camp. Its distance and height in comparison to the 10,000-foot-high ranges around the northeast end of the Bena Bena Valley must put it in the 14,000- to 15,000-foot level. Later on, traveling up the Wahgi Valley, we found it was the top peak of Mt. Wilhelm, 15,300 feet above sea level, occasionally snow covered and the northern boundary of the Wahgi Valley. I had seen its snow-covered top from Utu west of Madang in 1929.

The Korofagu people sent word through one of our now Pidgin-speaking followers that they wanted to come up and make peace with us about the theft of a knife earlier in the year. At the time we had shifted our camp to higher ground, a move that the natives interpreted as a retreat and so an invitation to attack. We paid for the casualties in tomahawks and trade and mumued (cooked) a killed pig in a hole lined with banana leaves and filled with hot stones. Under a local truce, these natives became regular visitors and never again underestimated our ability to defend ourselves.

On Christmas Day we had the strip about ready for landing. A heap of dry grass stood at each corner for smoke to signal all ready if and when a plane should come over. Anytime now Guinea Airways should fly over to check the landing strip. At about 10:00 A.M. we heard a plane approaching, and we scrambled to light the corner fires. Every local native promptly disappeared into the high grass and pitpit on both sides of the strip. Even our camp followers were tempted to join their one-talks. Their mentors reassured them, however, and they stayed in the camp area. A Gipsy Moth piloted by Bob Gurney and with Jim Taylor on board made a couple of low runs over the strip and dropped a Christmas cake, which disintegrated into acceptable crumbs. Gurney then decided to try a landing.

It was always an ordeal for us to watch an initial landing on a bush strip leveled off with sharp sticks and bare feet. We were petrified with fear and hoping that the plane would stay on its wheels once on the ground. Bob made a good landing, bumped a couple of hundred yards, and pulled up and swung around to taxi back to the camp on the side of the strip. We first took the pilot on a tour to inspect the strip so that we could shift responsibility for future landings onto his shoulders. By this time the locals were emerging from their hiding places and, reassured by our boys, were rather hesitantly approaching the plane, whispering assurances to each other but ready to stampede again should it make any move, suspicious or otherwise.

The natives regarded Bob Gurney and Jim Taylor with apprehension until physical contact had established that they were human beings, like us, and male human beings at that. We heard muttered the obscene greeting that they would like to eat the excreta and genitals of these visitors from the sky. The natives viewed the plane from a safe distance but could not be induced to touch it. They scattered to their hiding places with hands over their ears when the engine started and watched in amazement when it raced along the drome and took off. Gurney circled and flew back over the strip, causing them to rush back into their hiding places. The more courageous natives then stood up and watched in wonder as the plane gradually disappeared over the grass ranges and headed back to the Ramu. Geologist Kingsbury from New Guinea Goldfields Limited in Wau flew in on December 30. After looking over the river flats and some dish prospects from holes sunk in the gravel beds of the river, he went back to Wau to confer with his principals on his observations.

Guvaso, one of my key boys and a former police boy, and some of our other boys were surrounded and fired on by the Segosia people, who lived in a well-fortified village right on top of the high ridge above us at about 6,000 feet above sea level. None of the arrows hit anybody; this was the usual preliminary effort by primitives to test the fighting spirit of strangers in their area and the power of our weapons. Guvaso, who was in charge of the party, fired a few shots and answered all their queries. We sent word that we could not tolerate such episodes. We had no doubt that the experiment was being observed by the hundreds of natives who kept tabs on all camp activities from daylight until they were shooed home at dark. Any relaxation of our survival vigilance, including immediate acceptance of a challenge to our locally endowed supernatural powers, could bring a concerted assault on our small fenced-off outpost. We looked like easy meat. These people were cannibals, although the heavily timbered ranges above abounded in opossums, bush fowls, large carpet snakes, and other animals, all meat to a people hungry for animal protein. Their warring neighbors barred any hunting parties from the low country. A smoke from a warming fire in the high ranges sent an ambush party from the current occupiers of that area. Cannibalism supplied the need for animal protein, although it was subject to some tabus and restrictions; the young men or women were not supposed to eat human flesh. These restrictions simply gave the older men and women a larger share of the meat.

The next day the Segosia congregated on a rise above our camp and, waving bunches of leaves, indicated that they wanted to make peace. We received them not too cordially, as we did not want them to think us more relieved and happy to straighten things out than they evidently were. They brought two pigs, which we killed and cooked, sharing the meal with the donors. They intimated that our firearms were superior to their bows and arrows. To stress the point, we shot the two pigs with a .22 rimfire rifle. Not much noise but two dead pigs. We sacrificed an empty bottle to demonstrate the power of a rifle. It was put up about fifty yards away, and bows and arrows were brought in. Although the archers could hit the bottle, the arrows just glanced off the side. A .32 bullet shattered the bottle completely. Every particle of glass was retrieved and

Outside a cane-barricaded village, Bena Bena-Asaro Valley.

taken home, probably for its cutting value or for its contact with the unseen power that had shattered it.

By this time Dan and I had pegged out reward claims on a short stretch of the Goretufa Creek between the point where it emerged from a confined gorge and the point where it joined the main Bena Bena River. After making the airstrip operational for some of the best bush pilots in the world, we moved our base camp down onto a flat terrace on the claims, cut slots in the soft rock at the mouth of the gorge, and dropped in two pine logs to dam the creek and lift the water into a small race to work the gravels in box-and-dish fashion. A box ten feet long and twelve inches wide was hacked out of a pine log. Crude ripples were made out of pine slats two and one-half inches by one inch nailed one inch apart onto side slats three feet long. These were fitted into the box. A few stones at the top of the box took the gravel carried in dishes, and water from the race ran into the box, which was rigged on a one-in-twelve angle along the creek. We had entered the alluvial mining business.

A couple of old men brought a wife along for Naraward, one of our boys. Evidently negotiations had been going on between our boys and the locals for some time. With "marys" (women) in the line of carriers and boss boys, new people could assume that we were not looking for trouble but came in peace. A long line consisting only of men, although not armed with conventional spears, bows and arrows, or stone clubs, was always suspect to the bowstring-happy primitives, conditioned as they were to the incessant struggle for survival.

My brother Jim flew in with Bob Gurney on January 13, and we put down a few prospecting holes in the Bena Bena gravels. The dish prospects from the holes looked good enough to us for large-scale exploitation by dredges. Jim took back samples of the dish prospects with him to Major Harrison, New Guinea Goldfields' manager in Wau. Our mining in the Goretufa produced six and eight pennyweights in the first two days of boxing. The values on the bottom would determine whether we should continue. It does not improve the large-scale dredging prospects on the river flats. I always regard a rich feeder stream or streams as a guarantee of workable values in potential dredging areas. Still, mining is a gamble, and prospectors, whether individuals or organizations, must be chronic optimists.

New Guinea Goldfields in Wau were good prospectors. Charlie Marshall, chief surveyor, and Ken Spinks, his assistant, were sent out to peg the dredgeable area. They were interested in putting down test bore holes below the watertable level to test for values, depth of gravel, and bedrock qualities with a view to bucket dredging. Ian Grabowsky flew a Moth plane in with Marshall, and we spent a couple of busy days pegging the Bena Bena River flats from its junction with the Asaro up the Bena Bena above Goretufa Creek.

Ian Grabowsky, or "Grab," as we soon called him, became an enthusiastic supporter of our plan to have a look over the ranges to the northwest and promised any support that he could give as

Guinea Airways' chief pilot. New Guinea Goldfields put Dan and me and our boys back on the payroll, thus making it possible to plan an expedition into unexplored country beyond the northwest ranges. They also promised us £10,000 cash for each and every dredge required to dig the Bena Bena-Asaro gravels should the values warrant exploitation. In the end, they did not. Today they are a never ending source of income for the thousands of local natives who have the energy to work the gravels, but few can sustain that energy. As we worked to eliminate the potential auriferous streams and peg out dredging leases, members of various villages along our route attached themselves to us. We became more or less accepted inhabitants of the valley and were able to look after ourselves and our people quite competently. Thus we survived and became the subject of village conspiracies that sought to use our superior arms to annihilate age-old enemies. The natives understood that we wanted to be friends with everybody and that any natives in our line who wore a laplap rather than the bark, sweat- and grease-impregnated native dress represented one of our party and as such would be defended by us. Still, this did not eliminate wishful plans to recruit us as involuntary allies. One day as we returned to our base camp after a prospecting trip, the Sayonofe people met us in full war gear, warming up their courage with battle songs. We discovered before any hostilities started that another village, Mahometofe, had convinced the Sayonofe that we were now allies of Mahometofe and had been paid in pigs, food, and women to clean them out. They were sure that the Mahometofe were in the offing, ready to come in to loot and destroy their village and murder anyone unfortunate enough to be caught.

We squared off to the Sayonofe people and sent the marauding Mahometofes running with a few shots over their heads. The Mahometofes were apparently left quite happy to search for ways and means to be more convincing in their efforts to convert us to their mercenary plans. Baranuma, a former police boy, and some of the line boys were fired on by the Kropar people. Towa, a Waria boy, was hit in the shoulder with an arrow. We understood that this was just another test from still another village, but to ignore a challenge by primitive people is to invite extinction, and we knew we must respond immediately to avert full-scale war.

We doubled our night watch and issued extra ammunition. Our old Warias were emphatic that there would be an early morning attack and herded our local boys into one of the grass-and-stick houses as a precaution against arrow wounds. Daylight came without an attack. We decided to investigate the unwarranted hostility. The villagers were ready for us in ambushes on all approaches to the pitpit-surrounded barricaded village. We avoided ambush by approaching from a high ridge above the village, closing in from above, and following spurs down toward the village. With a few shots we flushed the warriors from their high grass hiding places. They paused briefly to shoot arrows at us as they stampeded back to their village. Through our local boys we eventually contacted some of the fight leaders and old warriors, who were very voluble in their explanations of the preceding day's unprovoked attack on Baranuma and Towa's party. A few of the young men had evidently resented our seeming indifference to their village and felt that we had slighted their status as an important fighting group in that area. Some of these young men had taken the opportunity to demonstrate their resentment when Baranuma and company encroached on their stamping ground. But the episode was all in a spirit of good clean sport, and no deep hostility was involved; we should not take a few arrows shot in our direction very seriously. We were beginning to agree.

But we could not take any risks—the thin line between good clean sport and complete extinction was very tenuous and did not give us the margin we required for survival. The locals' barricades, ever-present bows and arrows, and expertise with their weapons did not suggest that any use of arms was casual. We decided to investigate and meet each challenge as it came along. Our experience with Kukakuka treachery was still too vivid for us to be readily misled by inexperienced outsiders. We had by now rather many dependents, and we knew that the "Noble Savage" ideal was (and still is), under a very thin veneer of civilization.

We were surviving by virtue of our presumed magic, our superior mentality, and our firearms, in that order. The magic was not a permanent attribute. It was called into question when natural avarice and our apparent trust encouraged the old men and young warriors to huddle in small groups, earnestly discussing ways and

Yomo village, Chuavi area, limestone wall in background.

means to take over our camp. The loot was unique and the human material in tribal payback an added incentive. Eternal vigilance was the price of our survival.

Dan and I decided to look over the range to the northwest to see whether our sunshine valley existed or whether New Guinea's interior was really a vast jumble of bush-covered ranges. Marshall, New Guinea Goldfields' surveyor, decided to come with us to plot our route for Major Harrison. We were ready for departure early in February but needed more guns to leave with Ken Spinks and Jim at the base in case there was trouble while we were away. We proposed to make a wide circle, come back down into the headwaters of the Asaro, and return to our base on Bena Bena airstrip. Orm Denny brought in the single-engine Junker plane on Sunday with

Crowd around fishline fence at camp on Marifutiga River.

the extra guns and a local native, Hegegee-hegegee, whom we had sent out to see the wonders that Narmu had inspected a few weeks earlier. The plane made a forced landing on the outward trip on a kunai strip near the Markham River. It was a rough landing, but Hegegee-hegegee, who was a bright boy and full of enthusiasm, hopped out, thinking that the landing had been correct.

We crossed the Asaro, which we had called the Garfuku in 1930, with difficulty. It was in flood, and none of our local natives could swim. They were terrified of water in any shape or form, and we had to ferry every one of them across individually, clinging to one of our boys. We camped on the top of the grass-covered range 7,800 feet above sea level. Hundreds of natives met us and escorted us to the top of the ridge 8,300 feet above sea level, the easiest place to defend should this mob turn hostile. We were a short walk from the main village, and every man, woman, and child appeared to be around the fishline fence when pandemonium broke out. We thought, "Here it comes," but while everybody had been visiting us, a couple of the neighbors had sneaked into the village and skewered an old chap with barbed arrows. We were urged to join in the chase but could not be persuaded to interfere. We expected to head in that direction the next day and did not want a hostile reception from the killers, nor did we want to interfere or take sides in the age-old feuds. We explained that we just wanted to wander through the country, washing the stones in the creeks and rivers and looking for bits of metal to put in our teeth. Personal adornment made lots of sense to these colorful people, who were much given to decorating their persons with the scintillating plumage of New Guinea's birds of paradise and the no less brilliantly plumaged parrots. Fortunately, I was able to display a gold-filled tooth to back up our story. I called a halt to the demonstration when some old lapuns wanted to explore my mouth with their fingers, which had presumably never been washed. We trekked down a kunai spur toward the sloping side of the long limestone escarpment we had seen northwest from our 1930 trip down the Purari River and turned west through a gap along the foot of the slope. From the top of another grass-covered spur I looked into the Promised Land.

Beyond the thickly populated grass ridges in front of us stretched a wide, flat, grass-covered valley with clumps of trees planted by wood-hungry villagers. The western end was lost in the blue haze of distance and smoke from the hundreds of villages, new garden clearings, and grass fires. Could this be the country drained by the Marki we saw in 1930? If so, it is the main headwaters of the Purari River, which cuts across New Guinea and is its third largest stream. New Guinea's unknown interior was not, after all, an uninhabited jumble of cloud-shrouded mountain ranges but the most thickly populated and fertile area in New Guinea and, as we now know, supports in an eternal spring climate the most colorful and decorative primitives in the world.

We followed a native track down the ridge to where the stream disappeared into an underground channel in the limestone and found the usual well-armed first line of village defense waiting for us. No invaders had ever before walked into these villages without a fight, and the inhabitants were not sure that we should be allowed to break their age-old security rule. I have always found it safe to ignore any uncertainty and keep going before primitive minds have time to react in their accustomed ways.

Bellowed instructions came from the crowd that saw us off a safe distance from our new contacts. The new crowd, seeing that we carried only rifles—in their eyes mere sticks—broke off sticks and shouldered them, marching with us to their village. The mouth of a large limestone cave with stalactites dangling from the roof in long strips gave us an opportunity to show them what the sticks on our shoulders could do. We snapped off a few, and the reverberations from the rifle shots appeared to impress them. They put down their sticks, took a hard look at our firearms, accompanied us to their lookout boundary, and bellowed the news to their neighbors on their watch posts across a deep gulley.

We were met by hundreds of fine-looking people who timorously shouted the greeting "Wendoulee" at us. Beside a shallow, fast-running river, the Marifutiga, on an open flat near the spot where the Chuavi Police Post stands today, the Marli, as the natives pronounced its abbreviation, drained the southern side of the dividing range from the Asaro. The shrub- and grass-covered ranges, right up to the 9,000-foot frost level, were thickly populated by a friendly, rowdy, virile people. Some had mops of frizzed-out hair, in contrast to the greasy ringlets of the Asaro-Goroka people, and some were tattooed on the face and arms, so that they resembled the natives around Port Moresby. Their dress differed from that of the Gorokas. They wore a string sporran with long, wide dracena leaves tucked under a hard, narrow bark belt as a rear covering, and the usual string bilum over their backs for their extra arrows and bit of personal gear. Their noses, pierced in two to five places, held pieces of cooked sweet potatoes, sugarcane, bright-colored feathers, shaped bones, bamboo, or pieces of the conus shell passed through the septum. In no time people surrounded our camp by the hundreds, screaming their impressions to anyone not already busy screaming his own. A match struck a light on a rough surface and instantly silenced the chatter. Some natives put a finger out to see if it was real fire.

Our dogs, we were pleased to see, terrified them, particularly

Snowy, a short, blocky cross between a bulldog and a bull terrier but with the bulldog's wide head and compact build. Snowy was a most amiable animal until he was aroused. His best act, and I think he looked forward to it, was shooing the last of the sightseers from around the camp back to their villages, always a safe distance from the camp. He could be snoozing peacefully all day, just and only just tolerating the noisy rabble and the strange but rather attractive odors that went with them, when the time came to send the last of the sightseers home. We needed all the goodwill we could get for tomorrow's yodeled and shouted introductions to the next village group assembled on a boundary lookout. Snowy knew his stuff. It was necessary only to wake him up a bit and take a firm grip on his collar to pave the way for his act. He would then contort his never very handsome bulldog face into a most ferocious and terrifying aspect, send forth blood-curdling howls of apparent hate, and strain on his collar, pulling me toward the now stampeding warriors and apparently intent on tearing them apart. He was released when they were well scattered. Snowy never bit anyone in these stampedes, but his compact form zigzagging through fast-moving bodies sent them home with the impression that, even though we appeared unarmed, Snowy and Darky would always be there to contend with.

We picked from a native's belt an almost transparent dark green colored stone axe. The stone was fitted into the usual L-shaped holder with the side pieces of shaped timber extended to balance the heavy stone blade and bound into a strong compact working tool with orchid cane vines. It was sharpened on the bevel and differed from any of the floater rocks in the streams we had prospected. The locals pointed west toward the huge valley we had seen from the divide—another incentive for us to find out what minerals, if any, this apparently igneous rock promised us farther west.

We were "Wendouleed" into and out of each village group as we slowly climbed back up the dividing range above the Marli. At one place we picked up a fine-looking, very self-possessed warrior named Lobo-na-gui. We nicknamed him "Lobo." Lobo was one of those natives whom everybody appeared to know and to respect. His movements were quick, definite, and decisive. He was the fastest and most accurate archer we had seen, and he decided we needed him to manage our travels in this risky country. His shouted requests for food and firewood brought immediate responses, and for hours he harangued assembled villagers sitting quietly around our fishline fences. He answered all questions most decisively. I never did find out what he said, but he was certainly a personality in the area. Lobo came as far as his safety allowed, and he slipped away one night from a cold camp 7,800 feet above sea level, taking a steel tomahawk and a few beads we had given him. He was seen off by the watch boys and later became a good friend, philosopher, and guide whenever we were in his district. His philosophy became much too precipitate and bloodthirsty once we had left his sphere of influence and friends. He reckoned "open season" on any man, woman, or child outside his people. Lobo fully appreciated the power of firearms.

At 8,000 feet a heavy hailstorm hit us and pounded fine damp mist right through our fly and tent. At that altitude it was cold enough, even in the tropics, but the icy wind that accompanied the hail did not discourage the entranced sightseers huddled around our camp under their karuka or pandamus leaf capes. They sat out the storm, and when we shooed them home at dusk they just shook themselves and bounded off down their steep slippery track to the village. They were a tough people. We dropped down about 2,000 feet into a deep, timber-covered gorge along a wet slippery native track which from years of sharp stick-dug footholds and eroding rainwater was more deep trench than track. On top again we were piloted through a long row of village houses built on the top of the ridge for defensive purposes. A deep, wide trench had been dug at the approaches to each end of the village. A long log served as a bridge before the barricaded entrance. This was the last line of defense in the survival wars.

We crossed back into the headwaters of the Asaro at 9,100 feet above sea level. With a tight line to keep us together through the heavy cloud cover that shrouded the top of the divide, we slipped and fell down another trenchlike track through the clouds to a magnificent view of the Goroka Valley beneath us. We walked right into a massed sing-sing beside the Asaro and were well received by hundreds of decorated natives, who crowded around to examine the strange intruders. The line boys were plied with cooked pork, kaukau, taro, and the native asparagus.

The place where in 1930 we had broken through a gap in the range to leave this valley and go over the Bismarcks down to the Ramu River could be seen on the opposite side. These people must have heard about white skins and were friendly. Not wanting to push our luck too far, however, we crossed the river and camped on an open terrace overlooking the river. The river gravels looked promising, but a color or so right off the bottom was disappointing. El Dorado must be over the range in the sunshine valley into which we had looked.

Hundreds of rather cheeky young sing-sing-decorated warriors were on hand the next morning to test us but were too uncertain of our defensive power to open with their arrows. A few stones were thrown into a creek as we crossed it, and Charlie Marshall was hit with a rock. We immediately turned off the flat and up a knife-edged spur which gave us rifle control from all sides. Once we had reached the open grass terrace, no further attempts were made to start a brawl.

We pushed on down the valley, up and down the gullies out through the flat terraces, into country we had crossed in 1930. The people were friendly, and there was plenty of native food. The Ma-hometofe (west) people tried to persuade three of the young men who had joined our party higher up the valley to go with them to their village nearby. They were so obviously afraid of the Ma-hometofes that we refused to allow them away from the tent in which they were huddled. During the night the watch boys disturbed a nocturnal visitor. We let Darky, one of our really mean watchdogs, off the chain and he promptly drove him off. These people were really afraid of dogs. Darky was not very large, but he hated any native who did not wear a laplap. He could tolerate even the smell of stale pig grease under a laplap but would swing on one of the numerous dangling pieces of bark cloth on any local who approached the line boys on the march.

We met Jim Taylor, who had flown in from the Ramu Police Post and was doing a look-see patrol up the valley. He had at last persuaded the Administration to show some interest in this new highland country, which was thought to hold great promise for the future of New Guinea. Even if no gold or mineral deposit was initially found, high-priced tea and coffee could be grown here, as they were in the Kenya highlands. We told him of the great valley to the west, and he immediately decided to persuade the Administration in Rabaul to allow him to accompany us. We reached our Bena Bena base camp at 11:00 A.M. on Monday, February 2, 1933.

Our party consisted of New Guinea Goldfields' manager, Major Harrison, Dan, Jim, Ken Spinks, and Ian Grabowsky, who piloted the single-engine Junker plane. We flew out from Bena Bena at 9:40 A.M. on Wednesday, March 8, 1933, approximately west-northwest over and across the Asaro-Marifutiga divide and the thickly populated ranges we had crossed on foot the previous month, and up the wide limestone escarpment into the Wahgi Valley. We confirmed that the Wahgi River, flowing southeast through the ranges in a series of tremendous gorges after it meandered through the valley above, was the Marki which we had seen running into the Purari in 1930.

Before us lay the thickly populated valley supplying the apparently never-ending stream of bloated corpses we had seen floating down the river in 1930.

Here was another ideal gold-saving valley; any gold shed into these streams would still be here. It would not have been scoured out by frequent floods or swiftly running streams. We remembered the beautiful, greenstone axe the natives were using at the eastern end of the valley. The long grass-covered mountaintop which from the air appeared to form the western end of this valley and which later we erroneously decided must be the Mt. Hagen that Dr. Behrmann had seen in 1912 from the Sepik River appeared to be distinctly volcanic. Its symmetrical sides, if they had continued to a point of intersection, would have made it a 20,000-foot-high mountain in the ages of its activity. Looking down from the plane the valley fulfilled and exceeded the optimistic hopes of even a gold prospector. Bounded on both sides by towering mountain ranges up to 15,300 feet above sea level and twenty to thirty miles wide, the river meandered through the intensely populated grass-covered flats and terraces surrounded by distinctive gardens laid out in checkerboard squares with numerous thickets of cultivated yar trees, the natives' source of firewood and building material. We saw no natives; all were hidden from the strange and disturbing visitors who roared in swift travel up and then back down their valley to disappear over the ranges whence they had come.

Plans to explore and prospect this new area were entirely approved by Major Harrison. In the meantime, New Guinea Goldfields had flown in drilling equipment with Joe Sands, an old mining man, who was in charge of the drilling job. We managed to half float and half drag suitable lengths of rather crooked logs for the derrick legs, cut from the few yars growing beside the creeks that had survived the years of grass fires by virtue of their almost inaccessible position in the gorges or slip country, where grass is sparse and provides little heat for a tree-destroying fire. The eight-foot by six-foot sills were pitsawed out of pine logs after they had been maneuvered through the gorge of the Goretufa to a pitsaw platform built beside the stream. Sands rigged the drill and had it going before we started off into the west-southwest again.

The locals, or Bena Bena people, as we called them, had by now decided that we were a valuable asset to their district. Accordingly, they inundated us with food and pigs bartered for shell, beads, and steel. After observing their adornments, we brought in large white gum shells, spotted gum shells, the small cowrie, and the small tambu shell, which was the gold currency of the whole of New Guinea. These were avidly snapped up and then traded out to the surrounding shell-starved people at many times the price. The Bena Bena airstrip became an important trading center. We bought all we could, but we would have needed a couple of planeloads of shell and trade a day to keep up with the barter goods brought in by the trade-starved people. We sent a few of the young men out by plane to see the outside world and bring back stories they could tell their friends. Esagoer, a bright little chap, went back with Jim, who was constructing a road from Wau to Edie Creek. Esagoer's first trip in a truck must have been something of a disappointment. After Jim had driven him a few hundred yards down the road from his camp, Esagoer nudged him and wanted to know when the truck was going to take off. Airplanes represented his only known means of transport!

By this time some of our line boys had acquired brides, readily arranged by their trade-conscious men, and the pitpit girls were making great inroads into the precious stocks of shells and beads we were building up for the big push west. It was impossible to stop them from practicing the oldest profession in the world, preserve our trade goods, and avoid the most widespread cause of war. Seeing we could not stop it, we had to control the traffic. After discussion with our key boys, who knew what the consequences would be if the disgruntled father or brother of a touted daughter or sister did not get paid for his liaison efforts, we insisted that all liaisons be cleared with one of us to make sure that there was no rape. Our key boys also agreed that claimed abuses of this arrangement should be investigated by the key boys, with Dan or myself acting as referees. Penalties were rather severe—up to twenty strokes with a cane, administered by one of the boys themselves. This arrangement worked well enough. There was never any need for it to be otherwise, but the next year when Dan and I were prospecting the country to the southeast of Mt. Hagen, an old chap suddenly stormed into the camp enclosure and made a swing at one of the watch boys with his stone axe. The other watch boy was ready to shoot him, suspecting an attack. I happened to see the old man coming, however, and knew that he was alone. Some of our boys grabbed the old chap. Through interpreters from Mt. Hagen whom we had with us, we learned that his daughter had been raped by three of our boys. We calmed him down, and I lined up all our boys. The old boy then brought his daughter along to identify the culprits. She put the finger on three of our key Waria boys, and we put it up to the rest to decide punishment. They asked Dan and me to administer it, which we did. The natives immediately became sorry and asked that we stop. The incident was not so very important. After it was over, however, I gave the father a gold lip shell, a fabulous present in that society, and the girl a handful of small shells. Everybody appeared satisfied at our very proper sense of propriety and concern with preserving female chastity. Everyone crowded around the wronged father and daughter to examine and comment upon the magnificent payoff. Our camp believed that we had impressed these primitive people with the white man's integrity and justice and that our example of justice would long be remembered by these primitives. The next morning the old men brought along all the female youth and beauty of the village and said that if we had any more gold lip shells we could rape the lot.

Jim Taylor was anxious to have a look at the new country and chartered Tommy O'Dea, one of New Guinea's pioneer pilots, to fly over the valley from Bena Bena. Tommy had a DH 50 with wide tires that enabled him to use rain-softened strips. On Monday, March 27, 1933, Taylor, Spinks, Dan, and I flew out over the Wahgi again. In the clear morning air we confirmed our earlier opinions of the valley and became more enthusiastic than ever to prospect and explore it. We were ready to start the next day.

Leahy and Taylor
(Administration)
line leaving Bena
Bena drome,
March 28, 1933.

THE YEAR 1933

We moved out from Bena Bena airstrip at daylight on Tuesday, March 28, 1933, with our key boys and some of their wives, who decided that camp life was much more attractive than their villages with the constant threats of ambush and open wars. Those of our camp followers who understood and spoke Pidgin English made communication with the local people much easier. Their "place talk" was not understandable to the natives on the Marifutiga fall, but in time, with a chain of interpreters, we could communicate with most of them. We collected a few more "turn-im-talks" for our interpreter chain as we progressed through the country. The malaria-free highland people appeared to be much more intelligent and learned camp duties and Pidgin quicker than any of the coastal people I had known. Jim Taylor's party of police boys, carriers, and camp followers, with ours, made up an invasion force that seemed rather terrifying to primitives, who became suspicious of any long line of male marchers openly and purposefully walking into their domain. I am sure that the absence of bows and arrows, spears, and the shouted sendoffs from villages as we passed out of their territory, plus the presence of unarmed and undecorated men and women, saved us many introductory skirmishes as we progressed over the ranges and up the valley.

It took us almost two hours to move the line and cargo across the Asaro. This was the wet season in the Highlands, a bad time to start an expedition into this country of fast-running rivers and very slippery native tracks, but the country was open, sparsely timbered grass ridges except when the track led over the uninhabited, heavily timbered, cloud-shrouded ranges. Our boys were enjoying every moment. They had never been the centers of so much interest, they had never seen so much pig and so much food generally, and they had servants to do all the hard work of carrying their packs and doing camp jobs. They shamelessly exploited the shell- and trade-starved natives in barter for their beautifully worked bird of paradise, parrot, and cassowary feather headdresses. The colored labels from meat tins or bottles were eagerly accepted in trade.

We climbed the range out of the Asaro-Goroka Valley and crossed over into the Marifutiga-Wahgi fall at 8,200 feet above sea level and about 3,000 feet above the Goroka Valley floor. We took a more direct route over the steep ranges up and down the natives' trenchlike tracks in the general direction of our previous camp on the Marli, near today's Chuavi Police Post. We were welcomed back again by the hundreds of excited natives who had seen us before and hundreds more who apparently broke down traditional tabus and barged into enemy territory to see the sights. Our friendly invasion of this country with articles, implements, and white skins created enough interest to overshadow their individual animosities and served to weld them into one great group of amazed humanity. These people could not decide whether to laugh or cry, were at once terrified and amused, and were ready to stampede the moment anyone in our party made a suspicious movement.

Above the continuous chatter of the hundreds around the fishline fence came a voice from the top of a grassy knob. It stilled their noise, and Lobo literally stormed into the camp. He was welcomed by us all and was escorted into the inner sanctum, where he promptly took over. From the inside of the fence he harangued the crowd and laid down the law. We told him in sign language to come with us, indicating all our line and pointing in the direction of the northwest. We pointed to the sun and, with a hand on the side of our head and eyes closed, indicated with clenched fists brought together six or seven times that we would be away sixty or seventy days, or sleeps. Lobo had made up his mind before he arrived in the camp; he was not going to miss another opportunity to see the world in such apparently safe company. He would learn the magic secrets we evidently had, and God help his local enemies then. He would probably have become the Genghis Khan of New Guinea but for civilization's eventual establishment of a police post in his domain. He selected a few of his young men and insisted they have their hair trimmed coastal style. After a thorough washing in soap and water, they were free of all traces of pig grease and stale sweat for the first time in their lives. They were an attractive, smiling, willing people and, once out of their area, more interested in camp safety than our boys. They were closer to the hazards of survival in their primitive environment than we were.

From this camp we turned and went up the limestone corridor toward the northwest and to a country and people who had never seen or heard of white skins before, up and down along slippery native tracks studded with white limestone boulders with the whole countryside in an uproar. Groups of awed and curious people peered at us from the cover of prolific gardens and ornamental shrubs fenced against village pigs, which were led around on a bark rope tied to a front leg. We camped on a rise in a patch of yars but could not altogether escape from the tall matted pitpit and vines which grew in profusion in this incredibly verdant country. We were immediately surrounded by hundreds of boisterous villagers, who obediently parked their bows and arrows at a distance, as we asked.

The village houses in this country were not tightly grouped and surrounded by a barricade of cane, as in the Goroka Valley. Their houses were much bigger and better built, some round and some long and rounded at each end. They were built of saplings and bound together with vines with a very weatherproof grass-thatched roof, from the top of which as many as four or five long sticks with bunches of leaves, or bits of zamia tops, were tied. They resembled chimney pots. The sides were wide slabs of split timber with a low narrow doorway, through which entrants crawled on hands and knees, and were subdivided into rooms inside. The slow, smoky fires kept the occupants warm and reasonably comfortable if they reclined below the smoke level. Most of the cooking was done outside in a deep hole lined with leaves of the banana or any large bush. The food was layered in with red hot stones, and the top was covered with layers of leaves, grass, and a thick layer of soil. Inside the house a couple of pieces of sweet potato, yam, or green bananas were always cooking to provide a tasty baked snack when the charred outer skin was scraped off. Farther up the valley we heard that these one-door grass houses, their only entrance and exit barricaded to keep the warmth in and nocturnal raiders out, sometime became funeral pyres during dry times when night raiders applied a firestick, creating raging infernos in a matter of seconds.

Some of the large men's houses had shafts dug inside, that connected with an escape drive from the side of the ridge where the house stood and created a potential fire escape. The side of the ridge above and around the outlet was left well covered by shrubs and cane grass, and the area was used as a latrine to discourage too close inspection. No self-respecting warrior would foul his person with excreta and forfeit his place in the homecoming victory parade.

To these people everything of ours was endowed with some magic properties. Even the dogs had a magical allure, and a demand for a few hairs from Snowy and Darky became a craze until the dogs responded with anger when hairs were pulled out of them. Even their excreta were picked up and rolled into leafy packages that became conversation pieces. When nature called us, a bodyguard had to restrain natives eager to rush forward and package our body waste as well.

In primitive societies women are invariably excluded on pain of death from seeing or taking part in any secret tribal ceremonies. Women rushed with the rest of the whole village to see the strange visitors, however, and some of them reacted hysterically. Some fled screaming, later cautiously returning for a second look. Groups of men and women decided that some of our boys were a reincarna-

Man with ceremonial axe, middle Wahgi area.

tion of dead relatives. The smart Warias occasionally agreed if the widow was young and comely.

A .303 rifle bullet which tore through a yar tree puzzled these people. They could find no reason for the hole in the splintered tree but collected the splinters of wood and carefully wrapped them in leaves for discussion and examination at leisure in the secrecy of the men's houses and the confidence of the village elders and wise men.

Personal adornment, which varied from that of the Asaro-Goroka people, was colorful and included brilliant feathers of every bird that lived in the area artistically arranged in headdresses or drapes, each individual feather painstakingly sewn or tied into attractive geometrical patterns. Short lengths of cowrie and tambu shells stitched onto lengths of bark string were draped over the nose or from ear to ear across the face. Cowries arranged in rows or patterns and stitched onto narrow pieces of stiff karuka leaves were worn across the forehead. Birds' legs, whole wings of birds opened out and mounted on sharp pieces of palm, and bright beetles mounted on bark strips or tied pin style on the end of a sharp sliver of palm stood out from the woolly heads at any old angle. Scraps of twisted roots and sections of cane, smoked to add color, and opossums' tails complete with fur, dangled from their ears or were draped in strips around their head or body. Young women wore pigs' noses, some still rather smelly, worn bracelet fashion around their wrists. As with the Asaro-Goroka people, lost finger joints indicated grief for dead relatives.

The tattooing on face and limbs in this region was and remains an intriguing aspect of the natives' culture. We could find no definite or distinct patterns, just the usual lines and contour dots around the cheeks. The custom of tattooing could have followed a trade route up the Purari from the south coast of Papua and could have been introduced by the trading Lakatois from the Moresby area who through the centuries had made annual trips to the delta country. It would have taken centuries for the custom to reach this remote spot. The original primitive mechanical art of tattooing allows little latitude for distortion without loss of the pattern.

In this area and extending south, the green snail shell of iridescent colors competes with the gold lip shell for value. The common cowrie, or tambu shell, is good currency for food and services. We found no steel of any description; any coming in from the south or north would be kept and not traded by the people living in the heavy bush country south and north who had to hack out garden patches every year.

We pushed on, among farewells from mobs that were nearly hysterical but still self-possessed enough to scramble for souvenirs in our camp area as soon as we marched off. Small groups of awestruck natives greeted us with "E shon a" or "Wendoulee" as we progressed over their thickly populated ridges, up to 6,700 feet above sea level and down to 5,000 feet. Welcoming groups of men and women at each village through which we passed invited us to camp there.

From the top of a ridge under the precipitous limestone corridor near the village of China-Shiva, escorted by hundreds of chattering, rather smelly natives, we looked into the wide, flat valley with its broad, slow-running river meandering through. As far as our binoculars could penetrate through the haze, we saw clumps of yar trees, bananas in profusion, lines of fencing, and smoke curling up into the morning air, proclaiming the most thickly populated area in New Guinea. Years later a census count found more than 50,000 people in an eight-mile radius of Kundiawa Station near an airstrip originally named Chimbu, after the river which races along from the highest mountains in the Bismarcks to join the Wahgi.

We dropped down into the Chimbu and found a very frail vine suspension bridge anchored to trees on each side. It took hours for our Warias, whose people have for centuries made bridges with local cane, to reinforce this one with sash cord ropes carried for the purpose. Even then it was a slow job to get the cargo and boys across, especially the bush boys, who had never seen a vine bridge and were quite understandably terrified of the surging water below and the white water of the Wahgi it joined just below the bridge. The next year we found a fordable section of the Chimbu just above the bridge, but a bridge is still the only safe way to cross in the wet season.

We camped in the village of Mirani above, with the usual packed mob of sightseers. Food was plentiful and pigs were available by the dozen, but we could not barter for more than a couple from our rapidly dwindling shell supply. Feathers from birds of paradise,

Suspension bridge over Chimbu River.

both red and white, and the scalelike plumes of the Duke of Saxony bird of paradise were features of the native headdresses, some of them most artistically arranged. This was high terrace country with gravel beds exposed on the cutaway sides above the river. We managed to get a few colors of gold off the bottom of old beds, but there was so much New Guinea mixed up with it that separation was a nonpaying proposition. Perhaps higher up the river there might be a stream worth working.

We pushed on up the valley over undulating open country. As the country flattened out, checkerboard gardens, formed of ten- or twelve-foot squares and adapted for drainage in the high rainfall area, became common. Ditches had been dug around the squares with sharp sticks or long paddle-shaped wooden digging imple-

Burned-out village houses, Chimbu area.

ments. These were typically thrust into the soil and the sod levered out, on to the top of the square. The kaukau runner was planted in the soil; sugarcane grows in abundance and is a welcome goodwill gift from villagers who appreciate its almost immediate energy-reviving qualities after toiling up and down the ridges and gullies.

We pushed on up the valley under the shadow of Mt. Wilhelm, 15,400 feet on the north, and the central range, up to 13,000 feet on the south of the valley. We were escorted through villages and along garden paths lined with colorful hedges of plants and flowers of varieties known in civilized countries only in carefully tended

Man waving stone axe, Chimbu area. Dan Leahy stands at left.

pots or hothouses. The natives use dye from the variegated leaves and soft stems to color their bark-string bilums and the long strip of network the men wear as a frontal covering draped over the wide bark belt. Here, the men's belt was much wider, with patterns cut into its surface; a bunch of dracena leaves pushed up under the belt formed the rear covering. There were some big, fine-looking men among the woolly haired and black bearded. Hawks' wings protruding above their hair made them appear most impressive.

Here was probably the most powerful group in the valley. Its members lived in one of the best parts, not in grouped villages, but in rather isolated farmhouses evidently on their own farm plots amid a profusion of native food and fruit. The ever-present pigs wandered around or were tied to a stake outside the house.

Bows and arrows were not much in evidence; spears appeared to be the principal armaments, some of them works of art that were chipped and carved out of a single length of fine-grained timber up to ten feet long. They had three sharp points up to ten inches long and about thirty-six inches back from the tapered carved main point. These outward-slanted auxiliary points would compensate for a near miss by the main point. A piece of opossum fur and woven cane band ornamented the main shaft below the three smaller prongs, and there was beautiful carving between the prongs and the main point. I think that such a spear was never used for throwing but, like the intricately carved arrows of the Asaro-Goroka people, served to finish off a disabled enemy or was reserved for combat in very close quarters. In this area we found the best examples of primitive Stone Age art I have ever seen, now known as the Hagen axe. This is a stone blade of rhyolite slate, blue-white in color, about ten to twelve inches long, which tapers from up to six inches wide to two to three inches and is ground down to one-quarter to one-half inch in thickness. A smooth, flawless piece of stone, rounded on the cutting edge and with the bevel sharpened, it was mounted between two flat pieces of wood, the tips of which were slotted to fit the end of the stone blade. A balancing piece of carved wood was fitted unto the stone blade, and the whole was bound onto the usual L-shaped piece of branch with part of the trunk forming the short end of the L and carved down to fit. It was then bound into one compact whole by colored pieces of orchid cane and ornamented with pieces of fur or ringlets of cane dangling from it. The stone blade was pushed into the slotted end, and a keeper loop of bark string kept a loose blade from falling out and breaking. I do not think this axe would stand up to a single blow on a hard skull. It has probably degenerated from a utility battle axe into an ornamental or ceremonial axe.

Farther up the valley the natives' huge mops of hair were sometimes further padded with loose hair and packed into a covering of net woven from bark string that perhaps offered some protection from axe weapons. A victim of a stone axe attack carried into our camp at Mt. Hagen some weeks later showed narrow axe wounds on his back and hands and into the back of his head under his mop of matted hair, apparently the results of an upward swing with a

narrow-bladed work axe rather than a downward chop with a ceremonial or battle axe. The work axe was also here in greenstone. It is
more utilitarian than the ceremonial axe. It had the same overall
design and was bound into a compact work implement with heavy
bark rope. The stone blade was six to eight inches long, one-half to
one inch thick, and two to two and a half inches wide, with a sharp
bevel edge. It was the best stone work axe found in this country. I
think that it has now displaced the ceremonial axe as a weapon of
war.

We were conducted down a well-used track to a narrow part of
the river with a vine suspension bridge. Although here the river
was running through flat open country, it was a big stream swollen
by the wet season rains. It surged through this narrow channel,
constricted by hard mudstone outcrops on both sides. Vast quantities of deep water were boiling up and sucking down debris from
undercut gardens higher up. The bridge was extremely well constructed and sound from an engineering point of view. Rows of
long, strong posts were tied together and anchored to logs buried
under piles of rocks. The multiple strands of vine which formed the
handrails and footway were laced into a V-shaped passageway
across the water from each side, and long stay lines of vine tied to
tree stumps or anchored under stones kept the structure fairly
steady. The local vine did not appear to be as good bridging material as lawyer cane found at lower altitudes. It had too much "give"
in it, and after a few weeks of weathering and the weight of traffic
over it, it sagged into the current, which further strained the upriver sway lines.

From the hacked-off tree stumps along the narrow, bridgeable
strip of river, we concluded that years of enmity had cut all bridge
communications across the river. When an uneasy peace did come
the people had to supply their own bridge pylons in the form of
long posts and piles of rocks. Crossing the large, fast-running rivers
with long lines of natives who feared bodies of water and unstable,
frail-looking vine bridges was always a problem. The cargo could
not be taken across by swimmers without total loss or water
damage. Our emergency rope supply could do no more than reinforce the handholds and footway; even then hours were needed to
transfer our long lines of natives and cargo from one side to the

other. Rafts or canoes of any kind were unknown in this region. From just below the bridge where the river widened and the water was less turbulent, we cut down a long banana tree and tied our heavy sash cord ropes to each end. Some of the boys stood on opposite sides of the river holding the ropes. It was pulled in to the bank, and two of our water-wise boys held on to it as it was played out from their side. The current swung the very bouyant stalk and its human freight across to the opposite bank in a wide arc. The slack was then taken up, and the stalk, now held by the boys on the opposite bank, was played out into the current to the other side, taking back bridge-wise boys to bring another load of cargo over the suspended vines.

After we had cajoled, persuaded, and at last threatened to leave them on the opposite side, all our hydrophobic camp followers decided to venture out, hugging the banana tree and a water-wise boy accompanying each of them. Crossing eventually became routine and smoothly executed maneuvers in our excursions around the country. Once we had their confidence, the absolute trust our new recruits placed in us and their readiness to follow our orders or instructions were sometimes embarrassing. They were utterly dependent on us in their desire to see the country. Only punishment would discourage their inherent propensity to steal from new and momentarily demoralized natives. The responsibility of returning them safely to their villages weighed heavily on our small armed force and tested our ability to withstand treacherous ambushes or early morning raids.

We moved through the country as if we had been acknowledged its supremely powerful conquerors. Most of the Stone Age people accepted our assertion of status. Trouble usually came the second or third visit, after the wise men had had time to sit around and discuss our visits, our apparent lack of weapons for either offense or defense, and particularly our lootable assets, which must be very strong in magical qualities and well worth acquiring.

It was now time to start looking for an airstrip. The plane was due to fly over in three days, and we selected a long, flat terrace crisscrossed with old, shallow garden drainage channels. Jim Taylor calmed down a few of the men, who were puzzled at our leveling off operations in their country. Jim pantomimed, pointed, made the appropriate noises, and counted on his fingers the number of days before the plane would arrive. The message was understood after much repetition, and men, women, and children joined with our boys in leveling off and flattening out the area. With much hilarity and hard work, another homemade airstrip was built and made operational by the target date.

We all suffered the usual qualms as we watched the first landing on Monday, April 4, 1933. Heavy rain overnight had softened the strip, and we cut long lengths of pitpit to corduroy the wheels down-end. We sighted him a long way off near Mt. Irambadi, the prominent triangular-shaped mountain in the eastern end of the valley. The steady drone of the engine could be heard before the plane was sighted, and the continuous roar of the approaching plane became the dominant voice in the valley. The people were terrified of this strange bird that roared in from the sky and over their heads. It circled at no great height to examine the strip and our smoke signals and came in to land from the river end.

By the time the plane landed, the people were on their knees. They fearfully watched the landing, which was good, and saw the plane taxi up the strip to our camp. The unconcern shown by our boys encouraged some of the more adventurous to take their hands away from their eyes or peer through their fingers. Some were even back on their knees preparatory to edging in for a closer look when Ian Grabowsky, the six-foot-three-inch-tall pilot, stepped out in a brilliant white flying suit with a close-fitting skullcap and a pair of large green flying goggles. There was a long low moan of despair from the multitude. Everyone flattened, prone on the ground, not even daring to look up. Kingsbury, New Guinea Goldfields' geologist, emerged second from the cabin, and another moan went up. We coaxed the people into standing up and persuaded them to touch the wings and feel the warmth of the engine. A very subdued crowd watched as Grab took off for home. They fell to the ground when he circled low over the camp and then stood to watch the plane disappear beyond Irambadi.

The natives had been precipitated into the twentieth century without their knowledge. I have often wondered what sort of a legend the arrival of the first plane with its crew might have inspired had all future communication with the outside world been cut off.

Gardens and houses, Mt. Hagen area.

Grab brought in another two loads of stores, and we again moved up the valley, prospecting each stream as we crossed it. We had a Bena Bena boy, whose name I could never remember but who answered to "Pick, Shovel, Dish." As we approached a stream, the whole line took great pleasure in sending "Pick, Shovel, Dish" to the front to enable me to pan as we crossed. We found some mineralization, but no gold. We camped at about 2:00 P.M., in time for the local people to overcome their initial shock and bring in food from their gardens before dark.

The valley now had a slight west-southwest swing and widened out considerably. The wide, slow-running river meandered through it. There were thickly populated grass slopes up to 6,000 or 7,000 feet, and the grass-covered tops of mountains protruded at 12,000

to 13,000 feet above the early morning cloud layer. We were looking for the Mt. Hagen reported by Dr. Bohrmann from the Sepik
River in 1912 and had decided that the long, level, grass-covered
mountain sloping up from symmetrical bush-covered slopes must
be it. We climbed to the 12,600-foot top and camped there for two
days but were never able to sight the Sepik River. Nevertheless,
the name Mt. Hagen stuck.

Mt. Hagen is one of a group of extinct volcanoes which centuries
ago enriched the highlands with thick layers of lava and covered the
surrounding ranges above the lava level with thick layers of a soft,
soapy deposit impregnated with black sand. Even today, the people
recount a legend of dust coming from the sky which accumulated
on the roofs of their grass houses and eventually caused them to
collapse. After we had exhausted our supply of empty tins, bottles,
and bottle labels, we discovered that the small cowrie shell was
common currency for foodstuffs such as sweet potatoes, sugarcane,
pitpit tops, native asparagus, and bananas. Steel axes were scorned
in favor of the native stone axes, but knives exercised fascination.
Great effort was needed to cut and shape tools with pieces of stone,
shell, or opossum teeth. The sharp knives therefore began to seem
acceptable, but not immediately. Some sorcery might have been
associated with the knives. In any case, cowrie shell was cheap and
convenient and has been brought in by the ton since that time for
trading, always at a profit, with shell-starved villages. Today the
shell currency market has become saturated, and the natives want
hard cash or folding money.

The southwest turn of the river made us decide to cut across the
bends of the valley, leaving the roundabout north and northwest
side for later investigation above the Gumanche-Wahgi junction. It
was a knee-deep wade through slowly moving water to a very frail-
looking sapling bridge across the Gumanche channel and another
knee- to waist-deep wade to the large outcrop in the middle of the
valley that we promptly named "The Island." Our dogs were half
carried, half towed, suspended from lengths of laplap under their
bellies, across open water too wide for them to swim. We camped
on the bank of the Wahgi above the flood level of the surrounding
country in a wet and mosquito-infested camp, but I do not think we
could have avoided the usually noisy, chattering crowds of local vis-

itors. Here, in dozens instead of hundreds, they were more subdued and almost timid. They brought food enough for the boys, but
we were glad to reach higher ground next day out of the swamp
country, a feature of this area. The watertable in places was low
enough to allow the heaped-up spoil from the natives' checkerboard garden beds to produce good crops of sweet potatoes, the
staple food. The high, craggy summit of a most imposing-looking
mountain looming above the high ranges in the foreground was
seemingly volcanic in origin, like Hagen and other cone-shaped
mountains near the west and southwest end of the valley. The valley floor was still about 5,000 to 6,000 feet above sea level. This was
a magnificent country with prolific growth and thousands of well-
fed, friendly people living out their war-torn lives in a valley where
the temperature rarely goes below 45 degrees or above 80 degrees.

We crossed the Island at 6,600 feet and had a good view of our
surroundings. The craggy top of Keluwere dominated the country
to the southwest, standing out in bare rock isolation well above its
surrounding ranges. A large valley, the Nabilyer, ran south from the
southwest side of Mt. Hagen, and the Bismarck Range petered out
into a low divide on Hagen's northeast side down into the Sepik
River, probably a headwater of the Yuat, which we knew carried
gold in its lower reaches before joining the Sepik. The whole countryside was thickly populated in places, right up to the frost line at
about 8,000 feet. The country was definitely volcanic; the floor of
the valley showed typical hummocky lava bubbles here and there.
We camped on a good drome site called Keluwere where old
garden beds were thickly covered in pitpit and coarse kunai. A few
low trees in this area leaned across our proposed strip, but the lava
flow and later streams from Hagen had formed long narrow strips at
right angles to the direction of their lean. We had no time to find a
better strip area before the next plane was due to come looking for
us.

There were hundreds of natives, some carrying a smaller version
of the pronged spear of the middle Wahgi people and a rather poor
type of bow and arrow. Some of the arrows were tipped with lengths
of human bone filed down to needle points. Later we were to hear
of warriors dying from comparatively minor arrow wounds. The im-
plication was that the bone tips taken from partly decomposed bodies

Mt. Hagen men.

EXPLORATIONS INTO HIGHLAND NEW GUINEA

Mt. Hagen women.

were still carrying lethal infections. There were some very fine looking men almost six feet tall, shining with grease and decked out in plumage from birds of paradise, parrots, and dollar birds. Hawk wings, which were extended and mounted on a sharp sliver of palm and embedded in the tightly packed, net-covered hair of their heads, made them look even more impressive. Probing with long slivers of the black palm, somewhat resembling the hat pins of our society, kept the population of head lice on the move.

Hundreds of daily visitors brought in excessive quantities of all sorts of native foods and pigs and bartered for any camp refuse or shell, and so we had no trouble getting the strip cleared and leveled in time for the plane's arrival on Thursday, April 27. Grab brought in the Fox Moth and with him district officer Ted Taylor from Salamaua and geologist Kingsbury, who stayed a day or so and looked around the area. Grab again stupefied the locals into silence and subdued awe. His passengers were felt all over before they were acknowledged to be human. Geologist Kingsbury confirmed our conjectures about the geology of the local area and tentatively identified the blades of the natives' axes as rhyolite. He was a most enthusiastic prospector.

Kingsbury reported that the Bena Bena, where the drillers had found gold values too low to warrant dredging, was a washout. So were dreams of a fortune from the Bena Bena also, but we recovered quickly from the disappointment. We now had months of prospecting in new country ahead of us in probably the most interesting and attractive country into which prospectors ever walked— an eternal spring climate, lots of open country, and thousands of Stone Age people, whose armaments, tools, decorations, and reactions to first contact were even more intriguing than the first panned dish of gravel. We had no worries about food and meat for ourselves and the boys. Our boys rarely left camp without a lump of cooked pork dangling from some part of their gear, and we invariably left behind a heap of native foods that our party could not eat.

Gold lip shells were the most valuable trade in the interior, with slabs of bailer shells next. The tambu (a small cowrie) bought food and was good currency. We brought in bright shiny shells right from the reefs on which they occurred and used them in preference to old, traded-in poor-quality shell and shell fragments. Shells were mounted on a length of bark rope and worn in long ropes and coils around the neck. The bailer shells came from comparatively deep reefs off the Papuan coast from Moresby and were probably gathered on the annual Lakatoi trading cruise to the Gorrabari people in the gulf. They were then traded inland village by village. Years passed before their pride-of-possession value wore out, or a better specimen was traded in from the coast. Each piece ultimately reached the Highlands in fragments, each many times more valuable than the whole shell had been when the first native on the coast paid for it in barter. We brought in new bailer and gold lip shells straight from the sea. The bailers, used to bail out canoes, were the subjects of much discussion and planning by everybody.

How could they be cut into the most valuable pieces, along lines marked on the outside part of the shell? The natives knew all about cutting with sharp slakes of stone but did not know how to bleach shells to the dirty white color they liked. Our coast boys showed them how to bleach the cut pieces in hot ashes, being careful not to burn them until they disintegrated. The gold lips in their possession were poor specimens, having been discarded by hundreds of owners. They had been padded with gum from a tree, mounted on bark, and painted with red ochre. The thick muscle ends had been cut out to form a crescent shape. From the horns on the crescent tips, holes were drilled through which a rope could be threaded. The pendants were sometimes worn by young, unmarried girls. The gold lip we brought in by plane still had its rough scale exterior, and was straight from the sea. Gold lips were given out in payment for pigs or for work, and our boys showed the natives how to grind the scaly exteriors down to their white and gold surface. The natives had no idea where the shells came from or how they were produced. Among themselves they figured out that the shells grew on trees like fruit and that the sharp nails sticking out of the soles of our walking boots enabled us to climb the shell tree and kick them off when they were ripe.

Our Hagen base on Keluwere drome became the commercial center of the area, and its value increased enormously. The greater the distance from this center, the more people and trade passed through. There are profiteers among primitive races as in our culture. As the trade and talk moved out ahead of our probes into new country, we were welcomed for the trade we carried and our entertainment and prestige value to the group near which we happened to camp for the night. Hundreds milled around our fishline camp fence, and a continual babble of opinions addressed to no one in particular articulated each individual's thoughts and opinions. Having no gold lip shell at that stage, we tried china saucers and plates as a bright, shiny white substitute. These were snapped up, and we wrote Mrs. Wright, the cook at Guinea Airways' mess in Lae, to send us in any broken crockery or discarded plates. The shards went like hotcakes, and in a few days reappeared, with holes neatly drilled through them, as breast decorations worn suspended from the neck. Still, crockery never did become as valuable or as much treasured as the real gold lip shell. Synthetics even in that primitive society were suspect, and I never saw one exhibited in a Moga or shell-and-pig-exchange sing-sing.

Until our importation of shell was organized we depended on broken crockery, cups, and plates from Lae for pig buying and for the more valuable services performed by the locals around the camp. We encouraged this aspect of our contact with the locals in order to teach them that even in our society we had to work to pay for anything we owned. We did not want to perpetuate the Cargo Cult beliefs of New Guinea's semiprimitives that the spirits of their people showered the goods down from above.

Bob Gurney flew the Fox Moth in with a load of cargo and went back to Buasi's camp on the Wahgi to shuttle in the cargo left there. He advised that the natives had become threatening. Buasi thought that they were planning a raid, which would also mean the killing of everybody in the camp. Jim Taylor and Dan flew back with Bob and walked the boys and stores back along the south side of the river. They received a great welcome from the locals; each member of the party was well hugged and grease smeared. We were one big happy family, at least for the time being. Ken Spinks and I were flown around the Hagen area in the Fox Moth. The northeastern side of Mt. Hagen drained north; we thought that this must be Sepik water, probably the Yuat, a large tributary carrying traces of gold in its lower reaches. A long, narrow, thickly populated valley to the west, now known as the Wabag Valley, which drained into the Yuat headwaters, hinted at more prospecting country. Large grass-covered valleys at high altitudes, through which slow-running streams meandered, extended the populated areas as far as we could see to the south and southwest. The northwest-southeast folds and faults in what appeared to be limestone country south of the volcanic belt around Hagen could drain into the main Purari, which cuts right across the country farther east and drains the Wahgi and Goroka valleys. Around Mt. Keluwere, an extinct volcano, were small lakes and large areas of very swampy-looking country, probably old lake beds, their outlets still reducing and gradually draining the old beds. A vast area of heavily timbered country fell away to the south from these thickly populated grass-covered valleys, and the drop in

Fences, gardens, and homes, middle Wahgi area.

altitude was much more pronounced on the Sepik fall than on the Papuan side.

We were ready to probe the Sepik fall and left our base camp on May 9 to the accompaniment of wails of sorrow and distress that we were leaving. The natives dusted their bodies with ashes, and some of them made ready to cut off a finger with their stone axes to emphasize their grief after first making sure that one of us was on hand to dissuade them from the fatal chop. We left some boys and police boys at the camp to look after our stores while we were away. Although we could now tell the locals quite clearly that we would be back in a few weeks, they continued their antics for a few miles away from the base. They had little faith in our ability to survive a long trip through the country of their bloodthirsty neighbors.

We cut all the streams into the Wahgi coming off the Bismarck Range, which peters out before Mt. Hagen and is part of the north-south divide, but there was no gold in any of the streams we crossed. The Gumanche, a rather large stream, ran through a vast swampy area and, backed up by the flooded Wahgi in the wet season, flooded a large area on the northeastern end of the outcrop we called the "Island" in the middle of the valley. We spent a night on the top of a mountain the natives called Alt, 9,300 feet above sea level. Following the almost obliterated track up through kunai, then clambering over slippery roots and rocks in the wet, mossy forest country was a long slow job.

By an extraordinary piece of luck, while I was slowly plugging along, head down to pick the best foothold in that sort of country—preferably a root running across the track where the arch of a boot across the root gave a better grip than the sodden sole did in mossy soil—I found a stone pineapple club minus the handle. It would have rotted off years, probably centuries, before. This was a typical Kukakuka pineapple club head but somewhat cruder in construction than the present-day Kuka clubs. Although the people on both sides of the Bismarcks in this area are the local experts on stone axe-head manufacture we had never found any evidence of such a club in their present armory. A rare specimen that I found enshrined on the giant slab-sided pot plants in their sing-sing parks suggested their vague appreciation of its association with ancestors of whom they had never heard.

Clouds over the top of Alt obscured our reason for climbing it. We hacked out a very rough and uncomfortable camp among the tangled mass of moss- and lichen-covered growth. Our latest Stone Age recruits enjoyed hacking out a campsite and dropping some of the trees to give us a better view of the surrounding country if and when the clouds cleared. The steel axes, which cut through a tree rather than bruising through it, as their stone axes did, and the heavy steel knives or machetes, with which we sliced a thick vine or sapling at one blow, fascinated them. The utility value of their beautifully fashioned stone axes suffered accordingly. Every day we contacted new people who had never seen or heard of white skins

Mt. Hagen man with greenstone work axe and tambu (shell) headdress. Each cane rung represents ten gold lip shells or the equivalent.

before, and the reactions were much the same. There was initial fear. The group approached with whispered warnings among its members to be suspicious of us and everything with us. Then, gradually, everyone relaxed as fear gave way to curiosity and interest. Primitive people have limited reactions of fear, amazement, or appreciation and usually lapse into a negative dumbness after seemingly unbelievable events are thrust on them. They are overwhelmed and initially ready to see or believe anything. The inevitably abrupt introduction to our ordinary everyday tools, particularly those with a utilitarian application to cultural or survival needs, prompted immediate close examination and evaluation.

I am satisfied that these natives had not as yet developed the brain to cope with conditions commonplace that we, with our backgrounds of centuries of technology and culture, find commonplace. The adaptation necessary to survive snowed-in winters in the frigid zones or continual escalating warfare was beyond their ken. Black skins, a hallmark of the sun, have an evolutionary history in the hot tropics, where a bountiful nature rewards a modest effort with all the necessities of life. In contrast, white skins originated in the frigid zones of the world, where the threat of severe winters prompted the inhabitants to lay in a supply of food and firewood; otherwise they would freeze or starve to death. The wars of survival, which down through the ages were and still are common to all mankind regardless of color, have prodded the whites to the hydrogen bomb stage. Similar wars of survival have never prompted primitive thought to move beyond the bow-and-arrow stage in this country. The gap between the two cultures, which is inseparable from technological sophistication, is precisely the difference between a bow and arrow and the hydrogen bomb.

We decided to spend a second night on the top of Alt in hopes of looking around the countryside. Ken Spinks, our surveyor, had already compiled a cartographic record of our probes into this new country, and could tie in quite a few points we had already seen. He took his pick of new ones that formed a prickly serrated line right around the horizon in every direction, with valley depressions between. The clouds cleared for about half an hour in the morning. To the north and just below us lay a fairly big valley drained by a tributary of the Sepik which rose on the northwest flank of Mt. Wilhelm to stand more than 15,000 feet high. It was the highest mountain in the eastern end of New Guinea. Depressions between the mountains and open grass ranges to the west and south gave promise of more populated valleys.

Grass country always suggests population. With New Guinea's rainfall, the whole country would be bush covered in a few years, but fires started by natives in their migrations into areas identified by hunting parties or areas into which they moved as refugees restrained the bush. The garden patches of native foods casually established by travelers along their hunting routes become grassy patches in time and are ignited by a hungry native looking for a quick snack on his sometimes hungry hunts. Fire destroys all young trees but not the seeds or roots of the indigenous blady grass, which is always a sign of good soil and invades any old garden areas very quickly. Its ability to recover from a fire more rapidly than any other grass or shrub makes it dominant, and in the dry times it fuels a hot, growth-killing fire. Fire is responsible for most of the open grass areas. On the ranges in poorer soils, the indigenous kangaroo grass has the same ability to retain its dominance, working in tandem with native fires. Hunting parties systematically set fire to the huge areas of grass (kunai) to flush out pigs and small game, and they thereby perpetuate the cycle.

We cut our way down off Alt until we found an old hunting track which took us past some sort of native shrine—a small cleared area in which colored shrubs had been planted around a small shrub. Hanging from the center shrub were the jaw bones of many pigs. This could have been the mat mat (grave) of a hunter or a warrior, or it might have been a feasting place before a pig hunt. It took us until the next day to reach the river draining the valley below us, a headwater tributary of the Yuat. We found very few natives living on the valley floor, which was lava and through which the streams off the Bismarcks had cut deep, straight-sided channels. Colors of gold were in the main stream, which was mostly granite float stuff, and there was very little sedimentary gravel in evidence.

The natives were a poor lot; yaws and malaria, associated with low altitudes, had debilitated them. Their houses were poor structures. These natives appeared apathetic and dejected, in contrast to

Jimi River natives, poor types, malarial.

the virile, inquisitive, clean-skinned highlanders. The river was only 1,100 feet above sea level, and the valley was full of mosquitoes; this was a most uncomfortably hot and humid place after the salubrious climate of the higher country. We followed the main stream down the valley, running deep and fast a couple of hundred feet below the valley floor. The dogs cornered a pig, which we shot. It gave the line a good meal of strength-sustaining pork, but there was little else to eat in this sparsely populated area.

We had a plane coming in to our Hagen camp within the next week, and we began to worry about returning in time for its arrival. Sickness among the boys delayed us considerably. We found a few coarse colors in a small mud-bottomed stream, appropriately called the Yen by the natives. A prospector usually picks the most likely place and most favorable gold-holding conditions for the first few exploratory dishes of gravel. In time he learns not to become overly optimistic about a good initial dish prospect. This was the case with the Yen, a local concentration below a gorge. A clay or puggy false bottom held the occasional color shed from the gravel bed the stream was reworking. Like many of this country's northern streams, too much New Guinea was mixed up with the gold to make separating it a paying proposition.

We camped alongside the Yen on a low terrace, and a torrential downpour during the night had us listening to the roar of the rising water and wondering whether we would have to move to higher ground. It was not a very inviting prospect after a hard day's walk and respite inside a tightly tucked-in mosquito net with millions of insects waiting for a massed attack as soon as we touched the net. Wading around in a flooded stream on a pitch black night with no lights was not a happy prospect either. The storm blew over, and we moved on to the Gange, a fairly big stream coming off the Bismarcks. There was no gold of any consequence in the Gange, but the floater material in the stream provided the rocks for a large, flourishing stone axe industry. Littering the area were numerous small puddles of water with a piece of bark to sit on and lumps of sandstone grinding stones in various thicknesses of worn-down slivers. The crude pieces of rock picked up along the stream were selected for color and absence of flaws, then flaked down by battering first with heavy stones and then with smaller stones held in the

Mt. Hagen man with ceremonial axe.

Sharpening stone axe, Mt. Hagen area.

EXPLORATIONS INTO HIGHLAND NEW GUINEA

hand until the rough shape was ready for grinding into the smooth flawlessness of the finished article. We did not see any greenstone work axes; this area appeared to be essentially a ceremonial axe center. The stone blades were traded and mounted by the new owners in the villages, according to their taste and style. There was plenty of native food at this altitude, about 3,000 feet above the valley, where the enervating heat and pests no longer afflicted the people.

We crossed the divide into the Wahgi at 7,000 feet above sea level and dropped down a very wet and slippery bush track to a village on the Wahgi fall. We received a great reception from the people, who piloted us over the range on our way out and had food and pigs ready for barter on our return. We were within sight of our base camp area and with a lightly loaded line. Everybody wanted to go home. We left at 6:30 A.M. but lost some time passing through villages, where we refused pressing invitations to stay overnight politely as our anxiety to be on our way would allow. We made the base just at dark. It was a great relief to get back into a good camp and not have to think about rising before daylight, donning clothes that were usually very damp and cold from the day before, and being ready to go as soon as it was light enough to move.

Back at base, I urgently needed to develop Leica films taken during the trip. In this high country the water is almost static at 65 degrees and just right for the developer I used. Because of the frequent and sometimes torrential downpours, the water was relatively free of mineral contamination or was so diluted that minerals had no effect on the time and temperature of film development. Care in fixing plus thorough final washing gave me black-and-white negatives which over thirty years later are still good, as some of the photos in this book will show.

The usual crowd of local natives was with us all day. They drifted away or had to be shooed away each evening. An uproar on the other side of the airstrip had us worried during the night. The shouting and wailing was too far away for us to do anything other than wait to see the outcome. A little after daylight a long procession of fully armed men and some women, wailing sorrowfully, carried in the badly mutilated body of a warrior slung from a pole. He had been hacked by stone axes; the chop marks suggested the

Mt. Hagen man from Tuman River area. A greenstone work axe is poised over his shoulder, and a bailer shell segment hangs around his neck.

stone work axe rather than the ceremonial battle axe. The mourn-
ers unrolled him and laid him out for our inspection. I think that
they were expecting us to wave our hands over him and bring him
back to life whole and healed. If we had been able to do so, I am
sure that they would not have been surprised. He was packed up
and carried away to his village to be the object of lamentations and
pig feasts until his burial. Corpses were sometimes buried in a
squatting position with the head above ground.

Bob Gurney brought the Fox Moth in with stores and mail. Jim
Taylor had a radio set sent out to help us keep in touch with hap-
penings on the outside, but the batteries did not arrive with it, so
we had to wait until the following trip to hear news direct from the
outside world. The radio was a wonder to all the local people. Some
of their initial enthusiasm and surprise returned when they first
heard voice broadcasts, although the long-wave static frightened
them. The next evening I asked them if they were going to listen.
They rather disdainfully replied, "They had heard it finish." Once
was enough; so much for our science and invention.

There were more quail in the grass country here than I had seen
in other areas. There were two species, the small pretty colored
button quail and the common brown quail. An hour's shooting with
every small boy in the area flushing the birds out, then spoiling the
shot by getting in the line of fire, provided relaxation and quail on
toast. The small boys were good quail hunters; armed with long
bushy branches, they noted where a bird landed, surrounded it,
and closed in, branches at the ready. The quail, not being able to fly
straight up, were knocked down and pounced upon as they took off
at their usual angle.

Ken Spinks worked out our position as latitude 5.48.20, lon-
gitude 145 degrees. Dan and Jim Taylor had a fly around Mt.
Hagen over the Sepik-Wahgi divide. The western fall of Hagen
drains into the Sepik waters, and all water coming from the big
valley to the west is Sepik water.

The natives of Mogai villages surrounded and tried to hold a police boy and a work boy who were getting firewood and looking over
the country. Both of them eluded the natives and hotfooted it back
to the base to report the hostility toward our party. This was the
inevitable test made by primitive people to probe the reactions and

defenses of a totally unforeseen and unknown force in their lives. We trooped over immediately and were met by a considerable force lined up at the northern end of the Mt. Hagen airstrip, abandoned as an airstrip and now a main street. A few shots scattered them, and we went back to our camp to give them time to figure things out for themselves. We were awakened before daylight next morning by a watch report that a massed attack was imminent. Apparently there were plans to wipe us out save Snowy, the dog, whose prestige was high amongst the people. Our assembled local natives demonstrated how they would grieve for us by picking up handfuls of dirt and rubbing it on their chests. They watched us closely for signs of fear of the coming battle. Our apparent lack of concern evidently impressed them with our confidence in our ability to handle any attack which might eventuate. They arranged for the two axes stolen from the police boy and work boy to be returned, and later a big pig was brought along and presented as a peace offering. We were all pals again, for the time being anyway, but we were keeping our powder dry just the same.

This was evidently the dry season in the area. The airstrip was dusty and the air dry. The fine volcanic dust permeated everything and was, I think, responsible for a mild sickness running through the camp. The locals were a healthy lot and arrived in hundreds every day to sit around and observe camp activities. Each foreign member of our party had become an important personage. Observers spent hours gesticulating and explaining to small groups of enthralled locals in a language only they understood the background and history of white man's excursions into their country.

Long lines of new people were arriving every now and again. The new waves evidently reflected the relaxation of local security measures to enable them to visit our camp. They trooped in slowly, mostly with supplies of native foods—long sticks of sugarcane, bundles of native asparagus, pitpit heads, sweet potatoes, and pigs—all for barter shells, beads, salt, and matches. Personal adornment and strange items of interest were demanded first. The demand for utilitarian axes and knives came later, when the novelty had worn off.

We were rolled up, ready to move out again, after daylight on June 1. Some of the locals decided to come with us on this trip. We proposed to cross where the Bismarcks peter out into a low, grass-covered divide at the foot of Hagen and follow the stream down to the Yen and the Jimi, all evidently Yuat River headwaters and one of the main branches of the Sepik. One of the local bigwigs, Keluwere, could not resist the temptation to create a sensation and made ready to march off with us. Frantic screams and rolling on the ground by his numerous wives and family made us decide to persuade him from coming. Keluwere had made the safety of our base his special responsibility on our earlier trip, and he could have helped us communicate our peaceful intentions to the people in this district. He was a noted orator and could talk for hours about nothing. An extensive trip around the countryside would have given him almost inexhaustible material on which to draw in haranguing the mob. He insisted on accompanying us until he saw that we were inclined to let him come, but he was not sure about his own safety on the trip because, as a fight leader and bigwig, he would be a marked man. He finally decided to stay put at the base, and we were glad to have a few of his one-talks. They would be able to give Keluwere a full account when we returned and to reassure the new people that we did not aim to loot or make war.

Traveling was a pleasure in this high country with its eternal spring climate, magnificent mountains, and colorful people. There was plenty of food for our boys. Having plenty of help to carry their packs and wait on them, they were bursting with energy and fat. We formed our followers into small gangs, each under the charge of one boy who had specific duties with rigging or pulling down a camp and other camp jobs. Our followers became expert at their allotted tasks and I am sure enjoyed the life as much as we did.

Each gang dropped its pack or camp gear in the camp area. A fishline fence around the area kept the mob away. One gang pantomimed an act of hungry bellies and shell currency to pay for filling them. The cook group sometimes picked up pieces of dry firewood when it was near camp time and had a cup of tea ready before we had taken off our heavy, very often wet, boots. The dozens of people in our retinue, especially the newcomers, were anxious to carry something by which they could identify themselves with the party. We traveled with some comfort, having a collapsible table and chairs and china cups and saucers, but the wear and tear on fragile utensils hardly made them worthwhile. We could make

Mt. Hagen girl.

yeast bread in an afternoon; the dough was prepared in the usual way with dry yeast. Our oven was two large gold prospecting dishes and one small dish. A hole was dug and filled with hot coals, and the larger dish was placed on the coals in the hole; the second large dish with the dough in it sat on the run around the outside of the prospecting dishes, so that air could pass between the two dishes to keep the bread from being burned. A small dish over the dough was piled up with hot coals. This arrangement gave us bread for a couple of days—a luxury in the bush.

Our shower in the bush was a tin with a perforated shower hose screwed onto the bottom. Filled with warm water and suspended from the ridgepole of the tent, with a mat of grass underfoot instead of a puddle of mud, it revived us wonderfully after a hard day's traveling under a clear sky. Air at high altitudes intensified the sun's heat.

We traveled north by northwest over rolling downs country with swampy patches between the ridges. In this area we were right on the north-south watershed, into the Sepik, or, as we thought then, the Kikori. We did not know of the northeast-southwest faulting which channeled most of the western waters into the Purari. We camped in a large parklike sing-sing ground. Well-grown yars and tall bamboos ornamented and shaded a lawnlike strip about 25 yards wide and 100 yards long. Down the center of the park, large ornamental trees grew out of giant slab-sided pot plants like mounds. Flanking them were rows of sharpened saplings in perfect lines. Pigs were tied to these saplings and later slaughtered. A large, oval, grass-thatched house at one end probably gave the old men of the area a place to rest and keep warm during the sing-sing. The whole was an example of landscape gardening that would have been striking in any culture or environment. The country was mostly lava which flowed from Hagen when it was an active volcano, so we did not expect good prospects until we had left that cover and had reached the older Bismarck rocks.

We picked up the usual few locals after persuading dozens not to come with us and dropped over into Sepik water. We passed a recently burned-out village. The survivors appeared terrified of our long line of carriers and camp followers. After our locals had reassured them, we had to persuade some of them to stay home. Although primitives who came with us had a civilizing and broadening experience after having been restricted to the comparatively narrow limits of their areas, the availability of food in the Jimi Valley limited the numbers that we could safely take with us. Primitive man did not associate any such mundane considerations with us, and we had almost to restrain the natives forcibly from joining us. I am sure another

Jim Taylor looks down on a sing-sing ground, Mt. Hagen area.

loaves and fishes miracle would not have surprised them in the least—in fact, they would have expected it.

The country dropped away. We traveled down a wide, grass-covered tongue of lava country and camped at 3,000 feet in the open grass beside a small swamp where millions of mosquitoes reminded us that we were again in malaria country. We climbed back over a ridge up to 5,500 feet, where there was plenty of food and pigs and more of the beautifully landscaped sing-sing grounds. After descending again, at 2,000 feet we found a couple of sacsac palms growing in a small swamp, the special care of nearby villages, to whose inhabitants its processed pulpy core was a luxury consumed on special occasions. My boys welcomed the sight of sacsac trees. Ewunga told the story of how sacsac had supplied us with food in 1930 after we had left the high-country food areas.

We made our way up and down over deep gullies cut through the grass-covered valley floor. Once we surprised a lone man and his wife on a well-worn track. They were too dumbfounded to speak, but we prevented them from hurrying away until our Hagen people came along. Then we could not stop the man's flow of yabba. He decided to come with us and promptly gave the bit of gear he was carrying to his wife, who was already loaded down with their food and other gear; his wife had no choice but to go with us. He was ready to lead us into his domain, himself doing all the talking, an arrangement which suited us. It was difficult to keep contact between scattered isolated villages, and such a big-mouthed guide could save us from surprise complications from bowstring-happy villagers.

Bird life was plentiful in the patches of scrub. There were white cockatoos; hornbills, which have a juicy steak on each side of the breastbone; and birds of paradise, both red and white plumed. The feathers were in great demand among our high-country camp followers; any low-country feathers were mostly traded in. The Goroka and Hagen line boys had a brawl over who should have the sole right to the feathers of fallen birds. Wild dashes into the heavy scrub to retrieve them caused brawls. The Hagen and Goroka-Chimbu people threatened to walk out. A walkout by the Hagen people would have meant sure death at the hands of the natives through whose country they would have to travel, and we would have been blamed for their deaths. We were obligated to bring them back alive and well to their people. The unfortunate wounded birds suffered most from the natives' acquisitive savagery; they were torn into bloodstained scraps during scrambles for feathers.

We got a few colors of gold in some of the small streams and the main stream, which now ran fast and flat, and was spanned by a "bridge-kunda," a familiar sight to our Waria boys. The bridge-kunda was in pretty good shape, according to Ewunga. We took it easy, allowed only two at a time on it, and spent more than two hours crossing the river. Afterward we camped in an open patch of grass nearby. No natives or food appeared, but we had enough to feed everybody. The heat in this valley 1,500 feet above sea level and enclosed by mountains up to 15,000 feet was very trying for us, and almost unbearable for the highland people. The heat and clouds of mosquitoes interfered with our sleep, and we were glad to pack up and move on at daylight.

Our dogs were having the time of their lives, dashing into the scrub after game. Snowy made the mistake of tackling a muruk (cassowary), a powerful ostrichlike bird related to the emu that lives in heavy bush country and has a straight, pointed toe which makes an effective stabbing weapon. Snowy limped back to us with a hole in his side which we thought could have penetrated his lung. He recovered slowly and found the first day's walk quite painful. We entered the low tropical country where the houses were roofed with muratta instead of grass and high-country reeds. It was hot as hell, with millions of mosquitoes. There were very few people and little food. The few inhabitants were a poor lot, fever ridden, and pocked and scarred from yaws. There was quite a lot of "grillie," a ringworm that covers the whole body. We found a few colors of gold in some of the streams, but as on most of this country's northern side, there was too much New Guinea mixed with it to make separating profitable.

Our Markham River boy died rather suddenly during the night, and his one-talks, like us, were very distressed. He was buried far from his home and his people. We placed him in a deep hole, rolled up in his belongings on a bed of banana leaves. Banana and ginger leaves were piled on top of him before the earth was filled in. Ken Spinks carved his name on a rough bush cross—JOHNNES—and his village, Wankon. We pushed on down to the main Jimi River, which was running in a steep gorge and was only 1,100 feet above sea level. Towa, a Waria boy, and Eyou, an Aitape boy, were still sick and traveled slowly. Sickness and scarcity of food made us decide to leave the barren, fever country and return to the food areas of the ranges and our base at Hagen. We deferred further prospecting of the country across the river until some other time.

We crossed the valley and climbed back to 3,500 feet, where, after a long hard day of rain and slippery tracks, we camped in a garden. It was a pleasure to be in a cool climate again, but we could have done without the nonstop downpour of rain. On a fine clear morning the locals arrived with lots of food and pigs. We remained in camp to give the sick boys a chance to recover. We were very concerned about the sick and we decided to split the party. The sick, with Ken and Dan, would head back to base in easy stages as their strength allowed. Jim and I kept going to the Yen of our earlier trip. We spent a long hard day trudging up and down over slippery bush tracks and camped in a garden on dusk. From this camp we made short trips down to surrounding streams, but although there was gold in some of them, there was not enough. The boys' sickness had depressed us. At the junction of the Gange and Jimi we found the usual few colors in places where there would have been concentrations if there had been any significant gold shed. After making our tests, we turned back toward the base.

We headed back via the Yen, which had not lived up to our optimistic expectations. A few black and red beads spotted in the very sparse shell necklaces of the natives attested to contact with the outside world. The owners pointed toward the northeast across the Jimi and the range toward the Sepik. We knew that two prospectors named Exton and Green had been in that area in 1930 or 1931. The beads had probably been traded over the range from their party. In the Gange area here were some wonderful stone axes, but our shell trade was short, and we could not induce the locals to barter for a steel tomahawk. They had a rather poor opinion of our steel axes.

We managed to find a guide to the next village, but these natives were very apprehensive about the people toward whom they were guiding us. They bellowed an introduction for us, and hurried away before members of the new tribe had appeared. We were loaded down with food, and they implored us to camp in the place; we had previously stopped here only for a food break. We disappointed our hosts, however, and kept going, anticipating the comfort of an established camp. From the top of the range we could look across the wide and magnificent Wahgi Valley. The distance that we had covered in two or three days' walk with outgoing packs we managed in only one with our light loads on the homeward trip. As we passed through a village area a sing-sing was in progress, complete with sacrificial pigs tethered to straight rows of pegs the length of the sing-sing ground. The decorations were colorful, and we smelled the odor of bodies thickly smeared with rancid lard. We were offered food, a pig, sugarcane, and a place to camp, but we pushed on, camping at dusk about ten hours from home.

This appeared to be the dry season, if there was a dry season in this evergreen country, and the time for sing-sings. Many of the natives were partly decorated. In some cases the feathers and flowers had drooped and become discolored from a mixture of melted and smelly lard and ochre coloring. The natives appeared to let the decorations fall off rather than remove them after a song and dance. Their gold lip shell and valuables were carefully stowed away in their houses, but the rest of the daily adornments just fell off as they wilted or decayed.

We reached our base camp in early afternoon after a daylight start. It had been a pleasant day's walk except for the occasional swampy patch where we sank knee-deep in mud and slush. We received the usual vociferous reception which became cries of grief when Kowra, one of their big men who had started out with us, was not in the party. He was with Dan and Ken and they had not arrived home, which meant they were having a bad time with the sick boys. Kowra's absence was explained, and everybody was again happy.

It was good to have undisturbed rest and relief from the labor of breaking camp and putting it up again at the end of a hard day's walk. Quite a few new houses were being built inside our "banis," or fenced-off area, and in each, a very coy local maiden and one of our key boys had arranged a love nest. These people had decided the best way to keep us and our shell trade in the area was to marry our boys into the Hagen society. Our boys were all for the idea. The fact that all of them had wives and families in their own villages was of no consequence whatsoever. Responsibilities in village life were light. There was always plenty of food and shelter and affection for any issue, and in this polygamous society, wives came and went. Few natives anywhere ever consider tomorrow. There are no tomorrows. Only today matters.

Dan and Ken arrived with their party three days after us, carrying some of the sick. One of the Goroka natives, Haulaway, was in a semicomatose state, recognized nobody, and was very weak. Eyou died after a great fight to survive. He was carried across the range, determined to reach the base, but during the night passed out, so exhausted and weak that his going was easy and peaceful. Eyou was the only boy we ever lost on our wandering through this country, and we felt badly about it. The Markham boy was one of Jim Taylor's boys. The two deaths during our short trip depressed the rest of our line. If we did not pull Haulaway through his crisis, we would have to face his primitive relatives back in the Bena Bena-Goroka country when we went back without him. We dosed him up with the usual malarial quinine and aspirin and some castor oil. He was very sick, but appeared to be better and more comfortable in a settled camp.

A few natives came in and claimed that one of their married women had been raped by one of our boys. We lined up all our boys and she put her finger on Koipore, a boy from the Upper Waria. Legal proof was virtually impossible among these primitive people. She and her relatives were not interested in the moral side of the offense; compensation was the only consideration as far as they were concerned. To judge by the current value placed on the oldest profession in the world, we made everyone happy. The woman received a handful of shells, and Koipore a dozen strokes of the cane. We had to view the incident from the local natives' angle rather than from our own. Too much compensation would encourage abuse with a view to rewards, and by ignoring such an incident we could provoke an attack. The attack would be triggered by the breaking of a tribal law but would be actuated by the promise of priceless loot.

A single-engine Junker plane, the largest the locals had seen, came in with a load of cargo. They were rather frightened of the plane at first. The engine was much louder as it taxied in and the amount of cargo impressed them. Bob Gurney, the pilot, was by now well known; even the small children remembered his name. Food was growing scarce; our base camp had become the local metropolis. Before our arrival, trade, shell principally from the south coast and from the Sepik River, had entered into the area in very sparse quantities and on rare occasions after having passed through the hands of thousands of primitive natives in the process of being traded inland where the shell's value always increased by virtue of its scarcity. By flying in new, clean shell we had upset all trade and trade routes, and our camp had become the distributing center for miles around. The people in the area had become rich beyond their dreams. They had ransacked their gardens for produce to trade for shell, which they hoarded up in pride-of-ownership variety. They forgot that they needed a food supply until their denuded gardens had nothing left in them. They had wealth beyond their dreams but were hungry. They were reluctant to trade any of their wealth out for food but became enthusiastic when we explained that they could sell part of it to us at a large profit. The rudiments of our economic system had been introduced to primitive society.

We decided to climb Mt. Hagen to have a look around and map out future probes into this unknown and entrancing country. We left base camp Monday, July 3, 1933, with a few of our boys and a long line of locals. The locals were given farewells with tears and wails by relatives who evidently did not expect to see them again. We traveled over rolling downs—grass-covered country with picturesque patches of old trees here and there in sheltered places where the frequent grass fires could not reach them. There were people everywhere and food in abundance. We had a magnificent view of the Wahgi Valley below us. The gardens were now rounded beds up to eighteen inches high and nine or ten feet in diameter, with the rich volcanic soil heaped up for drainage purposes in this wet climate. We camped at 7,200 feet in a sing-sing ground. Plenty of pigs were brought in, and one with five toes interested our boys from outside. They were uncertain about the wisdom of eating it, but a hard day's walk and an appetite for pork overcame their scruples.

The track up the mountain was hard going, but the grade along the lava tongues was not bad. At about noon we reached what would be the scrub and bush line at 11,000 feet and camped in the sodden alpine grass of Hagen's bald-looking top. We were still more than 1,000 feet from the summit. We were compensated for the fog, rain, scarcity of firewood, and cold wet camp by a breathtaking view of the Wahgi Valley and the valleys running southeast. Next morning we reached the top early in order to have a look around before the clouds closed in. Hagen viewed from the top has a typical volcano shape; the symmetrical sides of lava angle up to the straight line of its present height of 12,400 feet above sea level. We estimated that the original peak must have been over 20,000 feet above sea level. Small water holes formed in the lava showed no sign of any fish, but a few wild ducks hurriedly departed when we appeared. South and southwest around to the north, row after row of timber-covered ranges, here and there dominated by grass-topped mountains and spire-topped peaks, made an awesome picture for prospectors hoping to probe the mineral content of its rocks. A large grass and bush valley in the headwaters of the Gai and a tributary of the Jimi appeared to be thickly populated and gave promise of food, access to more open grass ranges, and probably a populated valley nestling in the deep folds of the ranges.

To the south and southeast, large areas of grass and bush-covered ridges gave way to heavily bush-covered ranges away in the distance. The smoke from grass fires and scattered village fires warming up the chill morning air gave us an inkling of the importance of these eternal spring, highland areas and hinted at the great numbers of Stone Age people who were spending their lives in these remote and not very accessible hidden valleys. The series of northwest-southeast-trending faults in what appeared to be limestone ranges to the south and southeast were one-sided and sloped precipitously to the southwest and probably formed the northern boundary of the oil-bearing sedimentaries of Papua that could limit the auriferous country in that direction.

Mt. Keluwere was another extinct alpine grass-topped volcano. Its last thousand feet or more of bare craggy rock top towered above Hagen and dominated even this landscape where 10,000-foot mountains were common. East of us Mt. Wilhelm's 15,400-foot slope with its patches of sparkling snow appeared even higher, towering above the thick white cloud line which filled the Wahgi Valley to the level of 7,000 or 8,000 feet. Clouds imparted to the tops of the ranges and mountains an isolation that accentuated their height and stature. The great peaks resembled islands of dark rock floating on a sea of white cloud.

We could not pick up any landmarks on the Sepik River or the river itself away to the north and northeast of us, and we began to doubt that our Mt. Hagen was the Mt. Hagen that Dr. Bohrmann's expedition had seen from the Sepik River in 1912. Although our knowledge of his expedition was scanty, we knew that his party had climbed some ranges off the river and could have sighted the top of our Hagen at that time.

There were many flowering shrubs and some stunted trees above the 11,000-foot level. Our boys had spent one night in this freezing atmosphere and eagerly picked up dry dead trees in their determination to have a good pile of firewood to warm up their tent for that night and any further nights. Snowy, our short-haired dog, was very susceptible to cold, and his inherent preoccupation with comfort created some excitement among the boys. He took over a bed of hard-won dry alpine grass over which one boy had spread his blanket. Snowy, who always appeared to consider himself at least as important as any native and who was prepared to argue the issue with any of them, obstinately refused to vacate the bed. He had not been so comfortable for days. He fought off threatened blows and much abuse, but eventually the blankets were pulled from under him. He retained possession of the dry grass bed, but before dark wandered back to his usual camping place under my bunk and slept on a layer of dry grass there.

The distinct symmetry of many isolated mountains in this area, the lava flows which filled the valleys around them, and the great thickness of the ash that even today covers the country above the lava flow levels are ever-present reminders of volcanic violence in the past. The volcanic eruption must have occurred centuries ago; there is no trace of any recent activity in the district today apart from a rather violent earth tremor—"Guria," as it is called in New Guinea. I left our high house hurriedly amid the crashing of bottles and tins each time such a tremor shook the walls and knocked the dead tops off trees.

Our compasses went haywire on the summit, suggesting magnetic interference. Ken Spinks rigged his theodolite and mapped the surrounding country, tying his new observations in with those made earlier. He built a trig (triangulation) station on top at 12,600 feet. It would have lasted a long time if the locals had not used the timber for firewood. We had to carry a sick boy back down the mountain, another Markham River boy. The flat-country people had trouble with the hard going of the ranges. Their tall build, long legs, and quick short steps were not suitable for climbing either up or down, and they lacked the heart of the people from the rugged ranges and mountain valleys. They also found it difficult to cope with food scarcity or a survival challenge from primitives.

We received the usual surprised welcome from our friends at the base camp. They had heard or imagined that some of our people had died on the mountain, and they had plastered their bellies with mud to show their concern and sorrow.

The Markham boy died, and the locals asked that he be buried in their cemetery. They appeared in full mourning, with mud on their bodies and threatening to cut off fingers but always taking care to see that one of us was present to stay the fall of the stone axe. We assured them that the gesture was proof of their extreme sorrow. Buasi, Jim Taylor's boss boy, gave a short funeral oration in Pidgin. He told everyone we all had to die, some in the morning, some at bello (lunchtime), some in the afternoon, and others at night. We all face the same fate but will "come up gen" on the last day and meet each other again. The local natives were buried sitting up in a hole covered with earth and fenced in. Ornamental shrubs and flowers were planted in the enclosure. A small grass house was built in which a pig was cooked in memory of the departed one.

Ken and I went off with fourteen boys to prospect one of the Wahgi's main headwaters. We could raise colors, but the test proved only that there was gold in the area. The vast sheet of lava which would have covered earlier streambeds left only the more recent sheds, if any. Granites and slates with lots of quartz showed some promise of good gold somewhere in the area.

We were back at base next day. Wives were becoming a problem. These people were determined to see that every one of our boys had a wife. In this polygamous country each family seemed to want a female representative at court, so some boys had two or three wives. When we contacted new people, the sight of women in the line of approaching strangers reassured bowstring-happy warriors and gave us time to contact them and mollify them before a brawl started. Domestic affairs were another story. Even in savage society, the presence of more than one female ministering to a single male creates friction. Tension was especially likely if the rivals belonged to another "talk," or tribe; it had always been standard practice to destroy and in some cases to eat such foreigners. The ménage became a madhouse and always proved that the female of the species is much more deadly than the male. The distraught husband, in his extremity and as a last resort to prevent murder, hurriedly admitted to having flouted camp rules in acquiring more than one wife. He appealed to us to rouse the lot and give him back the peace he had known before he became entangled in primitive intrigues and female interpretations of these intrigues. In the wake of their pathetic appeals for peace, the husbands immediately fell prey to the same situation once again as new liaisons were proposed by designing papas, mamas, and shapely daughters.

This was a land of plenty, with food and pigs in such abundance that we could not cope with the supply. The people were beginning to see the value of steel axes and knives in contrast to the stone of their implements and were trading pigs for axes and kaukau for knives. This was the first stage in the degeneration of their beautifully fashioned stone implements. At this writing in 1964, the primitive tools, now technologically obsolete in the area, are produced for the trade by modern steel cutting devices and abrasive stones. They are still collector's items but are somewhat cruder in appearance.

Bob Gurney brought General Tom Griffiths of the Administration in the Fox Moth on July 15, 1933. Warden Taylour from the Wau was also on the plane. Both men were amazed at the extent, potential, and population density of this highland country. They saw, as we did, a very prosperous future for its land and its people. We proposed to look at the country to the south and southeast, toward the area marked on the map as the Papuan border. Advisers at our base camp again implored us not to go; they were fearful that we might establish another base camp away from their area. The Mogai people, a most bloodthirsty crew, were waiting to pay us back for the setback suffered at our hands a few weeks earlier. To attempt to go through their country would be suicide. We reassured our advisers, knowing that our words would be passed on by the trickle of gossip, even between hostile groups. We explained that we would not start anything if they did not, and we wished for a peaceful and if possible friendly passage through their area.

A few of our locally appointed guides did not arrive for the trip, probably because of last-minute doubts about the Mogais' reac-

Jim Leahy, Jim Taylor, and Ken Spinks prepare to leave Keluwere drome
(Mt. Hagen) to look over the country to the south.

tions. We left about eight in the morning on Monday, July 17, 1933.
A start from base camp is nearly always late; it takes a few days to
establish the camp routine of early starts. The Mogais met us without a spear, an axe, or a bow anywhere. Sticks of sugarcane and
cooked kaukau, even an occasional lump of cooked pig, which represented a considerable sacrifice on the part of a meat-hungry people expressed the Mogais' concern to let bygones be bygones. We
were escorted through their stamping grounds, and a couple of the
men decided to accompany our expedition. A small plateau on the
western end of the range, which formed a divide of as much as
13,000 feet between the Wahgi Valley and its parallel valley to the
south, showed the most encouraging gold prospects to date. There

were twenty-five to thirty colors of coarse gold to a dish. A thick overlay of soft, soapy volcanic ash impregnated with black sand covered the slaty bottom. The encouraging dish prospects made us decide to camp on the plateau on our way back and take a good look at the area.

We dropped down to 5,000 feet on to the Nabilyer River, confined in a gorge of 200- to 400-foot-thick lava overlay, which ran southeast to join the main Purari, which evidently collected the northwest-southeast drainage as it cut across New Guinea. We found some gold on the small migrating beaches but not enough to inspire any enthusiasm. We saw quite a few worn-down steel axes that had been traded in from the Papuan coast. The people in this semibush country were shy and less numerous than on the open grass valleys. Proceeding over grass and bush ridges, we camped at 3,860 feet beside the river, where a bedrock of slate was exposed under the lava. Before the eruption the river could have been anywhere under the volcanoes. There was very little mineralization on the present bedrock or "arse true," as my mining boys described bedrock. We saw no reason to intensify our search in this area.

The local people and their dress were, in comparison with those Hagen, rather drab. The people seemed relatively subdued or overawed. They wore a thin strip of bark as a belt and fine cane anklets and wrist covers. They carried bows, arrows, and shields; were smaller than the Hagen people; and were not nearly as volatile as natives of the kunai country. The women wore a short, rather narrow covering in front and a long, narrow rear covering that hung from a girdle of bark rope. Made from dried reeds rather than native bark strings, it somewhat resembled the Kukakuka apparel.

Here for the first time we saw a kunnunna, or courting get-together of the young women, young men, and not so young men, who were greased, painted, and decorated with feathers. The meeting place was a long house. A couple of fires gave off some light and great heat in the enclosed space. A man and a girl sat facing each other. To the subdued hum of a rather dirgelike song they gradually swayed their bodies from side to side, and moved forward until their noses touched. The head movement became a cheek-nose-cheek contact. They smeared each other with their pig grease and paint and disarranged their decorations. Seeing our interest, our Hagen people promised to take us to another such ritual when we were back in base camp. It is essentially a night ceremony, and the Hagen people were not as reserved in its performance as these newly contacted semibush natives were. Nose rubbing advanced to leg rubbing, the personal adornments and covering became disarranged, and the couple dashed outside to consummate the sing-sing despite the not very convincing remonstrations of the aged crones who acted as chaperones.

Ken Spinks and Dan took compass readings daily and tied them in with earlier observations. They marked a tree near the camp with the number 52.

We climbed down the gorge to where a single log bridge took us across the Nabilyer and then climbed back up to 5,200 feet. Open grass ridges, thickly populated away to the south and west, told us that we would have plenty of food and easy going. We admired the white-speckled craggy top of Keluwere, the bright yellow of the alpine grass top above the dark blue of the timber line, and the blue sky in the crisp early morning air. A few curls of smoke spiralled up from homes hidden in the bush. Pitpit and reeds grew abundantly in this prolific country. This spot in Hagen's and Keluwere's lava-covered highlands, which had made the soil even richer than that in the old lake bed areas, would certainly become the inland metropolis of New Guinea.

Back at Camp 49 on the small plateau, Dan and I were able to get gold in every dish. We were on top of the western end of the dividing range between the Wahgi and the Nabilyer, at 6,800 feet above sea level. The range petered out on the east side of the Nabilyer, and the lava flows from Keluwere and Ialibu cover the country on the western side. We decided that the small streams draining the plateau would be worth boxing. The concentrate obtained from the box was carefully washed by pushing it against a thin stream of water, which separated the dross (waste material) from the heavier gold. The gold settled in a yellow streak across the bottom of the box in front of the dross. The box concentrate of black sand and gold was then treated with quicksilver, which amalgamated the gold and allowed us to separate it from the black sands. We could get as much as a grain of gold to a dish in the sparse gravels of the small streams, some of it specimen stuff of quartz and gold. The sharp roughness suggested that it had not traveled far from its source or was a reef formation buried under the centuries-old volcanic ash deposit up to 100 feet thick, through which the present drainage had cut to a soft slate bottom in places.

The test was good enough for us to ask New Guinea Goldfields in Wau to send out our geologist friend Kingsbury. Ken Spinks and Jim Taylor returned to the base camp. Dan and I moved over to the southern side of the ridge and prospected the streams coming off the gold-bearing ridge back into the main range. There was gold in the creeks coming off the country directly opposite those on the northern fall, enough to keep us interested, but this was no second Edie Creek. It was a pot boiler to finance further probes and not much more.

The local natives were very happy to show us tracks and brought along plenty of food and more pigs than we could afford to buy. They became really enthusiastic when we indicated that we would come back and camp on the creeks later on. We decided to peg reward claims in order to hold the territory. We planned ten 100-by 200-foot claims along the bed of the creek plus one extra claim of the same dimensions for each of us. We did not want any false reports to start a gold rush before we had time to give the area a good going over and examine the lower reaches of the drainage streams for possible dredging ground. No large deposits of alluvial gold were ever found in the area. The shed was too limited in this area, unlike areas such as the Bulolo River gravel, where colossal amounts of gold were being produced by eight bucket dredges in river flats enriched by the Edie Creek-Koranga and other streams in that area. We had no difficulty in locating a terrace suitable for an aerodrome. The Mogai people were now very friendly and helpful, and they filled in and leveled old checkerboard-shaped garden squares. They were determined to have an airplane, valuable for the prestige it conferred, to bring in trade and stores to their tribal grounds. We called the strip Mogai, the tribal name for that particular area. The main gold-bearing creek we called Ewunga Creek after our old Waria boss boy.

It was now July 30, 1933. Jim Taylor and Ken Spinks were due back in Wau in ten days. In the meantime Dan and I would carry on with our boys and go over the country thoroughly to find out the extent and value of the deposit. I developed a couple of Leica films. The camera was a very important part of our equipment. I could unload and load it on the march, and the thirty-six frames on each film allowed me to shoot hundreds of pictures of the country and people. Their dress, their weapons, and their amazed and fearful expressions at first contact, in contrast to the stiff poses that they take today when a camera is pointed at them, were all recorded on dozens of strips of black-and-white 35mm film. The locals brought in a large eel which they had trapped in a cylindrical bark trap. We had also seen a small, scaled fish in the streams. The natives knew nothing about lines, but regularly speared and trapped fish and eels.

Jim, my brother, came out with Kingsbury to look over the gold with us. Jim Taylor and Ken Spinks left for Wau, and Jim, Dan, and I took Kingsbury across the valley and up the range to Ewunga Creek. From the standpoint of large-scale mining, the Ewunga Creek area was a flop. There was enough gold to make it worth working, and there was always the chance that the formation would shed the gold buried under the thick deposit of volcanic ash if and when we moved the overburden of ash and exposed it. A prospector is and must always remain an optimist, always believing in the shadow more than in the substance. The Ewunga Creek plateau, which yielded little more than the amount needed for sustenance, gave Dan and me a home and a base from which to sally forth in all directions to prospect and explore the highland wonderland which so enthralled us. In the end we knew more places where there was no gold than probably anyone else in the country.

Back at the base camp we heard that Jim Taylor and Ken Spinks had arrived at Bena Bena but not without incident. Along the Wahgi Valley, our volatile friends, no longer awed or cowed, could see no reason to permit unique equipment and wealth to leave the area. As far as they could tell, neither Taylor nor Spinks had any means of either defense or offense—no bows and arrows and no spears. They had axes perhaps, but they were outnumbered 100 or 200 to one, and if they were rushed by the hundreds surrounding their fishline fence victory would be easy. The loot was the objective and the annihilation of the party an everyday affair. They

View of the Wahgi Valley. Mt. Kubor across the Wahgi River
near Nondugl village.

brought bark ropes along to tie up and carry away the loot. They
had seriously miscalculated, however, and the lesson they received
guaranteed safe passage of any white-led party through the district
thereafter.

Jim and Kingsbury went back to Wau in a Fox Moth, and Jim
sent out some mining gear and a pit saw (a giant rip saw) to cut
boxing and building material right on the spot. A platform would be
arranged over a depression alongside the felled tree to be sawn or
on a steep slope: steep slopes were easy to find in the up-and-down
ranges. A log would be rolled out onto the three- or four-sapling
platform and wedged so that it stayed rigid. A wet fish line rubbed

in black ashes leaves a mark when it is stretched from the ends of lines drawn on the log ends with a spirit level and is flicked a couple of times on both sides of the log. The boy standing in the pit underneath the log, watching the mark each time he pulls the saw down, has the worst end of the pit saw job, and he usually becomes covered in sawdust and sweat. It is a slow up-and-down operation, but perfect boards and building material are turned out once the operators become proficient. All sharpening and setting had to be done by a white man. A bad set meant bad timber.

Dan and I lost no time getting back to Ewunga Creek once we were on our own again. We left a few of our boys with their newly acquired local wives to look after the base on the aerodrome. Their in-laws, who were now privileged to wander inside the base camp at will, shamelessly pilfered anything not nailed down. Fortunately they had a natural fear of things they did not understand, and so our tinned stores, tea, and so forth remained intact, but salt, shell, and axes and knives just disappeared if not kept locked up away even from our own tried and somewhat trustworthy boys. We camped on a small terrace above the creek and put in a tail race to take away the worked gravels from the discharge end of our gold-saving box. The stream here was running flat, and we had to put in a long race to bring in a drop lower down. We picked up several slugs or nuggets up to one pennyweight lodged in between the big onion-structure boulders which littered the streambed.

Dozens of local people sat around the open grass ridges all day, watching our every move. They had brought more food and pigs than we could afford to buy and more labor than we could employ. They had no understanding of this kind of work and were puzzled that we were interested in picking up pieces of yellow stones. They were quite happy with the idea that we wanted it to decorate our teeth—personal adornment made sense to them. This camp was more than 6,000 feet above sea level, right on the Papua-New Guinea divide, and cold. We insisted that the workers be there at daylight to start work. Their names were written on a length of toilet paper, writing paper being scarce, and unless their names were written down at daylight, they got no pay when the day's work was over. There was hardly standing room in our workings most of the time, and little could be done. The laborers came and went at will. The early morning start and the cold water in the creek discouraged the older men. Sightseers, who could see enough in sun-warmed daylight, preferred to wait until later but nevertheless held out their hands with the registered workers for the three small cowrie shells paid for day's work. They learned the first lesson of our economy, "no work, no pay," and they were quite happy to accept it but saw no harm in trying. Who knew what the strange white men might do?

The pay was minute in comparison to our wage scale. The small cowrie in these highlands represented the second most treasured or valuable small shell in their economy. The small tambu was their gold currency, with the large shells, the gold lip, green snail, and bailer the equivalent of our diamond jewelry trade. We could buy 300 to 400 small, dried-out cowries, giri giri to the Hagen people, for three shillings on the coast. The air freight from Lae to Hagen at that time was 2s. 3d. per pound, or 252 per ton. The rubbish men or slaves became owners of wealth beyond their dreams, and their patrons promptly confiscated any shells that could not be concealed from them.

The boys became careless and left their firearms in camp instead of keeping them within reach while there were working. Dan and I always wore the heavy .45 revolvers and carried a rifle with enough ammunition to get us back to the camp if we were jumped unexpectedly. We sacked a couple of workers from our base drome Keluwere for not working and ignoring directions. They were disturbed about being pushed off the job publicly, but the crowd enjoyed watching someone else's embarrassment. The episode speeded up the work, and the dismissed couple were back on the job the next morning. They worked well all day and appeared determined to earn their shells by a good day's labor.

The age-old intertribal wars, although suspended when we arrived, erupted in individual squabbles and gestured abuse. We strongly discouraged conflict on the job. The natives could either work or sit down and look, but there were to be no wars within the camp-work area. We were not altogether surprised when a shot from Ewunga and a shouted call warned us that the kanakas were attacking with bows and arrows from the kunai ridge above the workings. A few shots dispersed them, and we watched them carry one warrior away. We found out that one man had been killed in the test effort. The unprovoked attack shocked the more trusting and inexperienced of our boys. They could not understand why they should have been jumped like that and were horrified that their newly acquired wives and relatives did not sound the alarm. The incident cleared the air and made plain to everyone that, although surface appearances might be friendly, a test was inevitable.

The incident did not interfere with the daylight rush to work. We had a large area around the camp cleared of ambush hideouts, as we did not want to confuse men who were running to work with men who were mounting an attack. All weapons were strictly prohibited within sight of the camp or work. Ewunga alone was happy. The attack had confirmed and justified his warnings to them that primitive people were not to be trusted. In the future their arms must never be out of their reach. "Me talk finish," he told them rather triumphantly on the subject of safety. He wanted to be sure that the message took root and would be remembered.

It soon became apparent that we had to give preference to workers who showed interest in mining and who needed no everyday schooling on what to do. The daily signing on and payoff, with different people who had to be shown what to do and how to do it, was too time consuming. Gradually we introduced accrued pay for greater working efficiency, particularly a longer working period— weeks and then months and then a year or two rather than the one-day period as at present. For a start we selected the best and most intelligent and induced them to work for two days running before being paid. For them we built a labor camp consisting of grass houses beside our camp. By the time we had to move on some of them were working a full week and were being fed from our stock of native foods. They became the nucleus of our team when we started gold mining in earnest in 1934.

Dan walked back to our base to meet a plane with stores and shell. He took with him a well-armed half of our boys. The Mogai people were friendly and helpful, and our base was in good order. Our evident determination to counter with decisive action any hostilities from the natives had dampened any warlike plans they might be devising.

Dan or I prospected all the streams within a day's walk of

Ewunga Creek. The gold was limited and was shedding from the central ridge across the range. Both creeks on the north side were worth working in this area of cheap and plentiful labor, food, pigs, and housing. They would not have been a paying proposition on the coast, where labor and food are expensive. Most of the deposit was covered with up to 100 feet of soapy volcanic ash impregnated with black sand. It would have been very difficult to remove the over-burden to work the small creek deposit of gravel in the old pre-volcanic gravel beds buried beneath the ash.

The area was interesting and intriguing. We were looking forward to opening it up and establishing a base camp for future prospecting, a reason for living in this highland country. We worked twenty-two days, employed an average of thirty-one local natives, and averaged two and one-half ounces of gold, some of it solid gold up to nine pennyweights. Getting ready to return to the coast, Jim Taylor arrived back at our base from Bena Bena on foot and reported that the natives were no longer awed or peaceful along the route, but he had suffered no casualties.

The first white woman to come into the highlands arrived on Wednesday, November 4, 1933. She was Mrs. O'Dea, wife of the veteran pilot Tommy O'Dea. George Whittaker, a medical assistant from Salamaua, was also on the plane. The locals were dumb-founded. When they recovered from their initial amazement, they summoned all and sundry within shouting distance to come and see the white missus. They immediately organized a sing-sing for her and sang and danced around her during the evening. The local women were delighted to see one of their sex. The affectionate embraces and enthusiasm soon had Mrs. O'Dea well smeared with rather stale pig grease and sweat, which she took in her stride. Her bright good nature and interest made her oblivious to such minor inconveniences. There were more people on the strip to bid farewell to Mrs. O'Dea when she and Whittaker took off for Bena Bena the following day than there had been when we first came in.

Menumbe, a friendly little local who ingratiated himself with us from our arrival, and eight of his people, including women and children, were reported murdered by feuding neighbors. We went over to their village to make inquiries. The killers promptly identified themselves when their names were called and were delighted when we told them that they would be taken to Salamaua and charged with murder. In their estimation it was a reward with notoriety and a trip for the murders. They were disappointed when the incident was shelved.

We were ready to leave for Bena Bena and Wau on Saturday, November 7, 1933. The base camp people now knew that we were departing, and every conceivable manifestation of primitive man's grief and sorrow was displayed. Men, women, and children howled and tore their hair. This time there was no diversionary camp scrounging to occupy them when we moved away from our base. The head man and his family and relatives had done all the scrounging the evening before. We left quite a stock of tinned food and some tools stored in one heavily barred house in Kowra's charge. Still, a few dozen people hopefully searched the old camps just in case Kowra had missed something. The hair tearing, tears, and howling sendoff continued until we left the drome. We headed back to Bena Bena and Wau along the south side of the Wahgi Valley to prospect the streams coming off the main central block of mountains, the route taken by Jim Taylor and Ken Spinks when they traveled up and down to Bena Bena. This prolific country, with its small homesteads nestling in their fenced-in areas of bright-colored flowers and shrubs, long lengths of staked sugarcane towering above the grass-roofed houses, and pigs tethered to fat banana trees created a first impression of peace and security. At intervals devastated homes—the scorched gardens, the burned skeletons of homes, and in places the pigs still sniffing around the scattered remains of the owners and their defenders—reminded us, however, that we must remain cautious and vigilant in this paradise of plenty.

We found little gold in the streams coming off the south side of the range, but the Mingenda River gave a color to each dish. Perhaps somewhere in the alpine grass headwaters there would be a gold shed rock barred in, like Edie Creek, where the gold was held in the flat-running stream, dribbling down the few colors or tracers to induce people like us to follow it up. We kept the Mingenda in mind for future reference. The rather forbidding-looking mountain range which it drained did not promise easy going, but in this country the gold appeared to be in inaccessible, cold and barren places.

We camped among the people who had been hostile when Jim and Ken last passed through. They had learned their lesson and welcomed us with sticks of sugarcane to refresh our line. They also brought in plenty of food and pigs, which we had no hope of either eating that night or carrying with us. There would be plenty ahead of us. We promised to come back and buy them on the next trip. They showed us where two casualties had died in the fracas. Small ornamental shrubs had been planted on the spot and the grass cleared around them for a few feet. They appeared to be quite resigned to events and bellowed a friendly message to the next people that we were on our way in their direction, although the whole countryside must have known of our presence by then. Pryor, one of the big boys of the middle Wahgi, came across the river from Jimbunar to see us. He had looked after the camp on our first airstrip in the valley earlier in the year and had probably saved it from attack when his greedy one-talks wanted to sack it. A few spears were brought in to barter for shell, their lethal ends carefully wrapped in layers of banana leaves to indicate that they were for trade and would not be thrown at us.

We crossed the Wahgi over a rickety vine suspension bridge. It sagged a bit lower with each crossing until it was under water in the middle, where the fast-running flood current stretched the upriver vine-sided stays almost to the breaking point. Dan brought the last of the line into camp nearby at 9:00 P.M. Mt. Wilhelm, towering above the northern ranges and the valley, had a covering of snow the next morning and was brilliant in the early morning sun. It held no interest for our boys or the local people, who were huddled in little groups over small fires trying to burn some of the mountain chill out of their bones. We were now backtracking along our incoming route and were welcomed by earlier contacts. Most of them had done a test and were happy to sit around in unarmed but still boisterous groups, pronouncing upon each article of camp gear as it caught their attention. The shouting almost seemed necessary as a way of remembering the details. An attack of fever made the next day's walk an ordeal, but walking, if one can keep it up, is the quickest cure I know. A hard day's walk, copious sweating, and a light meal and drink before bedtime to prevent a reaction from quinine and aspirin taken on an empty stomach, usually left me rather shaky the next morning but free of fever.

Along the route back we began to deliver the lads who had accompanied us on the outward trip into the arms of their tearful relatives who I think had given up on the idea of seeing them again. With their axe, knife, shell, laplap, and glass looklook (mirror) the travelers became the center of interest. In no time they had nothing left but their memories of the trip, their payoff having been taken over by the relatives. For every villager brought safely back with his gear, the people wanted to send along many more to share in the experience. We could now explain through Pidgin-speaking returnees that we were going away. Next year when we came back, we said, we would take some more people with us.

The following day brought us into Lobo-na-gui's people. Lobo had been talking nonstop for days and in his own territory really put on a show. He bounded up and down his steep slippery tracks in and out of the houses, talking, gesticulating, and exhorting all and sundry to bring food, pigs, firewood, camp poles, and so on. I am sure that he described himself as a fighter and protector of each and every one of us during the months when he had traveled with us. His hoard of trade was taken to his home and was displayed for all to see and admire from a distance, watched over by a close relative. Old Lobo knew his people and trusted few of them.

We found the arms, legs, and decomposed parts of a native caught up in debris just outside the camp. We had our camp rigged before we found these remains, which gave off no objectionable smell. The local people showed no interest. They were utterly indifferent to a corpse—as long as it was someone else's.

We proceeded on the long, slow climb from the Marifutiga River, where the Chuavi Police Post now is, to the 8,000-foot top of the divide into the Goroka-Bena Bena Valley. Here and there sons and husbands rejoined their families, taking their trade and their much longer-lasting firsthand accounts of their travels, which were embellished with each retelling. A whole new world had opened up for all of these natives and one that might prove it not to be the best.

We camped on top and looked down into the Goroka-Bena Bena Valley. The veteran Bena Benas became excited upon seeing their

Passing through a village in the Marifutiga-Asaro Divide.

EXPLORATIONS INTO HIGHLAND NEW GUINEA

Asaro man in the Bena Bena-Asaro area.

homeland again after months of absence. They had such unpronounceable names that they now answered to abbreviations or to the names of the tools they carried. The safe return of villagers loaded up with pay and goodwill did not prevent some of the people from making the most of any opportunity to pilfer. A knife and an axe disappeared. The theft of property set a bad precedent unless restitution was made, and we found a village fight in progress between an old man who had stolen an axe and a younger man who had told us where the axe could be found. They were hard at it with sticks, and the old chap was faring worse. He was very annoyed with the younger man for telling us where the axe was, but we recovered both the axe and the knife with no further trouble. We dropped down onto the valley and waded across the Asaro River, which was running fast from recent rains, and camped at Mahometofe village, the home of "Pick, Shovel, Dish" and some of his one-talks. They were accorded a great reception, with the usual pig feast, which interested them little inasmuch as they had practically lived on pig for the past months.

Mick Irwin and Bob Runkel were still on the Bena Bena drome when we returned on November 19, 1933. They were awaiting a plane back to Wau after having tested the Bena Bena gravels for gold dredging areas. The testing had been a complete washout, and we would have to keep right on looking for our El Dorado, but in this highland country I could not imagine a more attractive or interesting future. We would have a holiday and then carry on, starting where we had left off if New Guinea Goldfields agreed. If not, we had Ewunga Creek to work and stake us should no more finances be available from Australia.

We spent Christmas 1933 at home in Toowoomba, Queensland, and enjoyed an overland trip by car to Sydney and on to Melbourne. Automobile travel represented quite a change from the trudging over New Guinea's mountains. In Melbourne I contacted General Evan Wisdom, retired Administrator of our half of New Guinea, who remained very interested in our new discoveries. He arranged for a new company to go back and prospect the still unknown interior north, south, east, and west from our base at Mt. Hagen. Like us, he was optimistic about finding another Edie Creek and Bulolo gold dredging area.

A village on a ridge
below Chimbu River
in the Wahgi Valley.

THE YEAR 1934

In 1934 there was no air service between New
Guinea and Australia, and the first boat, the
Macdhui, left Brisbane on Saturday, January 14,
1934, arriving at Moresby on January 18. From
there Dan and I flew over the range to Wau. Dan organized things
from the Wau-Salamaua base, and I flew over the range into the
Waria with Jack Jukes in a single-engine Junker plane, landing on
the airstrip that Mick Dwyer and I had put in a couple of years
earlier at Garaina. I rounded up all our boys. Ewunga and a few of
them were raring to go, but a couple claimed that they had had
enough of tramping around the ranges. I picked out replacements
from the dozens of young men whose warrior instincts were being
frustrated in the now controlled and peaceful valley. These young
men were only too eager to acquire a stock of thrills, risks, and
feats to recall with the older men around the fires in the men's
house each evening.

We grew accustomed to the tearful, wailing farewell from parents and relatives as we assembled our small line of carriers from various villages and walked over the mountains to the coast at Morobe. Some of the old people hated to see their sons or close relations go so far away and were fearful of not living long enough to see them again or of contracting some crippling disease of old age that might make them entirely dependent on outsiders for survival. I was well enough known on the Waria River, having prospected the country with the villagers' sons from 1927, and always arranged to leave one son or close relative with each family to look after the old people while one or two other sons tramped the country with me. I still have Kotram and Gaigobi after thirty years. They married highland girls and became so spirited and independent that neither was willing to live in the village of his birth. The girls never liked the Waria village life, and the men could not tolerate the highland village life. The girls are now clean and competent housemaids and the men boss boys of a line of flying gang recruits who can tackle practically any outdoor jobs or emergencies on the farm. Like all natives they forget quickly, and even now, after they have had years of practical training, on occasion I must outline the basic requirements of simple jobs which they have been doing well for years. Their environment restricted their thinking to a technology and culture foreign to ours. In the years ahead they and their people will have to work or starve, think or die, if they want to survive as a people.

Over the coastal range and down the Mo River on canoes to the old German station at Morobe, I picked up the last of our boys from the coastal villages. This last group brought along three big outrigger canoes to transport us and our cargo to Salamaua. Sitting on outrigger canoes for hours at a stretch with the tropical sun beating down and the sea reflecting its burning heat, I was almost cooked on the first day out. A launch on a charter trip to Morobe picked us up at Miami, and we arrived in Salamaua on February 2, 1934. Dan was waiting with all the gear packed and ready to shoulder. The boys were signed on next day and after we had all received medical injections, our arms and ammunition were checked by Administration Officers to make sure that we were not going into the country inadequately protected. We crossed the twenty miles of sea to Lae in another launch and were ready to start the long overland trek back into the Promised Land on Tuesday, February 6, 1934. Our companions were twenty Waria, Markham, and coastal boys, most of them veterans of years of bush work. Each had a gun or rifle of some sort—Winchester .32, .38, and .44 rifles or 12- and 16-gauge shotguns for riots at short range. A native can outdistance a shotgun with his bow and arrow, but in close-up attacks from the hundreds invariably packed around our fishline fence, the report would dominate the frenzied war cries and would perhaps buy us time. The shotgun's effectiveness in close quarters had been proved in the Kuka country. Dan and I had a trusty .45 revolver on our belts with a reload of bullets for the .45's and the 6.5mm Mauser rifles we both carried. We brought along telescopic sights for the Mausers which enabled us to see farther into surrounding bush country in the night or predawn semidarkness than any native could see out. With the help of such equipment we could perhaps nip a raid in the bud before it got too close. Given the range of our rifles, we did not fear war in open country; indeed the natives fought that way between themselves. Our contacts, however, of necessity occurred at close range, with guides, food providers, and sponsors for the next village or tribe. Isolation would have cut off our food supply and would have brought unending hostility. We would have become objects of suspicion and would automatically have had a war on our hands with each new contact. If there is one aspect of life primitive people understand, it is their primeval code of kill or be killed.

Alienation of the various tribes would have defeated our purpose of prospecting and exploring. Furthermore, we would probably not have had enough ammunition to shoot our way back to controlled districts if our initial introduction had been antagonistic rather than friendly. If the assembled hundreds could see that we never started a brawl and that our actions were retaliatory rather than aggressive, they would understand and accept the rebuff, even wryly admitting to surprise that the sticks which we carried on our shoulders could go off like thunder. "We thought you were going to be an easy victory."

This time we were better outfitted, even to gray flannel pajamas (less conspicuous than white). We had lightweight eiderdown mattresses, our time-tested canvas sleeve beds, and two lightweight woolen blankets. We also allowed ourselves the luxury of a pair of white sheets each. Dog fleas, of which there were hundreds in some of the villages, became a very elusive quarry in blankets but were easily trapped against a white sheet background. We had Guinea Airways fabricate a tucker box from the duralumin of their Junker planes, so that our tea and sugar would be available for a track snack without our having to take the shoulder blanket fastenings apart. Our tents, Japara cloth treated in a copper solution against rot, even wet were lighter than the ordinary tentwear, which soaked up any night moisture and became correspondingly heavier next morning. Utility without weight was and must always be the criterion for human porterage, particularly in the mountains of New Guinea.

Boots were a problem. We needed waterproof lightweight boots which would not acquire extra pounds of weight on early morning starts through long wet grass. Hard steel sprigs in the soles were needed for a grip on steep, slippery tracks or fine-grained rocks. Our boots had to let us cross ankle-deep creeks or trek along a shallow streambed without becoming waterlogged and without falling apart when the weight was all on one side around some of the steep grass-covered ranges. A boot also has to have sprigs in the sole which would not push through to the sole of one's foot with wear and wet. These problems were a challenge to some Australian shoe manufacturers, but the results had proven less than satisfactory. We heard that snow was a much more insidious wetting agent than water, and snow boots had not been a very important aspect of Australia's boot makers more than thirty years ago.

Through an American hunting magazine we read of moccasin-type boots made for engineers by the Russell Shoe Company of Berlin, Wisconsin. We asked for this company's help in keeping our feet dry and our foot weight down. A few extra pounds' weight of water to be lifted by each leg going step by step, up and down, over steep country hastens exhaustion. I often envied our boys their track-toughened bare feet; the only extra weight they carried was almost half an inch of calloused sole. The Russell Shoe Company solved all our boot problems. It sent us lightweight elk-hide engineers' lace-up boots, which reached to just below the knee. The soles were fitted with half-inch-long hard steel spikes with heads the size of a shilling piece. A couple on the instep guarded against a foot-wrenching slip on angled slippery roots in the moss forests of the ranges. They enabled us to negotiate rotting log bridges or steep tracks and to stay put on fine-grained rocks in the creeks. The uppers were high enough to prevent the heavy woolen stockings from sopping up the large moisture drops from wet grass. We had to be carried only over the knee-deep creeks, and we needed only one spare pair of extra footwear, not three or four.

The first day out of Lae, traveling along a narrow track through the thirty miles of coastal bush, we camped at Yalu village to ready ourselves and our cargo for the long, hot march up the flat mountain-rimmed floor of the rift valley which runs through New Guinea with Lae on its eastern sea end. After dark, Baranuma, one of our old Warias, walked in, having talked himself into passage by plane from Garaina on the Waria River to Lae without a penny to bless himself. He followed us up to Yalu. Baranuma was dependable and crafty in this country, but of course no one is perfect. He was a welcome addition to our line of boss boys. We could always be sure that his fatigue after hard work would never be such as to restrict or curtail his value as a camp guard. He always had a few stooges to do his more arduous chores. He was a cheerful rogue but was positively opposed to trusting any new natives in the interest of his safety. He reasoned that our motley crew of natives was safe. Their intertribal animosity and mutual fear of the outside kept them loyal to him. The arrangement suited Dan and myself and assured the safety of the whole party.

Jokurry, or Joe, as he became known to everybody, was a homeless refugee from the Bena Bena area whom we had brought out with us and left with Bill Tracy in Wau when we went on leave. He was now an efficient Pidgin speaker and a favorite with everybody. In 1932 he had attached himself to us while we were prospecting the Goroka Valley. His father and mother had been killed in a tribal war, and he was a forlorn little bloke when we noticed him and invited him, using sign language, to come with us. After a few good feeds and no worries, with his natural good nature and humor and his quick wit he joined the group of outside boys as if he had always belonged there. After he had been less than a week in his new laplap, had thoroughly washed, and had had his hair cut and combed into a frizzy mop, he could be heard making what we took for disparaging remarks about the dress and make up of his one-talks who were bringing in food.

Joe, like all the inland people, loved salt—a pinch on the palm of his hand was as good as a sweet. I put a powdering of quinine on his hand instead of salt to get his reaction. He spat it out and started to enjoy the joke but restrained himself and put up his hand to stop us from laughing. Then he brought in his bush friends, offered them the same powder, and laughed louder than anyone at their disappointment and distaste.

He trekked with us until Dan settled down to coffee growing near Mt. Hagen. Joe married a Hagen girl, is a grandfather today, and is an important part of Dan's coffee and farming enterprise there. We asked him what the Goroka Valley people thought when we first contacted them. He replied that they thought we had come down from the sky and also that, if we were attacked and killed, we would go back and kill them all from the heavens.

We crossed the open plain country from Yalu to Sangan, the first of the upper Markham villages, under the coconut trees in the night time. Boys with hurricane lamps led the way through the high grass which hemmed in the track on both sides. Heated by the sun during the day, the sharp grass leaves scratched sweat-softened skin. This was adder country. The short, sluggish reptile moved slowly but struck with lightning speed if it was molested. Our boys, much quicker than a white man, could spot the adders on their favorite hunting grounds—the narrow tracks, which were a highway for rodent and quail. The line, loaded up with their packs, strung out along the track behind. We rested during the heat of the day under a grass shed on the bank of Munum Creek, where the silt-charged water from the fast-running stream had to stand before the excess silt settled enough to be used to make a billy of tea.

Sangan, with its round, grass-thatched houses resembling rather untidy haystacks under its profusion of coconut palms, was always a welcome relief from the hot, open plain country. The big green coconuts straight off the tree were a thirst quencher with no parallel, or so it seemed after the long hot trek from Lae across the Markham Valley to Onga village. From Onga we climbed the range again into the cool highlands along bush-covered native tracks above the gorge of the Wanton River, which thundered along 2,000 feet below us. We were again among new people. They brought us all the food we needed for our boys. It was good once again to have warm clothes and to be able to sleep under a couple of blankets. We reached the airstrip early, now relocated at the present Kainantu Station, to pick up the cargo we expected in by air from Lae. We camped on the divide between the Ramu and the south-running Purari River, above the village of Komparie, on the divide between the Garfatina and Karmarmentina, which are both headwaters of the Purari.

Here we could get food and wait for the rest of our gear to arrive by air from Lae. After a couple of days of waiting, a line of Komparie natives brought in some trade items, an axe, and knives they readily admitted to having stolen from a missionary party. They did not believe that we were waiting for a plane: they thought we were just waiting to recover the stolen property, so they brought it back before a raid could occur. In 1930, I remembered, a dish had been taken, and we had insisted on its return. The lesson had stuck.

With our loads all tied up again, we moved down the steep, slippery track around and down the grass range into better walking along the Karmarmentina where we had found a few colors of gold in 1930. Prospectors from Lae had come in. We were looking forward to having a cup of tea with Bernie McGrath, whom we had never met, but were told that he was prospecting the Karmarmentina above Epunka village, now the Administration outstation of Henganofi. From a fast-running stream in a hard-rock bed, the Karmarmentina flattens out and meanders through narrow flats of deep, alluvial soil sitting on gravels which showed a color or so of fine gold but not enough to warrant destroying the rich overburden garden soil supporting hundreds of natives along its course before its junction with the Garfatina at Epunka. We were always well received by the people along its course, having chased the few colors of gold from its source in the Bismarcks right down to where it was a one- to two-ounce box-and-dish proposition on the small, protected beaches and through its swift-bedrock-exposed course across New Guinea. Instead of meeting us with short lengths of vitalizing sugarcane, the natives stood off, well out of bow-and-arrow range, calling to each other in agitated voices, and retreated off our path as we approached. We pulled up our strung-out line of boys on a grassy terrace, issued extra ammunition to all the armed boys, and in a tight single line carried on toward McGrath's camp, a couple of grass-thatched houses on a ridge and above the village of Finintugu.

The camp was surrounded by natives who suspiciously ran for the pitpit tracks across the creek flats when we appeared over a ridge above their gardens. Some of them were carrying large wooden shields, and all were armed with bows and arrows as usual but with stacks of extra arrows in net bags on their backs, the reed ends ready to hand over their shoulders. We pulled up. Jokurry, who understood their language, told us that the master had just been killed by the Finintugu people, who were at that very moment looting his camp. We crossed the narrow gully and climbed up the ridge end to McGrath's camp, keeping to high ground and avoiding the enclosed pitpit-bordered track. The short, indigenous kangaroo grass allowed us a clear all-round view. The camp was now deserted by all the villagers, who were still shouting to each other as they raced through the pitpit-enclosed tracks back to their barricaded village across the creek.

Bits and pieces of McGrath's gear were scattered around the house. In the frenzy, the grass sides of McGrath's house had been torn out so that everyone could freely raid the murdered prospector's property. Everything fragile had been torn apart by grasping hands in the semidarkness of the hut. Broken containers had left a trail of flour, tea, and rice as raiders sped away from the camp when we appeared without warning. Tinned meat and rice for the morning meal for McGrath's boys, simmering away in a kerosene tin on the fire in the boys' house, lacked interest for people who had never seen rice, much less eaten it. We found McGrath's .44-caliber revolver, its muzzle clogged with mud, a few yards away in front of his house, with two spent bullets, one misfired, and three live shells still in the chamber. He had evidently discarded it in his desperate rush back to his camp for a shotgun. The two shots, probably ineffective, followed by the misfire must have led him to panic, believing the rest of the shots were duds.

Ewunga and Baranuma, standing above the campsite to watch for attacks, called out that they had found the master. "E die finis," cried Baranuma. McGrath had abandoned the camp and was in retreat up the grass-covered ridge. His route was easily traced from the arrows still in the ground along his track. A single-barrel 12-gauge shotgun, a cartridge in the breach and the hammer cocked, ready to fire, remained firmly in the grasp of his left hand. Two reloads were in his right hand. He had not been dead long. The arrow wound, which had left a patch of blood just below his shoulder and above his heart, delivered as he turned on his attackers and stooped to fire at them, must have given him a paralyzing blow and a quick death. This arrow had been removed, but the rush to loot and our sudden appearance had prevented the raiders from recovering some of the other spent arrows for use again. Arrows still potruded from the sides and grass thatch of the house. McGrath had been under heavy fire before he started his retreat up the ridge.

We made camp on a rise above McGrath's camp and decided to get word back to patrol officer Tom Aitcheson at Kainantu right away. Dan and five of our boys headed back over the range on the long walk back to the post at Kainantu to report the killing. I rigged our camp and settled down to wait, sniping at suspicious movements in our direction. The village across the river was being abandoned. Women, children, and pigs were going back into the range behind the village. The men were milling around, hurrying their families away and preparing for what we did not know. We were ready for any emergency. My 6.5mm Mauser fitted with a telescopic sight enabled me to see farther into the dense growth of pitpit than any raiders could see out. It was doubly valuable at night or early morning, when concealed scouts could be flushed out by soft-nosed bullets fired into their pitpit hiding places.

During the afternoon a couple of unarmed natives called out from the downstream side of our camp. Jokurry informed me that they were from Fagonofe village and had talk. We allowed them to enter the camp. They reported that McGrath and his four boys had been preparing to move out across the range to the Dunantina River, where another prospector, Bob Dugan, was camped. When the Finintugu people attacked, McGrath's boys threw down their packs and beat it up the range, leaving McGrath to fight a rearguard action.

None of us slept very long or very well that night. A few arrows were fired into our darkened camp early in the night, but a shotgun blast spitting fire and pellets into the pitpit gave potential raiders no reason to think we were going to be caught off guard. We braced ourselves for a daylight raid, but nothing happened. Our binoculars showed armed natives in force around the village.

At about nine in the morning a single-engine Junker plane roared in over the narrow valley and dropped a note advising us that Tom Aitcheson and Dan were on their way and should arrive before dark. Ted Ubank, who was mining on the Ramu River, came in at about four in the afternoon. We saw a light approaching from down-river, and there was an inquiring rifle shot to ascertain that we were still there. A reply from us brought Bob Dugan and Lance Peden with their boys into the camp. Another inquiring shot from up-stream and a reply from us brought Dan and Tom Aitcheson into camp about eight in the evening. All were hungry and tired after long hours of forced marches over the ranges from Kainantu. The day's activities, from the roaring airplane to the assembling of force from all directions to a central point at McGrath's camp, must have unnerved primitive minds. The natives deserted the village and streamed away into the range behind. At daylight we saw the last of them, still carrying their shields and arms, leaving the area. We decided to bury McGrath on the grassy ridge alongside his camp. Bob Dugan, whose feet were showing the effects of his forced marches of the day before, supervised the preparations for burial. The rest of us, with our boys and police boys, spent the day in the ranges and drove the murderers over and down into the Garfatina River. Two of our boys were wounded by flying arrows, but the thick, bush-covered gullies and high cane grass plus rock outcrops and boulders restricted the casualties on either side. We burned their village to emphasize the white man's disapproval and ability to retaliate.

A DH 50 plane flew over the camp. The roar from its single engine reverberated from the ranges and must have impressed the now scattered villagers. The pilot dropped a note inquiring after Bob Dugan and Lance Peden. Both showed themselves and ac-knowledged the note. McGrath's boss boy, who had an arrow wound in his right knee, told us that McGrath and his four boys had been ready to move off over the range into the Dunantina when some of his gear was stolen. When he demanded it back from the assembled natives waiting to scramble for anything that the party left behind, they became threatening. McGrath fired his revolver into the air and retreated back into his grass house. He threw away his revolver as he retreated, thinking it empty after the misfire. From his doorway he held up a white gum shell, a prized item of native trade in this area, as a payoff for his safety. The gesture was something no native understands; to them it was surrender. Surrender in the native culture is death, and all assets become lootable.

McGrath fired three out of four .32-caliber rifle bullets, then grabbed a shotgun and cartridges from one of his boys and told them to flee up the range. He would fight a rearguard action with the shotgun. His boss boy took the .32 rifle and one bullet which he had hidden. With McGrath in the rear, the boy started to climb the range. As McGrath stooped to aim the shotgun, an arrow hit him, and he went down. The boss boy, wounded in the knee by an arrow, fired the last .32 bullet and, dumping all the gear, escaped over the range while the natives were busy looting the camp. We buried McGrath, rolled up in his blanket, on the grassy knoll where he died. Building a small cairn of white quartz, the mother stone of gold, we marked the last resting place of another prospector for gold who had gambled with his life and lost.

Dan and I left McGrath's camp on Tuesday, March 20, and camped at what had once been Gavitula village but was now a burned out ruin in which the inhabitants of villages nearby were searching for loot overlooked by their fighting men. We had to help ourselves to native food from gardens belonging to the victors. Still flushed from their victory over Gavitula, they fired a few arrows in protest and kept going to their villages upriver, chanting their victory songs. In camp we patched up a villager with an arrow wound in the fleshy part of his leg, a minor injury in these beautiful upland valleys of violence and death.

Back on Bena Bena drome, we cut the grass to prepare it for a plane bringing in the last of our gear before the next stage to Hagen. Isagoa, one of the small boys who had been staying with Jim in Wau and who had expected the truck taking the boys to work to take off like an airplane, was met with the news that his father had been killed by Sayonofe people. The body had apparently been hacked to pieces and scattered around the countryside and into cooking holes or bamboo pots. Isagoa's mother came along in her widow's weeds—or perhaps "seeds" would be more descriptive. Row upon row of the blue-white seeds were strung over her body. Her face was blackened with soot, and mud had been plastered on any parts of her body not covered by the long ropes of seed beads. She wailed and howled, demonstrating genuine grief, but murder and death were everyday events in those thickly populated valleys. She would soon become attached to someone else and forget her loss. Isagoa was not sure he wanted to stay home. He much preferred the safety of Wau or any association with white men who could protect him from the never-ending threat of death from ambushes or intertribal conflicts.

The liaison between Neshaw and a local girl was about to produce a child. As Neshaw was not now with us, it was casually announced that the baby would be killed at birth. Oolase's girlfriend was also pregnant, and she too announced her intention of killing the child, as the father had not returned. We paid for the unborn in trade and promised future largesse if the mothers looked after them. We also made dire threats to be carried out if the mothers executed their casually declared intentions to destroy the children.

Tupia, one of our Waria boys, was distressed to learn that his young girlfriend, on whom he had lavished presents of steel, beads, and other goods stolen from our store, had offended a male relative in the handout. The injured man had promptly killed her with an arrow through her heart. Many years will pass, and much violence will occur, before these savage primitives are civilized. Death from natural causes is to them suspect. Their casual acceptance of a violent death, and their "kill or be killed" attitude toward each other will take years to eradicate. Will we replace it with unquestioning acceptance of atomic killing en masse? Our smug righteousness with these primitives is open to the charge of hypocrisy.

We were now continually being invited to take part in intertribal wars, the rewards being pigs and marys—the natives' most valuable goods and chattels, in that order. We patiently explained again and again that we wished to be friends with everyone and pointed to the diverse population of natives in our camp to emphasize the fact. But the natives' animosity was purely local, involving hereditary feuds, individuals, and relatives of individuals who were targeted in revenge for some recent murder. Such a person would of course need the power and authority to enforce his ruling. These natives needed a firm authority, disinterested and unaffected by their deep-seated parochial prejudices, to control and enforce peace, law, and order—but so does our culture, for that matter.

Bob Gurney brought the single-engine Junker in on Sunday, February 25, with the last of our gear. We packed it in thirty- to forty-pound packets, with a blanket tied on for shoulder straps. On Tuesday we marched out from Bena Bena airstrip. We camped about an hour's walk away from the base so that we could send back for any articles we had forgotten, as we always missed some on the first camp. The first camp out of a base was really a rehearsal to make sure we had everything; if we did not, the base camp was close enough.

Jim came out on the plane, bringing a 16mm movie camera, 2,000 feet of film, and a blue cattle dog from Toowoomba, Queensland. They were renowned camp dogs, intelligent and savage when necessary. Natives were terrified of our dogs; theirs were mere caricatures of ours. Small pigs have more initiative than the native village dog, which has been starved for protein to the point of being helpless and stupid. The small wild dog living in the ranges and hunting his food is a compact little animal and tames quickly but cannot survive on a diet of sweet potatoes without meat and degenerates quickly with native owners.

We weeded out the surplus volunteers, taking just enough to carry the packs: a long line of men walking single file along the track is difficult to protect. We traveled slowly and kept the line tight. Lapoon and Malae, two local boys whom we had taken to Wau to look around, had difficulty locating their people. Their village had been destroyed, and grass was growing in the ashes of their former homes. They received a rather reserved welcome from relatives seemingly too overcome from recent tragedies to admire the presents their boys had brought them. Malae and Lapoon were disappointed.

A tomahawk was stolen and during the chase after it, in which warring factions joined under the protection of firearms, Baranuma and Tupia reported one casualty and a pig taken from the village of the chief. We considered it of paramount importance to run down stolen property even at the risk of violence. When a native succeeds in stealing from the white man, his initiative and enterprise become an inspiration to others. The next party to come along becomes fair prey for all and sundry. The worst part of forays to recover stolen property is the worry of a counterattack. As our camp was rigged in an area that would be hard to defend, we doubled the watch and during the night checked to make sure that the guards were changed every two hours and stayed awake. The last watch woke the camp just at daylight. We were packed and ready to go shortly thereafter.

The Asaro River was running strongly over the ford. It was a hand-holding crossing for the camp followers. The Waria and Markham men made escort trips back and forth until all had crossed. We climbed the range gardens and villages deserted by the men who were fighting a large-scale battle on the open ridge within shouting distance of our route. Shouting and screaming appears to be as much a part of battle as the bow and arrow. The warriors appeared to enjoy a skirmish much as our culture enjoys a football match. The natives' sport is of course much more deadly and earnest, to judge from the leaf-covered wounds. It must have taken weeks of pain and inconvenience for an arrow wound to heal.

We camped at 6,800 feet above sea level on an open space between villages. The fight stopped when we made camp, and the self-proclaimed victors came up to the camp. Some of them were old fellow travelers who had been with us to Hagen and back the year before. They claimed five enemy deaths and were elated with their success. These people, distinct from the Goroka Valley natives, were better fed. They apparently had more permanent gardens and villages, and their dress of fine bark strings differed from the coarser strings of the valley people below. Their talk was also different. Jokurry could not interpret, or "turn the talk," for us, but the boys who had been to Hagen gabbed on and on to emphasize their superior knowledge of Pidgin English.

We climbed up through the last village to the divide at 7,800 feet. A beautiful crisp morning gave us an unforgettable view of the cloud-covered valley below, with the irregular black outline of the mountains silhouetted against the clear sky. The rising sun gradually climbed down from their top, and by the time we had reached the divide had dissipated patches of the night mist blanketing the valley floor.

Mountainside villages were always much more attractive than those on the valley floor. The frequent rains and better drainage washed away the animal and human wastes, and the mud was never as deep or as smelly. The neat grass houses were nestled in small fenced-in garden plots of bananas and sugarcane. Any available space underneath was covered by the leaves of sweet potatoes and various special greens. The parklike plantations of casuarinas on old garden plots were more ornamental than utilitarian; the timber-covered range was part of their domain and on their back step. Near the top, snug watch houses with guards seemed more comfortable than cold outposts. It was probably too cold for much night raiding by either side.

We dropped down, in places literally almost into the headwaters of the Marifutiga River, onto a flat where three creeks met, or in Pidgin "bunged," to the Water Bung Camp, a small, grass-covered terrace that down through the ages had been the site of markets or murders, or so we were told.

A young woman had the jawbone of her husband hanging from a cord around her neck. He had been a battle casualty. The relic kept her grief alive. The bone was not old enough to be completely free of flesh or smell, but it did not prevent her from joining the merry troupe of good-time girls who entertained our boys, singing and dancing around the roped off camp area. Here we were, among many of the boys who had come with us into Hagen in 1933. We followed a rough track down the river, passing the partly decomposed body of a native rotting in an old cooking hole, but none of the locals gave it a second glance. We could not learn what event had finished him off. He must have been a foreigner to be so disdainfully discarded.

The next morning there was the sorting out and shooing back of the unwanted volunteers who wanted to join us. We went out of the narrow, range-rimmed river gorge into the more open but still very much up-and-down, thickly populated country skirting the foot of

Woman wearing her husband's jawbone and bracelets made from pigs' noses.

the great limestone corridor. Our route was in semibush country along wet and slippery tracks, lichen-festooned trees, rotten moss-covered logs, and across clear icy cold streams gushing from cracks in the limestone escarpment. We camped at Sina Sina village, over-looking the Chimbu River. Our camp is the site of today's flourishing township and airstrip of Kundiawa. All through this area we were greeted by natives with short sticks of sugarcane which our boys gratefully accepted. They were a welcome refresher for tired bodies. Food and pigs were in abundance and were bought for cowrie and gold lip shells. Like the old-time sailor with a girl in every port, the local girls shamelessly courted our boys over the fishline fence; this time there were no suggestions that they were reincarnations of dead relatives. They were acknowledged to be very virile human beings. We tightened the watch but knew we could not prevent some straying into the pitpit nearby. The old boy who the preceding year had thrown himself across the narrow track to try to induce us to camp on his place was in the forefront of the official welcoming committee. We restrained him from prostrating himself (the mud was too deep), assured him that we would camp at his place, and found a clean camp space in an open grass area away from the village, where human and animal excreta and village wastes had not fouled the ground.

The old boy, caked with years of grime, his long beard and mop of hair greasy from a recent application of pig fat, tears streaming down his cheeks and a continual whine in his voice, insisted on throwing himself down and curling up at our feet. We put him back on his feet and convinced him that he was much more attractive at a distance and erect than at close range. But the mournful whine went on and on and on. He wanted to be the center of interest and did not allow us to lose sight of the fact.

In these thickly populated valleys and ranges, it was impossible to find a camping ground far enough away from the villages and isolated homes to ensure that there would be no night marauders. The friendliness and hospitality of the people tended to break down our rigid safety measures, but we insisted on an all-night watch, with as many as four boys on duty. We continually checked and harangued these boys on the hazards of trusting primitive people too much. The natives generally thought we were from the heavens, and our boys were sure that it was heaven complete with houris.

From Sina Sina we swung southwest over the low range and down the side of a grass ridge to the Wahgi River, here a whitewater torrent racing through grass-covered ranges. It was spanned by a rickety vine suspension bridge anchored to the hardy trees which grew out of its boulder-edged shoreline. The cutoff stumps of the anchor trees along the narrows marked the periods of peace and war between the river villages. Our bridge-building Waria boys reinforced the vine stays with our rope gear, and we crossed over.

Man waves a welcome with a stone axe.

The people on this side were being contacted for the first time. The news had echoed and reechoed from the valley below the year before. We climbed up thickly populated and intensely cultivated ridges to 7,000 feet and trudged across the country.

The people were inclined to be timid and reserved on first contact but soon became just as exuberant and boisterous as their counterparts in the valley. They unfailingly parked their weapons—bows and arrows and spears—well away from our camp, for which we were thankful. Their gardens were checkerboard beds like those of the middle Wahgi-Hagen people, and their long houses nestled in a profusion of fenced-in edible growth. The roof

Saplings span a deep protective moat, Chimbu-Wahgi area.

thatching was different—tightly tied bundles were secured to the rafters by the small tips rather than the root ends, which were exposed in straight rows on the roof of the house. The main uprights extended three or four feet through and above the roof and were topped with a staghorn or other parasitic growth. The country appeared to be generally limestone, but I felt sure that the top of the range, which must have been 11,000 to 12,000 feet high, was volcanic or granitic. There was no gold in any of the fast-running streams we crossed.

Towa, a Waria, developed a bad back and slowed us down. We put two long saplings through a canvas bed sleeve, and the local natives carried him, singing and yelling in relays up to 7,000 feet and down to 5,500 feet across the 500- to 1,000-foot-deep water-scarred mountainside. We eventually reached a long sedimentary stratum which cut across the mountainside from 6,800 feet down into the valley floor, twenty to thirty miles from where we picked it up. This stratum had stabilized to some extent the country above and below, constricting the streams in deep, very narrow cracks where they cut across it. All were bridged with logs, some of them slippery and partly rotten.

We were happy to see the natives express concern and vehemently bawl out anyone carrying a weapon in our presence. All were well armed with their stone, work, and ceremonial axes. They were big men (some, I felt sure, were almost six feet tall), greased shiny, daubed with paint and feathers, and decorated with shells. These big, bearded men were as imposing as their counterparts across the river at our first landing ground at Nangamp. Numerous wounds, some still suppurating and sore looking, suggested that conflict had been more recent here than on the valley floor where the streams flattened out. We shooed village pigs away from a partly decomposed and dismembered body of a native, probably a war casualty from upstream. These people, unlike the Goroka people, appeared to be shocked at the suggestion of cannibalism.

We put a couple of holes down to the gravel alongside the main Wahgi. We got a few very fine colors of flood gold unlike the slightly heavier colors in the narrow channels of the Chimbu area. This could have been a prevolcanic shed, being reworked by the present river from under the thinned-out ends of the lava bed which covered the country around Hagen. The gold was not coming in from any of the feeder streams on either side of the valley. Mt. Wilhelm was topped with snow as we started up the valley back toward our base at the foot of Hagen.

Wily old Baranuma created a stir in the camp. He accused one of our small volunteers of seducing one of the girls during working hours and reported it as rape, an unconscionable offense to these highlanders. The small boy just as indignantly denied the charge. In desperation, when it appeared that all the evidence (perjured, as we later discovered) was against him, he exposed his very immature penis. "E no enough," he tearfully explained, and the proceedings

Dan Leahy is greeted south of Hagen country.

collapsed in laughter. Baranuma proved to have been the real culprit. He had become annoyed when the small boy, who was dutifully looking for camp sticks, discovered him and a girlfriend together. Baranuma had rushed to cover up his embarrassment by fabricating a charge against the boy.

We pushed on up the south side of the valley toward our base camp at Hagen, retracing our outward route of the previous year. In places we followed a wide war trail of flattened-out trampled grass and pitpit where the warriors advanced ten or so abreast, singing and screaming to boost their courage. All of the houses we passed were intact, so it must have been a victory for the defenders. There appeared to be some unrest among the Tuman River people. We met small groups carrying their weapons, but they were quite friendly to us. They parked their spears and bows and arrows well away from our camp and brought along supplies of native foodstuffs. They told us that war had intensified with the people on the range above; in some of the skirmishes they had killed five of the enemy. They claimed no casualties among their own warriors, a statement which of course was a cover-up. In these close-in man-to-man spear-jabbing contests, both sides inevitably have casualties. We were now back in the language we used in base camp, and there was much gossiping between our Hagen people and the locals. We were told that Kowra, the boss boy of our base camp, had been killed and the camp looted by the Benambi people, hereditary enemies of Kowra's mob. They had continued the age-old feud as soon as we left the area the previous year. The story highlighted the need for an outsider with authority and power who could say "finish" to these wars and make it stick.

Blow flies were very bad in this area. After I went to bed one night, I felt a movement on my neck and found small, active maggots looking for something other than the wool of the blankets they had hatched on. Unless all wool garments and blankets were completely rolled up in a cotton or canvas covering, the blow flies infiltrated the wool and deposited their eggs, which in the warmth of the sun hatched out in an hour or so. It was a shock to wake up and find maggots crawling over my skin, and I slept cold for the rest of the night.

We began hearing garbled gossip from our base, different stories from different people. All of them appeared pleased to see us back and wanted to tell us their version of events during our absence. The line had been well supplied with food, and all were anxious to make us welcome and comfortable, supplying necessary firewood and tent poles. We evidently left all of these people with good impressions of our sojourn among them.

We followed the Tuman, a fast-running stream that distributes its gravels across the surface of its rather confined inlet before widening out in the valley below. We wanted to see if we could find the greenstone work axe center, but gave up after it became a narrow confined torrent diffcult to follow. We camped on a small area of high ground above the surrounding swampy area. We would return to base the next day. We broke camp early. Everybody was anxious to reach the base and meet friends and relatives. Home is home even when it is a mud-floored smoke-filled grass house. The Marin headwaters of the Wahgi were running a banker, and our water-wise boys had to make several hand-holding trips back and forth before we had everyone across. The first of the Keluwere people to greet us was small Puko, a pleasant little bloke who was delighted to see us back again. Puko had a couple of long beans and bananas stuck in his bark belt, a stick of sugarcane over his shoulder, and a poor type of bow and arrow (poor in comparison to the bow and arrow of the Chimbu or Goroka people). He distributed his sugarcane in short lengths to his old friends and was prepared to cook the beans and bananas at the first stop, but nothing would stop the line now until we reached the base camp.

Some of the older men were a bit timid as we neared the strip. They probably felt somewhat responsible for the shambles that was our base camp. A patch of kaukau was almost ready to harvest where our houses had stood. All the steel, picks, shovels, mining dishes, and other equpment had been stolen. Every can of tinned food had a hole cut in it. The contents had been poured out on the ground. The assembled crowd all vehemently accused the Benambi people, their age-old tribal enemies. The men and some of the women pantomimed a fierce battle, naming each other as the doughty defenders of the stores they had assured us would be safe in their keeping. They reenacted their valiant man-to-man stone axe encounters, almost getting a sweat up in their realistic recreation of their doughty deeds in our interests. At the height of their obviously insincere performance, I asked them to explain why their homes were still standing while our camp alone had been looted and burned. Taken aback by the question, they spluttered to a full stop long enough for the assembled people to begin laughing at them. They disappeared to deplore the white man's lack of diplomatic decorum. They returned the next day, as large as life and as full of confidence as always, but the effort did not pay off. The sacking of our base had been the work of the people of the boss boy Kowra after he had been killed in a fight with the Benambi people.

Kowra's people had run amuck, and it became part of their grief to loot our place and burn it down. They had rationalized the deed by regarding the camp as a temptation to outside aggression which had caused Kowra's death.

A war party woke us at about two in the morning as it raced to a fracas not far from our camp. The whole line was alerted and ready. We spent the early morning hours listening to the hysterical voices of warriors fighting with primitive man's stone axe, bow and arrow, and spear. One raider was killed, and everyone had a chop at his body to associate themselves with the killing. We spent a rather uncomfortable few hours waiting in the dark before dawn for an attack we thought was coming. A beautiful crisp clear morning with the sun coming up over the serrated skyline of surrounding mountains somewhat made up for our anxious night. Only animated nature, including man, disturbs the peace and contradicts the serenity of these fabulous valleys.

We moved out across the valley to the foot of the range about 2,000 feet below the small plateau, where we proposed to work the small alluvial gold deposit we had discovered the preceding year. A flat grass-covered terrace was cleared and leveled to replace our base camp and airstrip, which would be too far away from our workings. Sharp sticks and bare feet cleaned and leveled the ground. The clearing was just over 500 yards long and 60 to 70 feet wide. The porous soil sopped up the heavy wet season rains we were having. The natives, the very friendly Mogai people, did all they could to help us in their area, inspired by the prospect of trade and prestige. The Keluwere people were devastated when we deserted their tribal areas. They blamed the looting of our camp and were quarreling among themselves about its destruction.

All our mining gear, picks, shovels, and dishes were still safe with the Mogai men. They brought everything back with a great flourish to demonstrate their superior honesty and ability to preserve our equipment from outsiders. We had all our followers on the airstrip job. They were expert with their traditional gardening tool, the sharpened stick, loosening the bump on the surface. They preferred shoveling earth with their hands onto improvised vine and stick transporters rather than using a shovel. We had only a few shovels, so we used primitive man's methods until more arrived. We had the strip ready by March 23. Dan had done a very good job. He had gone over it three times, removing bracken roots, leveling and filling, and clearing off the rubbish. The single-engine Junker plane with doughnut wheels would have no difficulty landing and taking off from this strip.

Koipore's local wife, Liklik, whom he had taken home, was very ill and did not respond to the usual malaria treatment. The locals and even our own semisophisticated boys were quite convinced that fish she had eaten months ago was responsible for her illness. Her people brought along an old codger who confirmed their belief, and he offered to cure her for one bailer shell, an exorbitant fee in that society, plus of course the usual good feed of pork and greens. Her people appeared to be quite sure of his ability to cure her. He diagnosed the cause of her complaint as some foreign matter in her stomach and a general collapse of her insides. The condition had, he said, been brought about by travels far from her people and protectors. She had seen too many new and unique things and places and had been allowed to see and partake of too much of the unknown world. She was just overwhelmed by it all. He proposed to exorcise her particular group of devils and restore her to the ignorance that was appropriate for a young woman in the village. Knowing the natives' faith in local sorcery, we gave him two shells and urged him to start immediately. A small pig was killed, and cooking was about to start when the old boy began his preliminary ritual.

He slapped Liklik (Pidgin for "small") rather heavily on her bare back a couple of times and then ordered a supply of water, into which he threw a few handfuls of dirt picked up from beside where he was squatting. This he carefully mixed into a mud pie, blowing on it and muttering incantations in a rather subdued tone. He then proceeded to paint lines of mud up and down her belly in the approximate area of pain. As he painted he pressed her stomach and blew. He then placed his ear over the affected area and announced that all was going according to plan. The interior devils were now sing-singing, and she would start to recover almost immediately. The old bastard then scuttled off with a gut full of pork and the

Brother Eugene building first church in Mt. Hagen area on the Mogai drome.
He is using shells to buy pitpit (cane stalks) for the walls.

shells. Liklik's temperature was still 104 degrees. I never sighted
him again; he kept in touch with his case through one-talks and
never risked another visit.

Much shouting and excitement from the countryside announced
the arrival of the first white missionaries in the area. Dan and I
walked out from our camp and met Fathers Ross, Schaefer,
Augenunger, and Tropper and Brother Eugene, a tall lay brother
from Mt. Carmel, Illinois. It was Wednesday, March 28, 1934,
when they arrived on Mogai airstrip. They brought back Rebier, a
small boy from Palinger whom we had taken out the previous year
and had lent to Father Ross so that he could learn the language.
They were very enthusiastic about the great highland valleys

through which they had traveled after crossing the Bismarck Range from their Gueabi station on the lower Ramu River side. As Dan and I were by now ready to move on to the small plateau above to start work on the alluvial gold in the small creeks, we handed over our partially built grass and pitpit camp to them so that they could start their missionary activities.

The first Mass was celebrated in a tent fly rigged on the still untried airstrip on Sunday, April 1, 1934. Perhaps it was not a very appropriate or propitious day, but given the energy and enthusiasm of Fathers Ross and Schaefer, the mission seemed certain to succeed. They later made their headquarters at Rabiemul near the present Mt. Hagen strip. Father Schaefer was about seventy to eighty miles down the valley at Mingenda. Fathers Augenunger and Tropper were later assigned to other stations away from the Highlands, and Brother Eugene busied himself with constructing new grass, pitpit, and vine-tied buildings for the temporary camp on the airstrip.

Liklik was still very ill despite the old thief's ministrations. Father Schaefer thought she had malaria. No malaria treatment could improve her condition, however, and she died early one morning. Koipore woke the camp with his lamentations. Her mother and father were with him. Unlike most natives, who make sure everyone within voice range hears their expressions of grief, they were weeping quietly and preparing for her burial. She was wrapped in a blanket and tied to a long pole for transport to her people's place—according to Koipore's people's custom—a concession to him. My effort to comfort Koipore and sympathize with him failed. My sympathy and grief seemed unconvincing to him, as I had not shed a tear. Like all natives, he counted flowing tears and loud lamentations the only proof of inner grief.

On Monday, March 26, 1934, Jokurry, after his travels and association with us, now regarded us as his permanent patrons and protectors. He wanted never to return to his ancestral acres. He knew no residential conditions other than the primitive's readiness to defend life and property. We had never met any people claiming relationship with him, even after he became one of our boys and was in an influential and key position to distribute largesse stolen from our stores. Evidently he was one of the last of a group who had been on the run before he was born and who were of little interest as poverty-stricken, wandering refugees. Such people did, however, become fair game once they acquired a few pigs and sustenance garden plots on alien acres. The proof of ownership was the ability to defend and hold property. Joe and his small group were decimated by primitive man's avaricious and acquisitive nature and his contempt for defenseless life. Joe told us that cannibalism was widespread in the Goroka-Bena Bena valley and that no human meat was wasted. A father had no objection to seeing his son, a battle casualty, cut up and cooked by villagers, but he himself refrained from eating and after the meal collected the cleaned bones for burial. Bodies were carried to water, and the black skin was burned off in an open fire down to the yellow-white layer. The flesh was then cut off in small pieces with bamboo knives, was cooked with water in bamboo sections on an open fire, and was eaten half raw. The bones were fire roasted and picked clean, then smashed for the marrow. Evidently human and animal flesh received the same culinary treatment. There was no recognition of death from natural causes; all deaths were caused by sorcery. An enemy had made poison, and the obligation to avenge the deceased fell on near relatives. It was just another rationalization, if one was ever needed, for what would be premeditated murder in our culture.

Dan and Brother Eugene, with a few boys, went across to the old base camp drome to direct the plane due in over here in case he did not see our fires. Brother Eugene was hoping for his first ride in an airplane over to this new strip. The four stacks of dry grass on each corner were ready to light when he was sighted. Father Ross counted more than 1,500 natives around the strip waiting for the plane. They were still coming from every direction, and there must have been another thousand or more by late morning. We were all disappointed that no plane arrived. In those days pilots flew by sight and the seat of their pants and in this case over miles of often wet tropical coastal country, along sometimes smoke-filled grassy plains, weaving around or under cloud-clogged mountain divides up to 9,000 to 10,000 feet high, then along narrow bare rock corridors with peaks up to 15,000 feet towering above them, and an uncertain welcome should the single-engine plane have to force land among the primitives below. We knew all the hazards and were content to leave it to the pioneer pilots who did so much to open up the unknown areas of our world. A Fox Moth was sighted Sunday morning north of Mogai, and smoke from our four grass fires brought him over to make a good landing. Jim was with Bob Gurney, the pilot. He handed me a billy can full of what I took to be water. It was a can of urine. The long flight and the high altitude together had forced him to use one of the billy cans in the cargo. I made a mental note to carry an empty beer bottle if I had to do much flying in and out to the coast!

The missionary party and the plane with Jim on board left the following morning. The missionaries would be back as soon as they could organize and establish themselves on the strip. We intended to be up on the plateau working the creeks by then. Dan and I spent the next few days prospecting both sides of the ridge shedding gold. We decided to move up as soon as the missionaries came back in a few weeks' time. Our next probe would be to the south-southwest to prospect the high, open country we saw from Mt. Hagen, around Mt. Keluwere, then south and back east around Mt. Yalbu or Ialibu as it is now known. We had to wait for another planeload of gear before setting out. From inquiries it appeared that quite a lot of the shell, particularly the tam or bailer shells, was traded in from the south, together with a few very worn-down steel axe heads.

I had been buying up some of the bows and arrows tipped with human bone. The natives' dead were put in a round hole in a sitting position. A few leaves and earth covered the top, and a bundle of grass was uppermost. When the flesh had rotted away, the bones were recovered and ground down for arrow tips. They were chock full of lethal infection for the unfortunate who got hit with one. It was known there that a wound from one was usually a slow painful death, but the natives attributed its killing qualities to the "spirit" of the former owner rather than to the infected bone-tipped arrow.

Sitting around waiting for the plane, we had time to tell our boys stories and to hear some of their long-winded, repetitious recitals of events of long ago as told by their old men in the warm comfort of the men's house. Such stories of course always exaggerated a bit and were never other than flattering to the recounter. Koipore, whose home village was Lamani on the headwaters of the Bubu

River, a tributary of the Waria and about 5,000 feet above sea level, had been a small boy when the German government on this side of the island decided to define and mark the border shown on the map between this side and Papua. The surveyors recruited dozens of coastal natives to carry their cargo over the coastal range into the Waria Valley, then up the Bubu River into the mountainous backbone of New Guinea, a task only mountain natives could efficiently accomplish. They battled through until they reached the bitterly cold open alpine grass country more than 8,000 feet above sea level, then dropped their packs and deserted. They had nowhere to go except back through the villages in the Bubu headwaters, where the natives were renowned warriors and practicing cannibals. The unarmed deserters fleeing for their lives became easy prey for the women and children, who slaughtered them like so many wild pigs or dogs. One was found hiding in a tree by a young woman of Koipore's village who, contrary to popular romantic fables about the noble savage, called all her female friends and children to make sure he did not get away.

They built a huge fire at the foot of his tree, not to smoke him out, but to enjoy his terror when they made him understand that it was to cook him. One of the men skewered him through the neck with an arrow, then climbed the tree and tomahawked him. He dropped like a dead opossum and was immediately roasted on the fire and eaten. A small portion was given to Koipore to eat. He still claimed it had tasted good. Some of the runaways eventually reached their villages on the coast to tell the story of the massacre of their one-talks. Some years ago deserting Bubu natives, recruited from their now government-controlled villages, ran away from the goldfields and in trying to make their way back home along the coast were murdered by relatives of the Bubu villagers' earlier victims. These coastal villages had been under Administration and missionary control for many years, but they could not resist an opportunity to "back," or avenge, a killing. I am quite certain that, even today, under the cloak of religion and civilization, they would revert, if and when the opportunity came, right back to the primitive savagery of their forefathers.

I had an old boy making one of the pronged spears. He brought in a long, straight length of sapling and roughed it out most effi-

Spear making among the Mogais.

ciently with a small sharp stone axe. Then, with various bone, stone, and tooth tools, he carved out the auxiliary prongs and scroll-like marking below the main point, smoothing off its roughness with sandpapery rough leaves growing in the area. It took him a couple of weeks to finish; he never stopped gossiping to his assembled one-talks, and his spear-making effort became almost mechanical but most efficient. He evidently was a master in the use of primitive tools.

Baranuma believed that he should have had first choice of the pork, certainly before any of our camp followers, who in turn thought it was first come, first served. He had a choice leg put aside for himself, and a Bena Bena who disputed his right to it promptly settled the question of ownership by urinating on it in front of him. The old boy was disgusted but only because he had not had the idea first. Although he loudly condemned this "all same pig" degenerate action, we would leave Baranuma in charge of the base camp when we moved out. He had built a ten-foot-high pitpit fence around the camp, and with a couple of his Waria mates and a few Bena Bena, given our present friendly relationship, they should be all right for a few weeks. The locals were there every day in hundreds and on a plane day a couple of thousand. They quite understood then that on some days the clouds block the road, and the plane cannot see its way in.

The men sat around in groups, discussing events of the past and present. The older women congregated in groups, showing off their plump babies and endlessly weaving bilums (long lengths of pubic coverings for their male relatives to wear draped over their wide bark belts), and arm and leg bands, and small bracelets for the children. A woman was rarely seen sitting down, doing nothing; her fingers started to work as soon as she settled down to gossip. The younger girls spent most of their time primping and painting themselves. Arm in arm they paraded and ogled our very receptive Warias and even the primitive Bena Benas.

Nauta, one of our really dependable Waria boys, never seemed the least bit concerned about the outcome of any seemingly sticky encounter with hostile natives. He was always most definite in his contempt for their fighting ability compared with that of his people in times past, who ranged the valleys on both sides of New Guinea's mountainous backbone and whose outsized bows and arrows were half as long again as the best in this highland country. Nauta's invariable reply to shouted challenges was, "you come try im mefella!" He told us that years ago an Ono River native had killed his brother while he was visiting a village on the main Waria River, about two days' walk from his village. Nauta and Lalai, another of our team, had immediately set out to avenge the killing of his brother. They charged into the men's house, and Nauta drove his axe through the killer's head down into his breastbone where it became wedged. He had to leave it in order to make a hurried getaway back to his village.

We moved out Saturday, April 21, 1934, following native paths

Men's house and sing-sing ground, Nabilyer Valley.

over open ridgy country which showed a massed growth of pitpit grass and canes, emphasizing the fertility of these lava ridges. We then descended to the Nabilyer River, which we followed, up-stream along a gradually rising track to the village of Diudar, where we camped. We were escorted onto the sing-sing ground and were made welcome with plenty of native food, pigs, and sticks to rig our camp. In this Hagen area a light-skinned native's name is prefixed with the word "Kundu," and these people had already heard our native names "Kundu Mek" and "Kundu Dan." They had also heard of the power of our firearms. In the evening they brought along one of their fight leaders, a loudmouthed rabble-rouser who had taken an arrow through his bottom lip up into the roof of his

Mt. Ialibu from 10,000 feet above sea level on Keluwere.

mouth. I felt no sympathy for him. I have often wanted to jam something down the throat of a loudmouthed native who holds up the whole line on a steep single-file track while he harangues his friends in the rear. They propositioned us to go along with them and with our superior firearms revenge big mouth's wound and a long string of other indignities. We patiently explained that we were going over the range in question the next day and would not take sides in their tribal brawls. After pantomiming the dreadful end in store for us if we crossed the range without their protection, we disappointed them by refusing to have any part of their wars. They appeared to accept this outcome quite happily and next morning showed us the track over the range, 8,300 feet from the top of which we looked down into a comparatively flat, grass-covered area resembling the crater of an extinct volcano. Here and there, almost hidden in the prolific growth of high cane grass, we could make out a few native houses. The tracks were narrow, about a foot wide, running through the massed growth. We were given a fond farewell by our late hosts, now congregated on a rock outcrop overlooking the valley.

We proceeded in single file down onto the flat along the narrow track on the valley floor, thinking that we had been given a complimentary introduction from our hosts on the outcrop to the new villagers we were approaching. Arrows started to drop around us before our local boys screamed a warning that the introduction from our late hosts had not been friendly at all. As soon as we were down on the valley floor, too far away to retreat to the track up the range and above the flat, they had "war cried" that we were going to attack them and pay back old scores. We could see nothing from the confined track, and Ewunga rushed forward along the track to a small group of houses in a clearing where Snowy, our camp dog, had some of the plumed, shield-carrying, bow-and-arrow-armed warriors perched on top of a house to escape his gunfire-induced hysterical fury. We calmed them down and sent the treacherous Divdars scampering back to their village with a few shots in their direction. We picked wooden splinters out of a bullet hole in one poor chap's shield-carrying arm and assured them that we had no intention of going along with their enemies and attacking them.

We pushed on across the valley, escorted by some of our new natives who assured the embarrassed armed reinforcements whom we met along the track that we were friends and not enemies, for the present anyway. As we were heading into their strongholds, they would have time to figure things out later. The small hole in the wood shield and the shattered armbone were evidence of a weapon far superior to anything they had ever heard of. We climbed out of the valley over heavily timbered, lichen-festooned trees at 8,750 feet and picked our way down into another lovely little valley 7,200 feet above sea level. The northern slopes of Keluwere drain into this valley and form the Gowil, a tributary of the Nabilyer River.

Mick Leahy demonstrates the use of the rifle south of Mt. Hagen. Snowy and Bluey look and wait for the crack.

There were quite a few people in the valley but nothing like the population density at lower altitudes of about 4,000 to 6,000 feet. It was cold, wet, and miserable when the clouds closed in, but on warm sunny days these high-altitude valleys seemed indescribably attractive to all of us. At this altitude the houses were roofed with coarse reeds, the usual blady grass roofing material not growing to roof-making lengths. Lignum reeds were dried and draped in two-foot-long narrow pull pulls, or front coverings for the women and girls. The bark belts of the men were fewer than on the lower valleys. Their front and rear coverings were suspended from a bark

Vine bridge over
Gowil River.

rope belt, and constant scratching made it seem that there were
lots of lice under them.

Torrential rain and a clay subsoil had made some parts of this
valley a quagmire. The river ran slowly and meandered through the
grassy terraces, here and there cascading over rocky bars. At this
height it would probably have been a good stream for the introduction of trout. We crossed the Gowil over the best native vine suspension bridge I had ever seen. Anchored to strong posts deep in
the ground, the heavy high-altitude vines were laced and stayed
into a structure from which it would have been difficult to fall. The
footway, a double row of split saplings, was laced into the structure.
It was practically new when we saw it, but local vine did not last

Skull shrines south of Mt. Hagen.

EXPLORATIONS INTO HIGHLAND NEW GUINEA

very long; it rotted quickly and became a hazard on bridges after about six months. Houses 90 to 100 yards long and divided into twelve-foot-wide compartments suggested that large sing-sing congregations had recently been in the area. There were small wooden shrines on posts in ornamental garden plots, some with a small peephole in the front, through which human skulls in varying stages of decay were visible. From others the doors or lids had fallen away, exposing the whitened skulls of former natives, some with cracked skulls, suggesting a violent death. The presence of quite a few very worn steel tomahawks and an occasional piece of a big knife or machete suggested that we were on the trade route from the south coast inland.

We traveled south around the eastern slope of Keluwere, up and down from 7,500 to 6,000 feet over grass-covered tableland country, fairly heavily populated and magnificently fertile, which must some day come into its own as a farming community. Native food was scarce, principally because the people appeared to be so overcome and stunned by our visit that they just did not bring it. There was some segregation of their womenfolk, who were the gardeners and the barterers. They quickly realized that food was always welcome to men—any men, spirit or ordinary—and produced it. We always managed to get enough for the line and a bit to carry along, but in quantity it was nothing like that which we invariably left behind in the more populated valleys. The people here were not a friendly lot. Some of the men were either showing off or trying to create an incident to demonstrate to the Hagens with us how they handled intruding strangers. They grinned when they were asked for food and demanded exorbitant prices for small emaciated pigs.

One of the loudmouthed men made a swing at Ewunga with his stone axe when he refused to pay his price for a small pig. We watched him closely to see whether he might exploit this seemingly successful breaching of our peaceful attitude. One of our Hagens, through an interpreter, had a harried conference with him. He then wanted to give us the pig for nothing, which we refused, but we offered to buy it for one gold lip or tambu shell. Before we moved out next morning, Big Head sent two of his young men with us, probably to report back on our activities and means of defense against his sort. They were good lads, merged into our team, and gave no trouble or cause for anxiety.

The next day's track was through a flat swamp forest from tree root to tree root in knee-deep mud. Painted, greased, and mud-plastered men in the next village suggested a sing-sing or ceremonial occasion, probably to place skulls straight out of the grave in the small shrinelike boxes perched on poles ready for them in small, cleared, lawnlike areas. This was a quiet, reserved people, living in inhospitable mud and forest surroundings which suggested that it was a refugee group glad to have a chance to survive, even in a swamp.

The farther south we went, the more evidence became apparent of a trade route from Papua. Steel tomahawk and axe heads, worn down almost to the eye, were seen more often and broken pieces of knives bound onto pieces of wood made serviceable cutting tools.

At a village called Nargube we carved the name "Leahy" and the date "1-5-34" on a tree alongside our camp.

About 200 to 300 people around the fishline fence were quietly gasping at our gear and gossiping when an old man pushed through them, under our fence, and aimed a blow with his stone axe at one of the watch boys patrolling inside the enclosure. The other watch boy was drawing a bead on him but was stopped before he fired a shot. I was watching the man's determined advance on the camp and could see that he was very annoyed and also that he was alone in his fury. The boys easily overpowered him and took his axe away from him. Through our interpreters we found out that one of his daughters had been raped by some of our boys. He had been hit with a stick and had the welt across his back to prove it. We calmed him down and sent him off to bring his daughter along to identify the culprits we lined up for him. She was not very concerned or distressed and picked out four of our Waria boys, who confessd to the rape. We called a council of their one-talks. Although they were annoyed and very critical of this entirely unnecessary incident, they were very reluctant to administer any punishment. Dan and I could not let the matter go at that, as we wished to discourage rape, the root cause of many tribal wars. We had to show the couple of hundred onlookers around the fence this was a serious offense in the eyes of our party. We therefore gave them twenty to twenty-five strokes with a piece of rubber shock absorber, which does not absorb any shocks when applied to the bare skin. The locals around the fence were horrified; in their eyes the crime did not warrant that sort of punishment. However, it passed, and even the four Warias admitted that the rape had been a stupid thing to do in new country and they deserved the punishment. We gave the old man and his daughter a gold lip shell, a valuable item of prestige property, to emphasize our disapproval of such actions. Everyone appeared very impressed, and the presents were passed around and admired by all. We felt we had impressed these people with our prompt action in punishing the offense and our willingness to pay a high compensation to the injured party.

When night came, a flashlight shown into a nearby open front men's house shocked the assembled gossipers into silence. They gingerly held their hands in its beam and tried to understand why it did not burn them. The simplest items of our equipment reduced them to stunned silence and amazement.

Another clear crisp morning saw us plodding along a wet and sloppy pitpit-walled track. Near a large lagoon, which the local natives called Karndige, the usual awed assembly gave us a quiet welcome to their village. An old chap made a speech in which, according to interpreters, he said he knew we came down from the sky where all the food came from. He hoped that we would not eat him and his people and that there would be no more fighting now. What a vain hope!

We camped alongside another big lagoon, Donimme. Such small lakes are really huge waterholes, dammed up by lava bars from the now extinct volcanoes. We demonstrated the range of rifles by dropping bullets into the water near a mob of wild ducks swimming about a thousand yards away. It took the natives some time to grow accustomed to the report. Most of them fell to the ground and had to be induced to stand up again. Then they would not open their eyes until after the splash showed where the bullet had hit the water. We eventually got the message to them, but a few shots were needed before they could stand firm and watch.

We came upon a round silo-shaped building with a conical karuka leaf-thatched roof, about twelve feet in diameter and twenty feet high with a platform about fifteen feet high inside and with two

Round house, south-southwest of Mt. Hagen.

ladders leading up to it. It was evidently a ceremonial house of some sort. It was the first one of that type we had seen, and we could not find out what went on when it was in use during their sing-sings.

Some of the men wanted us to stop over for another night, became rather threatening, and barred our track out when we insisted on moving on. A few shoves and pushes left no doubt that we were on our way. An exasperating and common feature of these rather poverty-stricken villagers was their stunned and seemingly shocked reaction to our first contact. Often we could not get enough to eat. Not until the next morning would they manage to bring in food for the boys. They would subsequently want us to stop for another night so that they could demonstrate their hospitality, and sometimes they became really annoyed when we insisted on moving on.

It was difficult to cross a big stream coming off Keluwere; the water was running fast and icy cold over slippery rocks. Some of the boys and their packs got a dunking. A native would never think of trying to save his pack; if he falls or slips, he believes in sacrificing anything to cushion his fall. A gun or camera is never held up so that it does not break on rocks as he falls. The equipment hits first and is sometimes damaged beyond repair.

There was no trace of any mineral in the comparatively recent lava country, but there might be oil in the sedimentaries to the south. We smelled kerosene in one of the bilums our Hagen boys were carrying. It turned out to be a leaking gourd full of what looked to us like rather dirty kerosene, but it burned as well as the real thing. The boy carrying it admitted to having stolen it from a native house but claimed that there was plenty of it in the villages hereabouts. Evidently there was a rather large seepage of kerosene somewhere not too far away. It would not have survived a long trading trip in a loosely stoppered, rather fragile gourd. This country was on the volcanic-sedimentary contact, and the upheavals cracked some of the oil strata, which explained how pure kerosene could be found so far inland and among people who had never seen whites before.

We passed at 7,000 feet through the Gowieryump people and camped at Porgubu among the Tarngige. The people were too overcome to bring food. The altitude made the climate not good for raising crops. It would take kaukau (sweet potatoes) almost a year to mature, and the people looked as though they sat around and waited for a vine to produce. They offered us a few very emaciated pigs but in an impersonal manner and did not actively barter as the Hagens had once they had come to know us. This was the valley of the Mabagai River, which was now running southeast and probably formed the headwaters of the Samberigi somewhere in that direction. We were coming into limestone country, judging by the gravel in the streams and the sheer cliffs of white rock to the south.

The Ejerri people just sat and stared blankly as we walked through their village. They had a very lousy little pig tied to a stake, which the boys scorned. The boys had had it too good until now, and a few meat-hungry days would not hurt them.

We camped at 6,600 feet among the Karudda people. One old chap had a spoon worn pendant fashion around his neck. When we asked where it came from, he pointed to the south. We were also told that laplaps or loincloths had been seen in this area, worn around the head rather than the waist. The laplap's migration, we observed, was somewhat like that of the bailer shell. Traded to the delta people as a pubic covering, it gradually moved up the body as it advanced farther inland, and the fragmented pieces finished up as forehead ornaments. The natives had a name for the white man—Binekar Boricle—probably originating in stories from the Samberigi Valley, visited by Stanford Smith years ago from the Papuan side.

There appeared to be a big valley to the west of us, and we might be able to have a look at it some other time.

From the top of a 6,000-foot ridge we were introduced to the next group across a deep ravine. We were not too sure of the introductory remarks yodeled across the gorge and had some bad moments as we made our way, almost crawling, through five split slab barricades which guarded the thick pitpit-walled approach to the houses. Our new hosts, armed to the teeth, appeared to be uncertain about the advisability of allowing us into their inner sanctum. We persuaded them to put down their spears, bows and arrows, and wooden shields, and released the bowstrings at one end to show them that we were not looking for trouble.

It was very difficult to make the first contacts, and I do not think that the last place had given us a very good reference. I noticed some of our Hagen people had quite a bit of kaukau in their bilums; having tired of our civil requests for food which never arrived, they had helped themselves at night, and our late hosts had found out. I reflected that a shower of bone-tipped arrows could wreak havoc among a line of defenseless carriers. We camped at a village called Pooa 6,000 feet above sea level among the Kaybige Warguar people, who brought along plenty of bananas, kaukau and even a few taro. Shells were eagerly accepted in payment for the food. The main stream, the Mabagai, flowed east over a wide rocky bed in limestone country. On Friday, May 4, 1934, we were at Camp 32, 5,700 feet above sea level. On the day before, we had heard that the Karudda people had sneaked in through the five barred slab barricades and had set fire to the village while the Pooas were watching us.

There was not a color of gold in any of the streams. We were now down to the 5,000-foot level in a gorge through which a stream called Yarlbu raced at great speed. We crossed on a vine bridge, after reinforcing it, and turned east to north to cut the streams coming off Yarlbu or Ialibu, but we found no trace of minerals anywhere. We camped among the Arbuguy people in a village named Warababe. We were greeted by about 300 to 400 men but no women. They gave us plenty of bananas and sugarcane but little of the native staff of life, kaukau, which meant that the women were forbidden to look on this visit of strangers. The women would have brought more kaukau than sugarcane or bananas. We cut "M.D." over "Leahy" and the date "4.5.34" into an old casuarina tree, which may be of some interest in the years to come.

The gardens in this area were rounded beds about four feet in diameter and six to eight inches high. The country was porous and did not require raised beds for drainage. Eight to ten slips of kaukau were planted in each bed. There was a high, level expanse of country to the northeast of us, but it appeared to fall right away to the east. We were told that a bark-tiled round grass house was a special cook house for preparing the last banquet for a renowned warrior killed in battle; the explanation might have accounted for the others we had seen.

A heavy storm with torrential rain broke over the camp during the afternoon. We heard what we thought was someone in trouble and found a small Hagen boy, one of our party, naked as the day he was born prancing around in the downpour, having a bath and singing at the top of his voice. We threw him out a piece of soap to make a good job of it.

We crossed the Nuyar Buram, a large creek, and climbed up a ridge to the Luluarbo people, all silently and solemnly lined up to meet us and evidently thinking we had come especially to visit them. We greeted some of the important-looking men, walked on through their long row of houses and were almost out of the village before they realized that we were not stopping. They rushed forward in an effort to stop us, but the lousy little pig they produced was of no interest to our line, and we carried on across a wide cane grass stretch of level country to the Pubu River which ran fast in a volcanic breccia gorge.

We climbed up to the Koomeana people and camped on the village lawn. Their agitated calls to each other sounded like a hen conversing with a rooster after having dropped an egg. The loud chatter went on for quite some time and was taken up by the mob, so that quite a racket developed. We were not sure what it meant but were ready for emergencies. Two small boys with their small bows and arrows showed us the track to the next village in the direction we wanted to go. We went out of the high grass country into the heavily forested ranges and camped at a place called Liuba, a small poverty-stricken village showing charred shapes of houses burned in recent wars. There was very little food here, and the people were too overcome to think about bringing any in. We noticed quite a few skull shrines with some rather smelly and bleached skulls in the little boxes.

During the night a raiding party shot a few arrows into the camp, and from that moment forward no one had any sleep. Torrential rain never made it any more pleasant to wait in the dark for something to happen. The natives yelled and called and howled all night, but the rain would have made some of the streams impassable for allies or reinforcements. Natives do not like getting wet, even to exploit an advantage in war.

We were very pleased when the dawn gave us an advantage and some light to break out of the high cane grass and bush trap our camp was in. We armed all our wild men, expert warriors all, with bows and arrows and spears taken from the village and left the village along a thick pitpit-bordered track which gradually became a trench hard to defend against an ambush. We made our way through the open bush ridges along hunting tracks that petered out after a while, then barged and cut our way through the bush in the direction we wanted to go. We camped at dark on a high ridge with no food but at least far enough away from villages so that we could catch up on sleep.

The next day we followed a faint track to a bush garden. A small boy was seen racing away from it, and in a short time a group of very timid men showed up. They were almost immobile for about an hour. They stood in the same spot throughout this time, flicking their teeth with their thumbnails and grunting in amazement. We eventually communicated to them that the boys wanted kaukau out of their garden, and after paying them an axe, small knives, a few mirrors (glass "look look") and shell, the boys helped themselves and had a great feast. The Hagen natives with us said we must be supernatural—we just looked at a needle floating in oil (a compass), and it found a garden for us. A stone axe head made from chert, which the natives said came from a place to the southeast, might have come from auriferous country worth investigating.

We were down to 4,000 feet above sea level, but heading back toward our base camp would put us back in the 5,000- to 6,000-foot level again. The bush people led us along a well-worn track through bush-covered ranges, crossing the Pubu, a fairly big stream which was flood swollen and dirty, and a bigger stream called the Kormer, over which we had to drop a tree before we could cross. We reinforced a suspension bridge over the main river, the Nabilyer, and stayed at an old campsite of last year. The area had now been cleared and transformed into a sing-sing ground to commemorate the event. The natives decided that they now knew us well enough to approach us to accompany them in attacking some of their enemies. Pigs and women were, to them, the irresistible barter. When we turned them down they asked our Hagens just what we considered to be the good things of life.

The houses of the people to the south and west of Hagen differed from those in that locality, having partitioned off sleeping rooms and an open front veranda area. The open front veranda, judging from the sugarcane and cooked kaukau skin debris, was a much-used family dining room around the perpetual fire in the center. A doorway led into compartmented sleeping cubicles on each side of a narrow passageway, about five feet square and three to four feet six inches high, with a fireplace in the center. The occupants reclined with their feet on a crosspiece about two feet above the fire or hot ashes. The whole interior was a shiny black, as if lacquered, and as there was no outlet for the smoke, it must have been hard on their eyes after a night's sleep.

It rained buckets. I do not think there is any definite wet or dry season in this country. We were right on the divide between the northwest and southeast. The moisture-laden clouds blew up from both sides of low equatorial steamy jungle and swamp country, precipitating their moisture in the cooler heights of New Guinea's bleak mountain ranges. We pulled up for a cup of tea at Gibinuit and arranged for a couple of locals to show us the shortest track down to the river to wash a few dishes. They gave us the runaround to show us off to their friends, perched on almost inaccessible terraces. We could not raise a color and were so tired that we decided to camp where we had left the boys. We spent another bad day in up-and-down traveling across the country over ravines cut deep in the lava flow from Hagen. The swirling waters of fast-flowing streams took hours to negotiate when there were no bridges.

The combined forces of Komile, Mogai, Injigi, and Yamgar warriors had recently defeated and routed the Benambi people. At Kuta where we had now located our camp to work the gold, the survivors were making new gardens and homes and were still licking some of the festering wounds of battle. They appeared to be continually engaged in a guerrilla-type killing of individual foreign natives. The bereaved relatives eventually organized a massed attack and devastation of the whole village and drove the inhabitants over the ridge down into the Nabilyer Valley. Later in the day we passed through the devastated village and saw gardens cut down and flattened, and the burned out skeletons of houses. We camped nearby in a longhouse used to shelter the attackers. Some of our Hagen men gave their version of the battle, even pointing out where they had skewered a Benambi fighting for his life. The tale had been padded a bit, of course, by time and by their fertile imaginations.

We went through the gear of our local carrier line and found quite a lot of shell, puspus (woven cane bracelets), oil, and paint pilfered from the village near which we had camped. They were very upset that we took exception to their pilfering. Looting was a legitimate activity for anyone who could get away with it. In the estimation of our boys the natives we had contacted were just wild dogs and fair prey. Our boys could not see that these natives were no different from themselves or that the same rules should apply to them.

On the home run there was much excitement about packing and preparing to leave. We had a long hard day ahead, but light packs, and bellies full of pork and kaukau, and anticipation of the pitpit girls who would be waiting for them, put everyone in high spirits. The girls were on hand to greet the line, some of them well perfumed with the musklike smell of a certain tree bark which has great allure for men. The Warias needed no lures. It was good to be back in the base again. We could relax, clean up, and forget the early morning roll up of beds and sails (tents and flies).

We moved up to Kuta and built our bush-timbered, bark-and-grass-thatched houses on top of the small plateau above the gold-bearing creeks. Looking out over the Sepik divide to the north of us and the Papuan fall to the south, we had a wonderful view of the surrounding country with Hagen, Keluwere, Ialibu, and inner mountains towering above the fertile, densely populated valleys. It was an easy camp to defend and close enough to the villages on each side for us to be supplied with native foods and pigs. Digging holes for the house posts, we found some bones of long-dead natives buried on what had been an old sing-sing ground. Our Warias refused to help with the bones or the hole, so Dan and I had to put in the post. The Purari boys in a couple of days built a very compact and warm oval-shaped house about twenty-five feet by fifteen feet with a double row of sticks four feet high. Grass was firmly packed between the sticks, and the thickly thatched roof had holes for three fireplaces. The structure made a snug sleeping house but was much too hot and smoke filled for Europeans.

Kuta was 6,500 feet above sea level and 1,000 feet above the

Panorama from 1934 Kuta camp.

Panorama from 1934 Kuta camp, showing peaks of Schrader range and Purari-Sepik divide.

Panorama from Kuta camp. We found some alluvial gold in the creek below.

drome and the valley. We could see any plane movements in the valley below but almost burned our lungs rushing down when one came in unexpectedly. It was a damp foggy camp; we seemed to get the clouds from both sides of New Guinea. The clear, cold, crisp mornings always compensated for the foggy evenings, and for the occasional foggy mornings as well.

We built a two-story grass-roofed and bark-sided house, mortising the ridgepoles into the tops of the uprights and lashing the purlins on with vines. A huge bark-sided fireplace capable of holding great chunks of firewood kept the building warm enough in the early part of the night, but because of the numerous holes and cracks in the bark, our hair in the morning was silvered with moisture and the top blanket and pillow were damp. The fireplace timber and bark gradually dried out and became a fire hazard, and so we kept buckets of water handy to dampen it down. Sometimes in the early hours of the morning we had to urinate on the smoldering logs to stop them from bursting into flames. The risk of fire became so great that we decided to fly in galvanized corrugated iron at £252.0.0 per ton air freight as an insurance against fire and the destruction of costly gear.

The locals came in to work, bringing in poles, grass, and other supplies for the building operations. We wrote their names down and called them in the afternoon for their couple of shells in payment for their day's work. We gradually increased the one day to two. Eventually we would have the locals working for a month or so without the daily pay in an effort to train a team to work the gold, which cannot be done with day-to-day casual labor.

Hundreds of visitors came day after day. The old men were intensely interested in our steel tools, particularly the saw. They collected the sawdust and examined it minutely, flicked the steel saw, and fingered the sharp teeth. They watched with interest the mortising and shaping of the uprights and ridgepoles and gave a great cheer when the ridgepole dropped over the upright and made a tight fit. The spirit level was something of a mystery, although these highland people understood a straight line or a level surface better than any other New Guinea natives. The auger was a great success. The natives grasped its use in making holes and threading vines to bind poles together during house construction. We had no nails, and our first building operation made sense to people who had never seen a nail.

Metar, a big good-humored man with a great black beard and woolly mop of hair, became a sort of adviser to the camp on local affairs. He told us that the first steel tomahawk, which was worn down almost to the eye, had been traded in from the Papuan side and had first reached the valley when he was a child, perhaps thirty years ago. The legend that accompanied it told of a hard, rocklike formation of ready shaped and handle-holed steel axe heads, sharp side up, that formed the walls of a great waterfall. A small boy playing near the water had pushed a stick into the eye of one of them and had started to cut saplings and sticks around the village. His father saw him and understood the device's value as a cutting tool. He began collecting and trading the axes to villages throughout the district. I myself would guess that the axe had come from the Samberigi Valley farther south or had been traded in from the Papuan coast. Metar also told us that he had seen the first plane fly into the valley. He and his companions had all been terrified. They imagined that it had come in to eat them up, and all of them dived into the nearest bush or grass to hide from it. In some places they used

Buying food with shell at the Kuta camp, Mt. Hagen area.

Lining cooking hole with banana leaves at the Kuta camp, Mt. Hagen area.

the plane as an excuse to slaughter and eat all their pigs before it devoured them.

Pigs were coming in in such numbers that we would have to start a pig farm to hold them until needed. We farmed them out to local natives, promising a gold lip shell (kinyer, or kin) when we called for meat issue. Pork was plentiful in the Highlands. Although it was almost unbelievably abundant, the Goroka Valley people just could not curb their hereditary propensity to steal and eat pieces left unguarded. Peterkai, a cheerful Madang boy, brought in one of our Goroka natives who had been making off with a chunk of his pork. He received ten whacks on his bare backside with the piece of shock absorber as a lesson to his one-talks that other people's pig should stay put. I was satisfied that the Goroka Valley bow-and-arrow people were a much more primitive people than the spear people of the Wahgi and Hagen areas. Some of these big, bearded, well-built and good-humored old men had a lot of savvy and seemed able to absorb our way of life without much pain or regret.

We went down to the strip again to wait for the plane. Everyone competed to see who could spot it first. The Sail-Ho call of the coastal people was a whisper compared with the pandemonium triggered by the initial sighting of an incoming plane and the "balus e come" (bird is coming) cry. There followed a cacophony of hoots and yodels and ululations that gave way to silence when it came in to land and pulled alongside the camp. The plane was then surrounded by a densely packed mass of whispering natives who stood away from it at a respectful distance, forming a laneway of packed people from the plane to the cargo shed. Each piece of freight was welcomed with a whoop and an amazed sigh of disbelief when bags of shell were carried from the plane to the shed. Shell in such quantities was beyond their imagining. Judging by the occasional shouts and screams coming from down the valley, there was a brawl going on below the strip between the Mogai and Kuli people. It was just the usual payback affair between them.

There was still no plane. After the first day's fruitless wait, we felt as if we did not care whether it ever came, but the next morning our hopes were renewed, and we watched until noon again. The waiting hundreds, who dwindled to dozens as the planeless days went by, anxiously scanned the sky and asked in anxiety, "Today

balus e come?" to which we replied disgustedly, "Today eno come."
One of our Goroka natives after waiting a few days with us claimed
that he had had a dream that the plane would come on one particular morning, and sure enough, it turned up. Next time we were
expecting one, we asked him to dream again and save us a walk
down the range to the drome. He announced the next morning that
two planes would be coming in that day. We hurried down to the
strip to be on hand when they arrived, but no plane arrived, and
another week elapsed before the next one came in. Our Goroka was
discredited as a prophet and became the butt of the other boys'
jeers. He really believed he could will planes to come in. His first
success would have established him as a prophet among his own
people, who would be too afraid of his powers to doubt them
openly. The good-humored ribbing he got from us, on which our
boys elaborated, prevented him from becoming a prophet.

We were out of shell. The locals were bringing produce in and
were trusting us to pay later, according to their names and the
weight of the kaukau we were keeping. They trusted us to at least
that extent.

Swapping stories with some of our Goroka Valley boys, we
learned that village life for women was rather a hazardous affair
especially if they became refugees from defeated clans. The Mahometofe warriors brought back young women captives from vanquished villages. If another Mahometofe wanted a given captive
and was refused, he killed her on the spot with an arrow. A rope was
then tied to one of her legs so that she could be dragged to the
river, cut up, and cooked for the adults and the big kids of the
village. Another Mahometofe had bought a young wife from another village. She did not like her new husband and made a break
for home. She was intercepted by a villager who killed her with
arrows, and she too was dismembered, cooked, and eaten. Apparently any defenseless people were fair game unless they had defenders in the area.

The plane came on Tuesday, May 29. It had been delayed while
new doughnut-tired wheels were fitted in place of the narrow
wheels which would sink in the soft ground on some of our primitive landing strips. Fathers Ross and Tropper and Brother Eugene
came in from Kuruguru, now known as Mingenda, to settle in our

old Mogai drome camp. A group of six Lutheran missionaries with a long line of natives was also settling in about four to five miles to the north of Mogai at a place called Ogelbeng. The missions thus established themselves before the Administration. I wondered how long it would be before they grasped the significance of this highland country, with its million or so of virile people, for the future of New Guinea.

On Wednesday, May 31, 1934, Bergmann and two of his fellow Lutheran missionaries came over from their base camp at Ogelbeng to look around the country. We gave them as much information as we could about the country and people in the surrounding highlands and valleys. They were very enthusiastic. These inland people were going to be evangelized and confused, just like the rest of us. As long as they threw Bibles at each other instead of arrows and spears, the change would be for the better. They pushed on down over the divide into the Nabilyer Valley and back up the river to Ogelbeng.

I was very annoyed to receive a copy of the Administration map and to find that we were described as accompanying the Administration party instead of leading it into this highland wonderland. I knew that Jim Taylor had had long, and at times acrimonious, arguments and correspondence with the Rabaul authorities to allow him to investigate these highland areas about which I had told him in 1932. For the Administration now to try to take all the credit was dismaying but typical. The Administration constantly tried to jump on a bandwagon that had already gotten under way. Jim had named a couple of mountains after us, but presumably the names would not stick. Some seat warmer somewhere else would have the honor.

We had a new Mauser 6.5mm rifle and a new Walther .22 long rifle. The Mauser was a beautiful weapon and, with its telescopic sight, gave us a very definite advantage in the early morning attacks on bush-lined trackside ambushes. The .22 was a handy gun for small game, and some of our boys could use it with deadly accuracy, stopping a cassowary with a bullet in the head or one of the very few pigeons we found in the trees along the riverbanks and in the heavy bush country. We could carry more than 1,000 .22 bullets for the long rifle and be packing the same weight as 100 cartridges for a 12-gauge shotgun. The bullets were also much cheaper to buy.

As opportunity presented itself, we set up targets, often a piece of toilet paper with a dab of ink as the bulls-eye, and encouraged the boys to compete against each other. They became very enthusiastic and brought the toilet paper to show us when they hit the bulls-eye. It was very important that the attacking natives perceive any necessary shooting as visibly effective. Noise without immediate and obvious results meant little to a people who could achieve the effect of firearms by setting fire to a clump of bamboos, which explodes when the moisture turns into steam and blows open the rungs.

Dan and I went down to Mass in a tent fly rigged on the airstrip. It seemed rather queer, going to church with a rifle and a revolver. The boys with us were all armed also. We parked our rifles outside the fly, to be watched by our "Tulla Tulla," Lutheran boys who did not attend "Popey" services.

Some fingers were being cut off for recent deaths. The cut was more a mash than the severing that a steel knife or tomahawk would make possible. The wound must have been very painful for a few days. The amputation of fingers was quite an established practice throughout the Highlands from the Ramu throughout the territory that we had explored. One of the locals almost cut his finger off with one of our axes. The boys did not initially realize how much sharper our axes were than their own stone blades. Koipore, who had cut up and kaikaied (eaten) his share of fellow men, just cut it right off with a razor blade and tied it up for him. He became the center of interest with a white bandage on his hand and his arm in a sling. Our method of bandaging differed greatly from theirs, which used a couple of leaves picked off the nearest bush, softened by being held over hot coals and tied on with vine.

With the plane in and our stores packed, we were ready to go the next day. Brother Eugene toiled up the range in the night to loan us his most treasured possession—a true relic of St. Terese—a sure protection from violent death. I would rather not have taken it; its loss would be a major tragedy for Brother Eugene. We could not refuse it, however, and thanked him for his thought.

We left our base on the range for the exploration of the country to the west and northwest, first climbing Keluwere to see what we could from its top, which Ken Spinks's map showed as more than

15,000 feet above sea level. We would then proceed to the head of the Gowil, break over the range into the Sepik water again, and try to reach the Dutch border. It was all new country, and some of the Sepik tributaries heading in the central ranges carried some gold in their lower reaches. If the country flattened out on top and the highlands were more extensive, there should be another Edie Creek somewhere along this country's flattened-out backbone.

We dropped down along a slippery native track to the home of Uga people and camped near one of their really beautiful sing-sing grounds. An old patriarch friend, whom the boys had nicknamed Cocky from the numerous bits of shell he wore around his nose, which jangled every time he spoke, complained that one of the Mogais had enticed a girl away from his place. He asked me to use our influence to have her sent back to him. We promised to see what could be done when we returned to camp but did not like the idea of involving ourselves in the locals' domestic affairs.

After crossing the Nabilyer over a very rickety bridge and climbing to 8,000 feet, we dropped down into the Gowil, which drains the northern slopes of the Keluwere and camped among the Torgowarnigar alongside the river, a slow-running stream which became a whitewater torrent in places where lava bars crossed it. It would be an ideal trout stream and at this altitude of 6,500 feet might be cold enough for trout to breed. A few fish would make a lot of difference to both native and prospector in this upland country of people starved for animal protein.

On Thursday, June 14, 1934, we climbed the Keluwere and camped at the 11,000-foot level on an open alpine grass ridge at the foot of the main peaks. A small patch of dead timber, the remains of a clump of stunted gnarled trees, gave us plenty of firewood and a warm fire in each tent all night. A long, uniform grade up a lava flow through the heavily timbered side of the mountain was easy going. At 9,000 feet we came out into the alpine grass and even flatter country near the foot of the main peaks. We saw a small black and tan dog, one of the wild dogs of this country. These dogs subsist on rodents and marmots, which apparently live in the patches of stunted trees, that are scattered over the undulating ridges between 9,000 and 12,000 feet. The whole top area appeared to be waterlogged. A few mountain ducks swam at some of the water-holes.

We were out before daylight to watch the most magnificent sunrise ever over the top of New Guinea. The temperature was 33 degrees. Every mountain and peak for more than 100 miles around was visible above cloud-filled valleys. The morning sun created stark contrasts as it rose. At 12,000 feet we began the final climb through clumpy grass. The rare air slowed us, and we climbed in bursts of forty or fifty feet before collapsing onto the grass for a rest. The last 1,500 feet were the hardest and steepest.

Our aneroid registered 4,100 meters on the top, a rubbly platform with a hard core of bare, weathered rock. The southwest side fell away in a steep drop, down which the loose rubbly gravel which littered the top fell away and bounced out of sight into the cloud bank coming up below us. The space between the two topmost peaks or crags suggested an old crater area. It must have been a tremendous mountain in its active days. The whole Hagen district must have been a frightening, awe-inspiring area when Hagen, Keluwere, and Ialibu, three points of a volcanic triangle, were active. The local legend of dust from above, which accumulated on the roofs of the houses and made them collapse, was amply supported by physical evidence in the present ash beds above lava flow level. Still, the country appeared to have been free from such activity for so long that the legend seemed unbelievable. The saga had not been sufficiently exaggerated by storytellers to seem plausible at this distance.

The country to the northwest was a series of ranges topped by peaks and alpine grass-covered mountaintops brightened by the long rays of the rising sun. The dark, cloud-filled narrow valleys and gorges would be hard going on our northwest trip but also promised contact with new people. We hoped that there would be enough gold to justify our optimism to the shareholders of our prospecting company, New Territory New Guinea. We were having the time of our lives and just wanted to keep going, but the end of the rainbow was not yet in sight. We would have been mortified to have a new goldfield stop us up before we had had a look beyond the ranges in front of us.

A strong, cold wind kept the clouds away until we had photographed the surrounding ranges on infrared film. We climbed down again to our 12,000-foot camp. The boys set fire to the dry, tufty grass. The flames quickly climbed to the craggy top, sending up a great cloud of smoke that would tell Baranuma and company back at the base that we had reached the top. They were on the alert and sent up smoke in reply. The sight pleased our half-frozen team and got all of them on their feet to start down again. The well-used native tracks suggested quite a highway for local natives crossing and undulating uplands between the 9,000- and 12,000-foot levels.

Back in camp the boys reported some attempt to steal during the night, but a shot in the dark scared off the thieves. They turned up the next morning to show us a shortcut over the rim of the range that formed one wall of an old crater and put us on a more direct track in the direction we wanted to go upriver.

We passed through the Yarlbulgar, Barbargul and Kunjugle people, all very friendly, who urged us to sleep in their villages. Keluwere, the native we were taking back who had been with us on our last trip, did not want to stop anywhere. He was in too big a hurry to get home to tell his one-talks all about his wanderings. His people gave us a great welcome with all the food and pigs we could afford to buy. The boys happily sat around cooking holes, bursting with pig and every variety of native food. These boys would become the greatest storytellers of all time when they returned to their villages with their fund of experiences. We stayed a day in Keluwere's village to wash and dry out our clothes and gear. All day we were touched, mauled, and examined any time we moved beyond our fishline fence.

We broke camp early. With another of Keluwere's one-talks, whom he selected for us, we went up the river over flat and sometimes swampy terraces, some of them big enough for an airstrip. There were more people in this valley than we had at first reckoned. We camped at the foot of the Gowil-Yuat divide at 7,100 feet. The round kaukau beds were heaped up two feet six inches to three feet for drainage. We were well supplied with food for the line.

Breaking camp at daylight before too many of the locals invaded the camp area to scavenge, we began the steady climb up the bush-

Bridge over the Gai River, Wabag area.

covered range. We reached the top at about 10 in the morning. We were 9,350 feet above sea level. We went down into the headwaters of the Meeump, a tributary of the Yuat running into the Sepik, and camped among the Wileyair people, who lived in steep limestone and volcanic country on the western flank of Hagen, 7,100 feet above sea level. From our camp in the narrow headwaters we could see stretches of grass country, where there would presumably be people and food to enable us to live off the country and continue our probes.

Some of the women were wearing a long rear covering of lignum stalks which trailed along the ground as they walked. The style may have had to do with a marriage or mourning. The men were rather drab in a front covering of string net suspended from strands of rope, with a few leaves suspended in the rear. The boys wore no front covering, just a few back leaves. They were fine big men, with great mops of hair tailored into different shapes, some with a few feathers and plumes further decorating their heads. Long slivers of thin black palm, like the old-fashioned hatpins, were used to keep the head lice moving. Some of the lice could be seen crawling around their necks below the hair line. We discovered later that some of the mops were false wigs, pinned to real mops of matted hair with hatpins of palm, a fashion which could have evolved from the need for protection from axe blows.

Skirting limestone cliffs and detouring around the side of the range where the stream raced through confined gorges, we followed the Meeump down. The going improved when we reached the long tongues of lava alongside the stream. A new type of rickety-looking log bridge spanned the main stream, called the Gai. Long logs reached out over the stream from each side in an arc, the end gap spanned by long saplings that had been vine tied to the log ends. The anchor ends of the logs were resting on heavy log crosspieces, and great rocks stacked on top of the ends held the logs in position. The white water in the boulder-strewn stream below gave no hope for anyone in the event that the bridge collapsed, and we reinforced the tie ropes before venturing across one at a time.

We camped among the Marabay people at 6,100 feet, and their amazement was such that we could not buy much native food. Although this was a rather narrow valley, it appeared to be the most densely populated area into which we had walked. There were gardens wherever we could see. The last watch at 4:00 A.M. woke the camp and gave us time to pull down, pack up, and eat. Also, of course, it spoiled any plans for an early morning ambush that the locals might have entertained during the night.

We again found ourselves surrounded by a frenzied, howling, tearful people who screamed their pent-up emotions and leaped back with a horrified shout when we tried to shake hands or touch them. Hundreds of well-armed men, women, and children joined in our march up the valley, crossing and recrossing the river over their

Dan greeted by the Gai River people, Wabag area.

cantilever-type bridges. Their distinctive sing-sing or war cry, we
did not know which, was a most impressive serenade—a full-
throated chant to the up-and-down beat of their long bows and
spears. The roar cut off into abrupt silence, there was a pause, and
the chant was renewed with the same abrupt roar. I am sure that
these wild-eyed people did not know whether they were dreaming
or we were real. Little outside trade reached this valley. The
natives' decorative talent was expressed in their fantastic wigs of
human hair, added to their own hair, trimmed in different shapes,
and decorated with plumes from the bird of paradise and with colored leaves. In some cases a net covering was worn over the wide

Gai River people before attack at the Doye camp.

and floppy wigs and attached to their own hair with hatpins to prevent it from falling off.

We camped at 6,400 feet. During the night the dogs chased a few marauders away. The watch claimed that they had been trying to steal into the camp. The episode ruined our night's sleep and alerted us to the fact that we were again among a difficult people evidently prepared to probe for any weaknesses in our security arrangements. Our wakening at the last watch and daylight start did not save us from the noisy procession which joined us and marched along amid the same commotion as before. This was landscaped country along the flats on both sides of the now slow-running river. Roadways with wide borders of wildflower and colored shrubs led up to beautifully kept sing-sing grounds, and on through wide, deep sunken highways. Our marchers dropped away in enemy territory and were replaced as we passed through new villages. The houses were different from the Hagen houses, having a distinct hump in the back and a low entrance. They were scattered over the countryside, some of them behind barricades of split slabs across the narrow track through the massed growth of cane grass.

The Gai branched into two streams, and we camped on the top of a rather narrow ridge now much wider than our fishline-fenced camp area above the two streams at a place called Doye, 7,800 feet above sea level. A tightly packed crowd of more than 1,000 sightseers massed around our fence. The narrow ridge enabled us to ask politely that all spears and bows and arrows arriving with the owners be parked at a reasonable distance away from our camp. This request brought grudging compliance. I feared spears at close quarters even more than bows and arrows. An arrow must be fitted to the bow, but a spear can deliver a crippling quick jab.

Our camp was rigged fore and aft with the ridge. There a slight rise on the western end to a small knoll overlooking the camp. Toward evening I became aware of a lull in the babble of voices on the western end of the camp. Everyone appeared to be listening to a fine-looking native whose great mop of hair with the long black tail feathers of a bird of paradise further accentuated his height and authority. Twirling his stone axe above his head and swinging it from side to side, he appeared to be delivering a harangue neither complimentary nor favorable to us. I remarked to Dan, who was sitting on the opposite bunk, "There is a loudmouthed bastard parading up and down outside the banis (fence), who is looking for trouble and badly needs a lesson!" He finished his harangue, turned, and dashed off along the ridge to the small knoll overlooking the camp. Calling to the multitude below, he broke off a leafy twig, the universal peace sign, waved it above his head, then threw it on the ground and stamped on it. He disappeared down the side of the ridge. A few minutes later he reappeared with a long spear in his right hand and two spares in his left and called to the crowd to open a lane so that he could reach our fence, where Ewunga was on guard. I had time to say to Dan, "Here it comes," as I hurriedly grabbed the rifle and stood up outside the tent waiting for him to commit himself to killing or being killed. He dashed through the

Doye camp. The marker shows the spot where the spear thrower was stopped. Our team is on its way back to the base.

gap in the crowd. I was too late for a precise stopping shot before he released the spear at Ewunga to precipitate the massacre. As he whirled his body to throw I hit him with a soft-nosed bullet in the guts, the biggest target. As he went down, I lifted the top of his head off with a second shot. My shot was the signal for all the boys around the camp to shoot. I roared, "finish, finish im, that's all," indicating the casualty. They shouted back, "No got, no got, Master. Altogether he like killum youmi." However, the shooting stopped as abruptly as it had started.

Dan never even fired a shot, but the boys were quivering with rage and fear. Through interpreters with us they had followed the broadcast plot to close in by surreptitiously moving our fishline fence stakes until the camp area consisted of little more than the tents. A quick sortie with stone axes would have wiped out the camp; the diversionary spear thrust had been intended to precipitate an earlier massacre. The natives were so sure of an easy victory that they refused to take any shell in payment. Instead they threw kaukau over the fence and announced that they did not want any payment as they would soon have all our gear anyway. I soundly punished the boys for not telling us what was cooking. Ewunga replied that I would have called them a lot of bloody old marys (women) if they had told me.

I had stopped the shooting before the people had time to get too far away. I called to some of them to stop and tried to find out what had inspired the plot. They cheerfully admitted to having thought that we were an unarmed and defenseless party with a most intriguing lot of loot. They had not known that the damned sticks we carried would go off like that. They had thought that we would be very easy to wipe out. We had disappointed them badly. We patched up bullet wounds and picked out shotgun pellets. They carried away their dead.

The next morning along our track we attended to more wounds and picked out more pellets. A few of the old men were anxious to assure us that Big Mouth, who had had his brains blown out, had been the instigator of the attack. I am sure all would have had a chop at us had the plan not misfired. No one wanted to accompany us, and we pushed on along the ridge without the usual introducing committee. We had to start all over again to get in touch with new people. Our intrusion was resisted, and we had to fend off two very aggressive spearmen, who raced at the line with spears raised. One of them was badly wounded, and the other hurriedly retreated to talk it over with his one-talks who were massed in war array on a ridge behind. They took off, and we did not see them again.

According to a legend, a white man and his party had been driven out of the country on the Sepik side. This was probably a distorted account of an early German expedition up the river. The story might have affected our hostile reception, but these people were much more warlike than those whom we had contacted before.

We camped at a place called Taryoak and the next day pushed on to Rondeldai through intensely cultivated hillsides. The gardens were marked off by long lengths of vines suspended high up from dead ringbarked yars (trees) that resembled wireless aerials. Another great rabble of people surrounded the camping area, bellowing and shouting to each other. Word of the usual conspiracy reached us through our interpreters. We precipitated a scene by kicking one insolent big head under the chin and causing the lot to rush off. The natives were an impossible mob in this valley, and we could not but think the garbled version of a victory over a white man on the Sepik River side must have had something to do with their unusually brazen attitude.

The opportunity to loot any white man's gear would be considered a bonanza by these primitive people. News of such a raid would travel far and fast, inciting their natural cupidity, which would be intensified by the impression that, having no bows and arrows, spears, or stone weapons, we were without any means of protection and as such would be easy victims of a rush attack. Our interpreters were terrified, almost to the babbling stage. I was not so sure they were not adding something to what they heard before they passed it on. So far we could find no trace of any European articles anywhere in the valley. The men were very poorly decorated. They had the legs, claws, and paws of birds and animals around their wrists and smoked a small, conical-shaped cigarette, the pointed end stuck in a hole in a length of bamboo. Smoking was not too widespread through the Highlands and could have come in from the Sepik area.

We stood by all night, expecting an attack, but nothing on a large scale eventuated. We fired a few shots during the night to let the natives know that we were prepared to defend the camp. Our responsibilities to the defenseless primitives and our own boys was demonstrated when we saw a massed group of men warming up their courage with a war whoop. Our boys, believing an attack to be imminent, asked us to stay back out of the first line of defense to let them handle it. I said "To hell with that! Dan and I are better shots than all of you blokes." Old Ewunga said, "We know that, but if anything happen to you or Master Dan, we will never get home again!"

Dan had developed malaria fever. He had also taken a bad fall and had injured his back. His back had stiffened so that he could not walk and was in some pain. We camped at Rondeldai to see if he would recover so that we could carry on. This was a good camp almost 8,000 feet on top of a clear hilltop in pitpit and cane grass with patches of scrub country below the heavily timbered ranges behind. A corpse was still lying across the track from the main population areas. The cheerful, friendly appearance of visitors from the Sepik side suggested that they were enjoying the discomfiture of their probable current enemies. We were getting sufficient food and an occasional pig from these people, so we would stay until Dan was all right again. A few stragglers came in from the hostile side, their curiosity having outweighed their caution. We were very pleased to give them a friendly welcome. Our food traders from the Sepik side reassured them, and they started to bring in some food also. We asked them to take away the corpse, which had started to putrify. They just dragged it down the track a bit, scooped out a shallow hole, dumped it in, and threw a few handfuls of dirt on top. It was just another corpse on the track as far as they were concerned. An offer of a couple of guides to show us the track in the direction we were headed suggested that these natives were either anxious for us to leave the district or were cooking up a surprise reception somewhere along the road.

Dan was still too ill to move. We had just about decided to head back to our base. We could not delay seeking a doctor's advice too much longer. We were gradually establishing friendly relations with all the natives within the camp area, and I preferred to leave them as friends rather than as bewildered enemies. In heavy rain we pulled down our camp and started back to our base. Dan was carried on his canvas bedsleeve, swung from two long strong saplings, with a pillow under his knees to act as a spreader. Four boys took turns carrying him up and down over steep slippery tracks and across the fast-running creeks. He managed to walk across the rickety bridges, as more than one person at a time would have collapsed them. The local natives assisted us now in carrying Dan instead of wanting to kill us. We were grateful for the opportunity to give our boys a rest and save their energy for the really steep climb back over the 9,000-foot Sepik-Wahgi divide. Up and down from 8,000 feet down to 6,000 feet, we retraced our steps back to the base. Rain, rain, and more rain made the steep tracks so slippery that we had to cut footholds with our shovels.

Bamboo flares which appeared to be converging on our camp had us all out, waiting for an attack, but they passed on away from us. One of our locals from Meeump said it was a crowd returning from a sing-sing. We could not afford to take any chance, and I told the watch to shoot first and talk later. No native would be wandering around in the night rain just to visit with us.

We were well received through the Doye area. No weapons were in sight or derisive marchers or songs. The natives helped carry Dan through their territory, and we parted good friends. Once we had left the Doye people and the news of their abortive attempt to annihilate us, some of the people whose villages we passed through guessed that we had been attacked and that Dan was badly wounded and was being carried back to wherever we had come from. Some of the more adventurous young men decided to finish us off, starting from the back of the line guarded by Ewunga and company, who looked quite defenseless, having no bows or spears. A couple of shots sent them running. They flattened a patch of sugarcane in the effort to put as much distance as they could between them and our Waria rear guard.

A big branch of the Gai that came in from the south was called the Wobindamondai. I would have liked to wash a few dishes from it, but we left it until our next trip this way. Inasmuch as it headed in the limestone south of us, it was probably a dud where gold was concerned. These extraordinarily rich, intensely cultivated soils presumably lost their root crop fertility after years of cropping. We saw the first evidence of an effort to mulch and fallow garden areas. The mounds had been hollowed out, filled with grass and rubbish, then covered over so that it might rot.

It rained heavily all night. We were on the track again by daylight, down more than 1,000 feet, into the river. The river was an awe-inspiring torrent of dirty water, down which great boulders caromed, rounding off their rough edges or shattering into jagged pieces to be rounded off again as they were carried downstream.

We camped early at a place called Warit, the last place before the climb over the divide to the Mt. Hagen country. At least, so our current friend, philosopher, and guide assured us. He said we were on a shortcut back over the range to Hagen. The next morning as we made our way up and down over deep lava gorges, we found ourselves back on our old track alongside the Meeump. Our plausible guide claimed that he had been misled, but in fact he just wanted to show us off to his one-talks in Warit. There was no consideration for the inconvenience or the extra effort involved in transporting a sick man miles off a much easier track. We made him carry Dan without a break over some of his gullies to teach him not to tell lies.

The divide on the southern side of Mt. Hagen was about one of the worst stretches of track to carry our stretcher case; we climbed by hand and foot along roots and toeholds cut in the mountainside that was almost vertical in places. A long arduous day brought us over the 9,300-foot divide and on to the open alpine grass country where the grades were easy but the mud much deeper. Icy rain fell in torrents, and by late afternoon we were very glad to crawl into a few hunting houses alongside the track where the dry firewood that the boys had been carrying dried them out and food filled their bellies.

We puddled through open country along sloppy tracks from over 8,000 feet down through bush patches of root and stone pads to 6,500 feet and the village of our old friend Krobar, who had had the arrow in the roof of his mouth. They gave us a great reception and never mentioned the attempted doublecross of a few weeks earlier (nor did we). Some of our boys found out that no one had been hit by the retaliatory shots directed at them when we had also been under fire from their current enemies. A sing-sing was about to start, and more than 100 pigs, their skins for some reason painted white, were tied to stakes uniformly spaced in straight lines on the sing-sing ground ready for the slaughter. We could not find out what rite was involved. Hundreds of villagers were decked out in their paint, grease, and feathers.

There was very little sleep that night. The sing-sing was an all-night affair, and we were not too sure what it might turn into from our security angle. Some of the boys were too exhausted to accept the hospitality freely extended and after a feed of pig went off to sleep, leaving only the night watch on their job and a few of our local camp followers to celebrate. The main event was postponed until after our departure the next day, but there could not have been much more noise had the activities been in full swing.

We traveled fast over the home stretch. Dozens of sympathetic hand-wringing men helped carry Dan at a great pace back to the Mogai drome, which we reached at 1:00 P.M. on Tuesday, July 10. Father Ross had gone back to Kuruguru, or Mingenda, as it is now known, and Tom and Jack Fox were camped on the strip, having recently arrived from Bena Bena, prospecting the country as they came. Brother Eugene was on our original drome across the valley, building a mission station. We sent word over to him that we had returned and suggested he come over, as we were anxious to return his relic of St. Terese.

Our Kuta mountain camp kept out the rain from above, but the numerous cracks and gaps in our back walls allowed the wet, wind-driven mist to seep in through every hole. We still awakened with frosted hair and damp top blankets. Dan was much better and had started a line of boys gold mining in the creeks below. He was to go out to Salamaua on the first plane.

The streams draining the country on the southern fall of the central mountain range, between the Wahgi Valley and the Nabilyer River, through which the main Purari River had cut its way on the southeast end of this range, had always interested me. From various points south of Hagen I had studied the country through binoculars. The grass uplands gave way to heavy jungle. Although the contours of numerous gullies could be seen, the general outline gave the impression of a more undulating country, with the two volcanic cones the most prominent landmarks in that area. Dan and I knew them as 111 and 122, their compass bearings as taken from the top of Keluwere. The Fox brothers were waiting for the plane to bring in their stores, and they decided to come with me and cut all the streams coming off the south side of the central range, cross over the Irambadi-Chuavi or Chimbu country, then back up the Wahgi Valley.

The area on the Nabilyer side appeared to be sparsely populated.

We could detect very little smoke from cooking fires, and there were no areas of grass or even native gardens discernible on any of the slopes. Without local natives we would not be able to feed our boys or find the tracks in the direction we wished to go. Dan did not feel up to the trip and stayed back to develop the gold on the Kuta Plateau.

Lobo-na-gui and the Chimbu-Sheani people with us were getting excited about returning home, and were spinning the stories which would keep them eating pig for a long time to come. Lobo was emphatic that he would not stay home but would come with us wherever we might wish to go. It was a great comfort to have him, and he would always have a place alongside our campfires. Most of the lads from the Chimbu country could now talk some Pidgin English and would be a great help when the authorities took over later on. Dozens of the local natives wanted to come, but the problem of feeding everyone would drastically limit the number we could take with us.

We got away on Monday, July 16, and went over the ridge and down into the Nabilyer fall, camping at Gwaymil. Over the next few days we were in bush country along the side of the range on wet, slippery root-and-mud tracks. Some of the larger streams were too deep and fast running for us to wade across, and we dropped trees across the narrows. A few colors in some of the larger streams kept us going, but the villages gradually became smaller, and it became less likely that we would be able to feed our too long line of boys.

The people of Kailgu at 4,000 feet above sea level where we camped on July 20 told us we would not be able to cross or bridge a big stream called the Vildai. We rested the line for a day while Tom and I went ahead to look at it. It surely was a torrent, swollen by the almost continual torrential rains. We dropped a couple of the big trees growing along its banks, but the current caught the head branches and tore them apart on the rocks. With the main trunk stripped, they went sailing downstream at a great rate. We decided to turn back to the base camp and tackle that stretch of country some other time. There must be a dry period in between the day-and-night downpours we experienced.

From Camp 68, 6,250 feet above sea level and on top of a range above the cloud-filled lowlands, on our first really clear morning since we had left the base camp, we had a spectacular view of the country to the east, south, and west, with the bare tops of the central mountain range protruding above the ranges to the north. Volcanic cones 111 and 122 dominated the surrounding, comparatively level, cloud-covered bush country. To the south, small knolls or hillocks, typical of limestone country, stretched away for miles, with no high mountains breaking the continuity of the almost level skyline. Keluwere and Ialibu dominated the high limestone and steep walls of old craters, dividing the rivers to the west of us. The craggy topmost peaks of Keluwere, with a white cloud sitting just above its twin tops and illuminated by the first rays of the rising sun, relieved the darkness of early morning. Its craggy top and symmetrical shape would always dominate the surrounding country. In August and September, when the snow whitens its last 2,000 feet, it presents an unforgettable sight.

We left the Fox brothers in a camp with plenty of native food and reached our base to find Dan quite happy with his gold mining and very optimistic about the future prospects. We passed through a remnant of the Benambi people, now living in a small village called Millegar. Their old homes on the flat grass terraces below had been completely devastated. Bananas, sugarcane, and even ornamental shrubs had been cut down or flattened by a combined force of the Mogai and their neighbors. Imbil, a Mogai with us, proudly showed us where he had killed one of the Benambi people and indicated other places where some of his warrior friends had speared and tomahawked the men, women, and children of the vanquished village.

One of our Chimbu-Sheani boys ran away and created a stir for a day or so. We thought the locals might have killed him. The casualty would have been difficult to explain to his people at home and would reflect poorly on our ability to protect him while in our care. Lobo assured us that he would explain the incident to his people. The boy came back after hiding in the bush and stealing some kaukau from a nearby garden. He had apparently decided that he would have little hope of returning home safely through the Wahgi and Chimbu people, some of whom were hereditary enemies. We lined up the team and had Lobo tell him what a stupid thing he had done. Lobo painted a horrible picture of the fate of runaways. It was no use appealing to runaways from the viewpoint of bereaved parents. Personal pain put the message in its correct form for them. We had one of our outside boys give him a few cuts across his backside. If Lobo had done so, another intertribal conflict might have started.

Brother Eugene came up and spent the night with us. He was very excited; one would have thought he had won a lottery. The bishop in Sek on the coast had appointed Father Ross and him to the newly created district of Mt. Hagen. He was enthusiastic and hopeful for the future success of the mission and was happy about the opportunity to spend the rest of his life among the primitive people. He had no thought of any comfort or remuneration other than the privilege of serving God and the Catholic church and saving his own soul. Men and women must be born with such an outlook; I know I would not last very long as a missionary. I managed to dish wash him a few small specimens of gold, which pleased him. He went back to his camp very happy in his plans for the future in the highland country.

Our gramophone was a source of unending wonder and the laughing record (a recording of sound effects, mostly laughter, popular on Australian radio at the time) an amusement to all primitives. The first shock of hearing a human voice coming from it usually sent them running away. Later they would edge back slowly to see where the sound came from. Natives frequently asked us to play a record for one-talks who had not heard the gramophone and whose invariably agitated reaction amused their more knowledgeable friends. Consequently we had just about worn out our few records. Many of the sound grooves were so worn that the needle had to be moved manually. We asked Johnny, our by now sophisticated Bena Bena, what his favorite tune was. He proceeded to hum an imitation of a voice repeating the same few bars over and over from a worn groove.

Lea and Sid Ashton, Frank McKee, and his brother arrived in from Lae, having followed the Lae, Markham, Kainantu, Goroka, and Wahgi route. We were very pleased to see them. They stopped for a day or so, then headed over the Bismarcks toward the Sepik and Ramu and back to Lae.

Mt. Hagen's first gramophone.

Dan had a good team of gold-mining boys now. They would be expert miners and would probably work some of the creeks in their own district once they knew the value of gold and had acquired a taste for the commodities it would buy. I do not know which life was the best for them: the one they were being forced to abandon or our so-called civilized culture that was being inflicted on them.

Dan had a couple of teams of pit saw boys cutting some excellent planks out of the red cedar, semihardwoods, and pine trees from the great old trees in the nearby bush country. We would put a sawed timber wall around the house as soon as we cut enough planks. Throughout August rain and moisture-laden fog blew up from the south and through every crack in our bark walls. The house would have been unbearable without the fire we kept going day and night. I would wall it up when the nails came in and sawed boards were available.

I took Frank McKee over the ridge onto the southern fall to try out a creek which showed a few colors to the dish. We put a couple of holes down through the shallow bouldery gravel to the lava bottom. Frank thought there was enough gold to pay if he could get some water above the gravel and ground sluice the deposit instead of using the slower method of carrying it to the sluice box in dishes.

The creeks in this range country lent themselves to ground sluicing, having plenty of fall, or drop, in their levels as they cascaded down. Water was brought onto the top of the gravel bed, a wide trench was dug in the creek bottom if the bedrock was soft enough to pick, and this was paved with flat and rounded rocks, which sat on coarse seaweed or on rough bark off the zamia which grows in grass country. As the gold-bearing gravel was washed over the sluice, the coarser gold was trapped under the rocks and the fine gold in the cracks and crevices of the weed or bark. The water was channeled off, the rocks and weed and bark carefully washed, stacked up, and later burned, the ashes "dish washed," and the gold rubbed clean of stain, then amalgamated with mercury. The bottom of the sluice was scraped and set up once more for another month or so before it was cleaned up again. Floodwaters sometimes took the lot if it was not well away from the main channel.

Ewunga was haranguing the local natives about hygiene. They would not use the toilet holes dug for them but would dash out in the dark and relieve themselves alongside their sleeping quarters. In the absence of village pigs to clean up, human waste could be the cause of disease in the camp. No one would claim the offensive deposits, so Ewunga lined all the boys up and made them carry the excrement away in their hands. Afterward he took them down to the creek to wash themselves. It was a most effective means of teaching them elementary hygiene.

It had been two months since a plane had come in. We were looking forward to the arrival of mail, some reading material, and stores. Supplies of tea and sugar were low. No one would ever starve in this country, but the native diet would be hard to endure for long. Bob Gurney brought the single-engine Junker plane in. The peaceful airstrip always exploded into a volcano of noise and activity when it appeared. The novelty had not worn off for the locals, and they had many friends from remote villages on hand for a first close-up view of it. It was their show, and I would not have been surprised to learn that they were charging admittance to the drome. Jim came in and would stay until Wednesday, when Gurney would come in again with the rest of the cargo.

Brother Eugene had built the first church in the Highlands, a pitpit and kunai structure lashed to round timber with strips of bark. Round logs laid on the earth floor were a bit hard to kneel on so most of the congregation sat on them. Those in attendance were mostly locals consumed with curiosity about the church ritual. The church was packed right out to the open back awning. The comings and goings and whispered commentaries on the different parts of the Mass had the primitives intrigued.

Jim Taylor decided to come along with me for the second attempt to eliminate from consideration the streams coming off the southern fall of the central mountain range and cross over to the Wahgi Valley. We left our base Monday, August 27, 1934, and headed back around the range. It took us until the following Saturday to reach Kailgu, our earlier "turn back camp." The weather had been reasonably good, and we had a better chance of bridging the Vildai than we had had with the continual rains during our last attempt.

The second tree we dropped across a narrow part of the Vildai held. The line crossed without incident. We went up and down across the country and camped at a small village of Bargai about 4:30 P.M. The boys were exhausted from the hard going. One of the Mogai natives had spread out his karuka leaf mat on the side of the track and refused to take another step. I got him going. A little further along I saw him earnestly addressing a handful of stinging tree leaves that he held in his hand. He then flogged himself with the leaves and, rejuvenated, galloped off up the steep track in great style, apparently a new man. It took us over an hour to cross a lawyer cane suspension bridge over the Bargai. A single-man structure, it was somewhat risky even for one at a time.

Cloudy weather prevented us from getting a view of the country from some of the cleared "lookouts" we passed, and we were glad to camp at Orratar, a small village composed of a few houses and garden patches hacked out of the surrounding bush country. There was not enough food to fill the bellies of our boys, and the natives asked us to stop for another day so that they could call in all their friends from the bush villages to bring food and pigs. We were glad to rest. We spent the day drying out; the boys filled their empty bellies. We carried away any surplus to see us through the foodless days ahead when we would be above a food-producing altitude.

We crossed the Drou and Paldi, which were big streams, over log bridges where they narrowed. I feel sure we detoured down to a few houses in the village of Muru only 3,900 feet above sea level where our guide had some friends whom he wanted to see us. There was little one could do about these detours except to feel very annoyed. To disregard existing tracks would mean cutting new ones through heavy bush and isolating ourselves from food supplies. Consequently we just kept making frantic signs in the direction we wanted to go and followed the leader.

The streams so far showed no gold. The beds were granite and volcanic, some hungry-looking quartz and hard schisty rock, with little evidence of mineralization of any description. We climbed to 8,000 feet along an overgrown track through thick bush country and followed the top of a ridge to a mountain crossing camp called Koidendenoil, a small clearing surrounded by a thick growth of bamboos. We camped at Gibbitjebubu on the same ridge top 7,265 feet above sea level. Sodden moss, wet, rotten firewood, and mud made it a very uncomfortable camp. The boys located some dry firewood hidden by overlanders and made themselves reasonably comfortable for the night. Rice was on the menu tonight for the boys, and they appeared to enjoy the change. The Bena Bena and Hagen people were eating it for the first time.

Every rock and root had a thick coating of green, water-sodden moss covering it as we went on and up along the same ridge through stunted timber and coarse bushes on a wet and sloppy track. We reached a small clearing about nine in the morning. From the depths below in the timbered ranges we could hear the mountain torrents roaring along through their gorges. Through breaks in the clouds we caught a glimpse of bare, sunlit mountaintops a few thousand feet above us, and here and there we saw white streaks of water catapulting down the dark mountainside.

We reached the Wahgi-Nabilyer divide 10,000 feet above sea

level at noon and camped. It was a cold, cheerless camp, and the sodden firewood smoldered. There was little heat from the smoky fires. The boys squatted for most of the night wrapped in their blankets. Jim and I were not much better off with no fire in the tent and only as many blankets as we needed in a warm climate.

We were up before dawn and climbed a nearby knoll to take a few compass bearings before the clouds closed in and blotted out the surrounding country. From a peak 10,500 feet above sea level we had a superb view. South and southwest in Papua there was much more open grass country than I had estimated, and the smoke rising from houses suggested a greater population than I had thought earlier. There were still thousands of Stone Age people tucked away in isolated villages who had never been contacted by Europeans.

On the northern side we looked down through a narrow gap in the mountains into the Wahgi Valley in the vicinity of Mingenda. Mts. Herbert and Wilhelm stood out, their height isolating them above the surrounding ranges. Here and there small areas of glittering white could have been snow trapped in areas protected from the sun's rays. The early morning mist moved up from the valley, gradually blotted out our view, and left us isolated in a sea of clouds.

We pushed on down the mountainside and camped at Korgar, 6,700 feet above sea level, among the Kwilgar people who were seeing whites skins for the first time and—if they must come over the bloody awful track from the Nabilyer to visit them—probably the last. Everybody caught up on sleep during the afternoon and night, and we were again in a land of plenty—food, firewood, and meat. The boys gorged themselves and collected stacks of dry firewood. Most of them were exhausted, but we never allowed our camp security to want, however friendly the locals might appear.

We were on the track again at daylight. A cold, biting breeze from the top of the range made it difficult to leave the warmth of the campfires. The local people led us along tracks on which it was a pleasure to travel after the mud, slush, slippery roots, mossy stones, and wet stunted bushes that had confronted us as we scrambled across the mountain range. Here and there from isolated lookouts were magnificent panoramas of the country below, lit up by the early morning sun fringing the cloud-filled valley with red and exaggerating the height of the mountain peaks towering above the cloud banks.

We followed the Mingenda down and, where it narrowed, crossed and recrossed it over log bridges. In some places, where it cut deep through the sandstone belt, it was only seven to ten feet across and was spanned by a couple of logs thrown across the gap above the point where it surged through a bellied-out channel more than thirty feet below. We crossed the wide grass stretches of the Wahgi Valley and camped at Jimbunar. We heard that Father Schaefer was somewhere on the other side, but unfortunately the natives were having one of their frequent brawls with the people in that area, the bridge had been cut down, and we could not cross the Wahgi to see him.

We broke camp at daylight. Five of the Jimbunar people came along with us to look around the country. Jim Taylor would bring them back with him on his way back to Bena Bena. We followed Father Ross's track along the floor of the valley, which was much easier going than ours near the foothills. Passing through Kumar we saw a corpse trussed onto a carrying sapling, ready to be transported back home for burial. All the men were in decorated battle array—gold lip shells dangling from their necks, shell pieces adorning their bark belts, faces painted red on one side and graphite blue on the other, their bodies smeared with a mixture of pig grease; charcoal; the feathers of parrots, muruks (cassowaries), and birds of paradise; bits of shell; and an empty tin lid here and there. Bananas, sugarcane, and pawpaw trees had been flattened and houses burned. We camped at Mungar in the grass country. The natives asked us to wait until they crossed swords with the Kumar people, who had followed behind us. They were telling the Mungar people, I felt sure, that we would avenge the killing and devastation in their place.

The Mungars rushed toward the Kumars, apparently full of fight. We watched their antics for a couple of hours. Although they yelled at each other, sidestepped, pranced like corn-fed ponies, and rushed about in a great show of aggressiveness, no spears were thrown or arrows shot. They exhausted themselves with their antics, and a drop of rain gave them all an excuse to call it off. We bought a few spears and bows and arrows from the Mungars and pushed on next day to Binegar among the Guley people. Food and pigs were plentiful, and all were anxious to trade for shell.

A heavy storm during the night almost lifted our tent off us, and a stream of water wet some of our cargo. The big stream on the south side of the Tuman was running a banker. Our swimming boys had to make numerous trips back and forth with the cargo and nonswimmers. Jim and I had to swim across. It was a cold swim in the mountain water, but all of us warmed up in the sunny walk across open grass country.

We reached Kuta mining base camp at about two in the afternoon on Tuesday, September 12. All were very glad to be home again to relax and rest for a few days. A new kunai (grass) house on the most prominent point overlooking the Sepik fall on Hagen's northeast flank was probably one of Brother Eugene's constructions to bring the Gospel to these people. It was good that Father Ross was a champion walker; otherwise he would never have been able to visit his widely separated congregations in this area very often. He was a short man with short legs, but he could cover ground faster than any missionary I have ever known.

Some of the infrared and pan films had been ruined in the developing process, and an air bubble was discovered in the thermometer, probably from the high altitude. We were disappointed, as some of the pictures had been panoramas from the cross over the central range.

We tried to grow vegetables, including potatoes, but the thick layer of soft, soapy black sand impregnated with volcanic ash did not break down into very fertile soil. We could produce only very small spuds and stunted cabbages and lettuce. Even the kaukau, which mature in around nine months, were small and often inedible.

Kevin Parer came in in his Fokker, a great, lumbering single-engine plane and something new for the locals to see. The countryside was in an uproar with calls to come and see the new "balus." Dan was back, looking fit and well; with him were my old cross-country traveling companion Mick Dwyer, and a retired bank manager, Groves, from Japan. Mick would have a look around to see if there was anything worth working; Groves was just on a sightseeing tour. Jim Taylor and Kevin Parer would stay another night to hear any news from the goldfields and Salamaua and would fly back the following day.

We received word that air freights from Lae to Hagen had been cut to a shilling a pound for a full 1,800-pound Junker load. That halved the freight rate and could make this rather poor gold deposit a paying proposition. Our principals wanted us to eliminate the country east from our base before we again headed toward the Dutch border. We would go down the Wahgi Valley as far as China-Shiva, then south over the Wahgi River, and continue on to the Kaugel or Purari, if the population could keep supplying enough food for our boys.

The Fox brothers headed northwest toward the Dutch border and were likely to find mineral along the backbone of this country. They were good prospectors and could live off the country, so they would probably go far if the population persisted and the land was not a jumble of uninhabited ranges.

We were packed up, ready to head down the Wahgi on October 3, but rain and wind blowing up from the Sepik gap over New Guinea's backbone and down into Papua's swamps to the south delayed us for a few hours. Visualizing the pig feasts that any contact with new people usually meant, and wanting to look beyond the restricted boundaries of their village areas, more than 100 locals tried to accompany us. We shooed most of them back, but a couple of the more adventurous youths sneaked in at night. In the morning they claimed that they would be killed if we left them isolated so far from home. We reluctantly added them to a line of pack carriers and hangers on that was already too long. We found out that Salamaua, the post for the goldfields, was Mecca to all and sundry. If we were going there, everyone wanted to come. The tales of the few we had taken out and brought back had evidently fired the imaginations of all the men who heard them. They now wanted to see for themselves the outside wonders, especially the vast expanse of water, salted to their salt-starved taste. They evidently placed lots of confidence and trust in us and believed in our ability to bring them safely back to their homes.

We traveled down the Wahgi, crossing it to the north side via a very swampy track. A seven-foot-long slab of columnar volcanic rock, planted in a deep hole, seemed to be a boundary marking similar to the rows of stones in the native gardens, separating the garden plots of individuals. The locals with us told of a legend of many men carrying it, evidently from an outcrop of this rock, to its present site, where they planted it, but the locals could not suggest why.

We camped on a patch of high ground near the Island alongside the river, and Dan decided to build a couple of rafts to float downstream to Mingenda and disembark above the start of the gorges. He built two good rafts of light dry logs, lashed them together with vine and our sash cord, and launched them on the flood-swollen river with the best of our water boys, all of whom could swim. The rest of us sogged through the swamp country toward the village of Drogarka. The water table, lower than in April 1933, was only knee-deep in the soft ooze, but the unstable matted grass surface which moved up and down was rather disconcerting. I expected some of the rear boys to break through and disappear.

We were settled in camp that evening when Dan and his band of rafters broke through the pitpit along the side of the river just about exhausted. The river had become full of snags against which the force of the current pushed their rafts, pinning them against the octopus-armed trees. One turned over against a snag, and although the gear had been securely tied down, some of it was lost. One of the boys had almost drowned. A raft was an unwieldy craft and impossible to steer or maneuver in a flooded river full of snags. It was a good effort, but all preferred to walk in the future.

We pushed on down to Jimbunar, where our old friends from 1933 always gave us a welcome with plenty of food and pig; they were shell-hungry people. They could not imagine that shell would ever become a drug on the market and were availing themselves of every opportunity to acquire it and store it against the time when it would again become a very rare and practically priceless item in their culture.

Jim Taylor had delivered the few locals who had visited our base at Kuta. They had the female youth and beauty lined up with full decorations for a sing-sing. They appeared to have kept up the festivities all night; certainly each time we checked our watch it was in full swing. A very groggy, worn-out team shouldered packs for the

Above the Wahgi gorge downstream from the Chimbu River junction.

trek, by now well known, to the Kimbe River, where we camped. There was a big war in progress on the terraces across the Wahgi. New smokes from burning houses spiraling up at frequent intervals marked the advance of the invaders and the house-to-house rear guard action being staged by the retreating villagers. Through the glasses we could see the women and young children loaded down with salvaged bundles and leading the pigs on a foot rope away into the ranges behind. At least they would have some firewood for the cold and bitter times ahead to help prevent their people from being wiped out.

We camped with Father Morscheuser at Mingenda; Father

Schaefer came in like a whirlwind from an outstation he was building. We had a drink of tea with Pastors Bergmann and Helbig and two other white Lutheran missionaries at their camp on today's Chimbu airstrip which was then being constructed on top of a high terrace above the river. They were the most dedicated and enthusiastic lot of missionaries I have ever seen. These primitive people would be confused later on, trying to figure out why the rewards for the good life were the same while the approach roads were many and devious; for primitive minds here would be a source of conflict.

We went back over the Chimbu, wading across it instead of spending hours reinforcing their vine bridges for single man crossings, and climbed the ridge to China-Shiva. We passed a recently burned out village, devastated even to the bananas and sugarcane, which had been flattened and trampled into the soil, their alignment indicating the direction of the final massed attack.

We turned off the main Bena Bena track out of China-Shiva, climbed the range to 8,000 feet, and then followed a steep slippery track down to the Wahgi about 3,000 feet below. Running through the southeast end of the sedimentary belt on the south side of the valley, it constricted the north-running streams off the central mountain block. The river, churned into foam, was tearing along through the bellied-out rock gorge about forty feet below the vine bridge which spanned the narrows. It would be a great site for some future hydroelectric dam and was an awe-inspiring sight when viewed from above on a flimsy vine bridge.

We camped at 7,000 feet among the Dunar people, who fed the line and bartered pigs for shell. They had recently been cleaned out by another crowd and were rebuilding on top of a steep ridge with only one approach. It could easily be defended, and so they would presumably be safe for a while. The Wahgi continued through the steep gorge about 2,000 feet below us, and there was no doubt that it was the Marki which Mick Dwyer and I had seen in 1933. None of the Dunar people wanted to come with us. Their old homes, which we later passed, had recently been burned and destroyed by the Seanor people even to the complete destruction by ringbarking of groves of yar trees. We thought we were in trouble as we approached the Arbay people; they, thinking that we were the Youvais

Camp, Chuavi area, Mt. Irambadi at the left.

or Dunars coming to attack, sent up a war howl. A few arrows and a few bullets were exchanged, but no one appeared hurt. We passed through their villages and, in open grass ranges as hot as Hades, camped among the Seanors about 2,000 feet above the Wahgi. They seemed to be the bosses of this particular area, were quite friendly once we had made contact with them, and brought along enough food and pig for the line.

We circled back and slipped and fell down the grass range to where the Wahgi, a torrent of dirty brown-white water, roared over a series of bouldery rapids. It took us the rest of the day to reinforce and cross another rickety vine bridge. Even the dogs had to be carried over, their front legs tied around the boy's neck to allow him to use both hands to steady his crossing, his back protected by a blanket so that the dog could not scratch his back while it was being carried across. No man or dog would ever have survived a fall into the torrent below.

A steep climb up to 7,200 feet through hundreds of curious villagers took us toward Mt. Irambadi and our original track from Bena Bena to Chimbu. We camped among the Tamamuru people, all one-talks and almost by definition deadly enemies of the Yomos, whom we had first contacted in February 1933. A roadblock or barricade of split slabs fifteen feet high across a walled-in pitpit track protected a newly constructed group of houses against attack from one direction at least. The whole area appeared to be in an uproar, with armed men rushing around aimlessly and shouting at people whom we could not see. We were told that some of the Yomo people had recently raided and killed some of their men. Ewunga said that the Yomo had probably eaten them also, but we could find no evidence of cannibalism among these very volatile and fine-looking people.

Our Hagen camp followers were cutting firewood when one of the locals made off with an axe. In the uproar, Lowai, one of our Bubu-Waria boys, stopped him with a shot and recovered the axe. A group of girls in mourning for five of their men who had been killed by the thief's people a day or so earlier took the opportunity to finish off the offender by chopping holes in him with stone axes. By the time we got the story it was all over, but the preliminary uproar had us worried, and we stood by, ready to defend the camp in case our firewood line was attacked. Our boys told us a man and his mary had tacked themselves onto our line the day before. They knew that he was coming into enemy territory and tried to send him back. He sent his mary back but came on himself under their protection, then went out with the firewood line, evidently with the intention of stealing an axe and running the gauntlet of his enemies to escape with it.

A bright little boy, one of the hundreds of all ages congregated about ten deep around our fence, was brought inside by Ewunga, who said he wanted to come with us. His father, a rather important-looking old chap, also wanted to go with us to see something of the outside world. The boys trimmed his hair, washed most of the smelly pig grease off him, and put a laplap on him. He was given the run of the camp until we found him combing his hair with a table fork. We then discovered that Dan's watch and chain and the small boy were missing. He had admired the silver chain and had draped it across his nose, latching it over the peg stumps protruding from the holes around that organ. Lobo, whom Jim Taylor had brought back home and who was now in complete charge of everybody and everything, was informed of the theft. Lobo wasted no time. He exploded in howls of horror and with a few of his bodyguards bounded up the track to the kid's village. The father returned the watch and chain plus a few more articles that the small boy had pilfered. The old man was very anxious to hand back everything and avoid any further complications. Lobo must have told a hair-raising story to elicit such a quick response.

Not two hours later another native grabbed a lump of pork and a few presents we had given to one of our camp followers. Lobo quickly repeated his performance and came back with the loot. He was the big boss in these parts. He was also the most convincing demagogue, haranguing the hundreds around the fence, who appeared to listen entranced to his every word. He must have told a wonderful story and told it well, with all the necessary pantomime. The small watch thief duly appeared with the fence spectators the next morning and was grabbed by one of our boys. He most convincingly denied that he was the same boy whom we had brought in and cleaned up. Iparawar was very impressed with his denials but he had cut the boy's hair the previous day, and there was no hiding the haircut. We explained his theft to all and sundry and then gave him a hammering on his bare backside with a cane.

That morning the decorated, shield-carrying, and heavily armed warriors were wending their way up the rocky limestone ridge toward Irambadi to swoop down on an enemy village which had recently killed some of their men. Anticipating some good action pictures of the fighting below from the bare rocky crest of the knife-edge ridge, I asked them to wait while I packed a telephoto lens and tripod. With a couple of boys and Snowy, the dog, we went up and along the gradually rising ridge, which commanded a view of the surrounding country and the enemy village below. I set up the Leica camera with the telephoto lens among the rocks on the top of the ridge above the village. The shield-protected inhabitants were even then making a pretty good effort to defend their homes and gardens while screaming for more reinforcements from their outstations and ultimately began to drive the invaders back up the ridge.

As I was peacefully photographing the action below, I thought I would be exempt from attack, but arrows began to hit the rocks around us, so I picked up the rifle and bounced a few bullets off rocks close to the bow-and-arrow men. I had forgotten about Snowy, the dog, who went into frenzied action as soon as a shot was fired. With a yelp, away he went, after the now rapidly retreating villagers. The retreating invaders in turn were quick to take advantage of the stampede and followed as close to Snowy and the retreating villagers as they could, adding their hoots and shouts to Snowy's wild howls. One chased the other right through the village, whose houses went up in smoke as they went through. Only exhaustion on Snowy's part stopped the mad rush.

I sat on top of the ridge and felt sure that I would never see Snowy again. The natives would surely fell him with arrows, I thought, but big dogs terrified them even more than enemy arrows, which they were accustomed to dodging. I waited on top of the ridge, taking a few photographs of the now fiercely burning village. About half an hour later, Snowy came panting back up the ridge, leading a line of chanting victorious warriors. He squatted down exhausted, oblivious to the sensation he had created, and was a warrior of warriors. The next morning a long procession of men delivered a big pig and the biggest yam I had ever seen to the camp for Snowy, who had to be dragged out from under my bed where he was still recovering from his war-winning exertions. He received the offering like a prima donna and went back to sleep under the bunk.

Fathers Schaefer and Morscheuser were camped across the river, having a look around that end of the valley. Father Morscheuser was a fine-looking dedicated young priest just out from Europe, enthusiastic and delighted with every aspect of the country and people in these highland valleys. He looked forward to years of labor among them and prayed that his principals would assign him to the area for life. I camped with Father Morscheuser back at the mission station at Mirani beside the Chimbu drome constructed by the Lutheran missionaries, waiting for a plane to go to Wau. At their main station, Mingenda, Father Schaefer was incensed—his trusted local boss boy had been stealing pigs. Father Schaefer intended to collect them or their pork equivalent. It was good to see his wrath driving him into action.

Unless they were firm and just, and unless they demonstrated above all that they were the bosses and intended to remain so, no missionaries or anyone else would ever bring these highland people under control and mold them into civilized members of the world community. Right or wrong, we had to be the boss and remain so. As far as I could see, there were no ethics of law or order other than force and the ability to use it.

The Lutheran missionaries were great workers; they built the airstrip in quick time. Gardens, houses, and fences gradually transformed the hitherto semiswampy flat grass area nearby into a busy, thriving community. We had a drink of tea with Pastor Harold, recently out from Germany and just the sort of missionary that these new people needed to give them an initial grounding in our so-called civilization. He was full of energy, ideas, and drive—the right man in the right place.

The plane did not arrive. Sitting and gazing down the valley through binoculars became an early morning chore on (and always after) the day the plane was due. The wait for the plane coming in for these missionaries was no exception. I rolled my bed each morning and walked over to the strip to wait. At about midday, when all hope of it coming in had been abandoned, I went back to the camp and unrolled the bed. The routine might continue for up to three weeks. Then suddenly the plane would appear, and we would forget the annoyances and disappointments in the excitement of its arrival with mail, papers, and stores. There was a rather good reason for the delay. A village knock-down, drag-out fight with long sticks among a few of the local women suggested that the female of the species was as deadly as the male when her blood was up.

Back at the Mt. Hagen base after visiting Wau and Salamaua, we heard an even stronger rumor that the Fox brothers and all their boys had been killed out near Wabag. Some of the local people from Injigi had been wailing around the camp, mourning the death of one of their one-talks whom they claimed had been killed with the Fox brothers. We could do little apart from advising the Administration in Salamaua. The nearest police post was about 200 miles away at Kainantu, and the officers were kept busy with the local turmoil there. If we went to investigate and the rumour was true, we were sure to encounter more trouble with the killers, who would by now, with the victory and loot, be full of confidence and fight.

Brother Eugene came up and was quite sure that the rumor was true. The onus seemed to be on us to do something about it. We planned to investigate on our next trip toward the Dutch border. If they were dead, all we could do would be to verify their deaths. If they were still alive, they would drift back here in their own good time.

Some of the Lutheran missionaries came over from Ogelbeng, their base and drome. Bergmann did not think our Mt. Hagen was the same Mt. Hagen sighted by the German expedition up the Sepik River in the early part of this century. He thought it too far inland to be seen from the low country; Mt. Hagen, he said, would have been hidden behind the range nearer the Sepik, a continuation of the Schrader Range.

We started out with a line of more than eighty boys to find the Fox brothers, most of them locals who wanted to bring their arms to "back" the killing of friends and relatives who had been with Jack and Tom Fox. Before we reached the Nabilyer River, we were told "two fella Masta Fokis" had arrived from the direction of the Gowil the day before, had camped at Ougar, and were now back at the mission station on the airstrip. We turned back and found them being fed by Father Ross and Brother Eugene. They looked well and reported many populated valleys to the west and northwest. They had lived off the country, and their twenty boys looked fit and well. They thought they had almost reached the Dutch border but had no means of establishing their position.

The Fox brothers were a remarkable pair and had made one of the most noteworthy trips to date in this country. They found no gold and could not raise a color in any of the streams they crossed. In effect, they had just about eliminated the possibility of another El Dorado like Edie Creek in the Morobe District. Dan and I felt that we had been robbed of our principal interest in life and trudged back to Kuta rather depressed and wondering what to do next. We could not go over the same country that Tom and Jack Fox had been over; they knew too much about alluvial gold to miss any in the streams crossed. Somewhere along their route they had cut every stream running into the Sepik River off the backbone, or backbones, of this country, and most of the lower reaches of the drainage channels had been prospected from the river itself.

Brother Eugene came up in the evening to borrow a rifle for his yearly trek back to mission headquarters on the coast at Alexishaven for their annual retreat of prayer and fasting. I gave him a .22-caliber Walther and bullets to shoot pigeons on his way out. He refused a heavier rifle in case of attack. He was sure he would have no trouble with the natives and refused to take it.

I flew into Wau and was waiting on a plane back to Hagen to wind up the affairs of our prospecting company, whose principals had taken my advice and, like us, were disappointed that New Guinea had not lived up to the romantic legends of gold in every river.

A victorious warrior watches the village burning.

THE YEAR 1935

On January 3 I heard of the murder of Father Morscheuser by Chimbu natives upriver from the strip. The death of the missionary horrified us, but missionaries are a race apart. They believe their own inherent kindliness and goodwill is telepathically transferable to primitive man, whose way of life from the beginning of time is completely foreign and whose values directly conflict with our centuries of civilized behavior. The missionaries' route in from their headquarters on the coast at Alexishaven lay over the Bismarck Range and down the Chimbu River to the Wahgi Valley. They had traveled it quite a few times since 1934, and familiarity had bred contempt for their friendliness. Their steel tools and camp gear aroused the natives' acquisitive instincts. The missionaries hesitated to defend themselves, and Father Morscheuser was killed by an arrow through the throat. The Madang boys threw away their gear and packs and with the rest of the white missionaries escaped to a camp higher up the river while the natives tore their gear apart and looted it. As ever, the killing was incidental. The natives had no hereditary feud with the missionaries and no reason to attack other than the desire to loot.

My brother Jim, who was mining on the Watut River, needed labor. I planned to fly back to Hagen, bring out all our local natives and return them to their homes, and then continue on down to the Markham Valley to recruit a line of boys for Jim. I could not get a plane back until January 8. Bob Gurney, who flew me in, headed back to Lae and put down on the new strip at Chimbu, where he learned that Brother Eugene had also been killed not far from where Father Morscheuser had died. Instead of going on to Lae, Bob flew back to Hagen to tell us the news and camped with us that night.

This was bad news for the few whites and their boys in the area. The native reaction after the novelty of their looted gear had worn off would be anxiety about the white man's reaction to their looting and murder. Unfortunately no Administration action, punitive or otherwise, occurred. As the days passed, the surrounding natives, jealous of the loot so easily acquired, and the entire absence of any reprisal from any white man, felt new confidence in their ability to murder and loot any white party traveling through the area. Brother Eugene and his small line of Madang boys were attacked before they reached the people who had murdered Father Morscheuser. The locals were not going to miss such a bonanza twice. In effect, the rot had set in. The white man was easily stampeded, and his boys panicked and threw away their packs and gear in a terrified scramble to escape.

Dan and I realized that the end result could be a general attack to sack and loot all white stations as the word trickled down from the Chimbu. It was now January 8, and no move had been made to investigate Father Morscheuser's murder earlier in the month. To the natives, this delay suggested a fear of their fighting ability, and their trepidation decreased as their confidence increased. When Brother Eugene came along, they were waiting for him.

Tom and Jack Fox readily consented to come down with us and march into the murder areas. With our well-armed, experienced boys we could take care of any attack, and we were certain that there would be hostility. The locals' confidence had been boosted by two successful sorties. Tom Fox and I flew down to the Chimbu drome with Bob Gurney in the morning. The weather closed in. He could not take off that day but flew off the next morning to Lae to report Brother Eugene's murder. Tom and I walked back to the empty Catholic mission station at Kuruguru (now Mingenda) to wait for Dan and Jack, who were taking the boys with our camping gear down overland, to pick us up.

We planned to cross the limestone barrier at the back of the mission station. With this barrier between us and the Chimbu drome, we would avoid contact with any official party flying in from Salamaua. The remnants of Brother Eugene's line of carriers were nursing various arrow wounds on their backs, arms, and legs, none too serious but all suggesting that they had been in full retreat when they were hit. The Madang natives are not a warrior type; they are a rather cowardly crew who will desert and run when the pressure is on and their skins are in danger. They are furtive conspirators and demagogues rather than fighters. They assured us that they had seen Brother Eugene killed before they fled. "Plenty spear belong bowanarrow fas long skin belong im E die finis long ground." They convinced us that Brother Eugene was dead. All we could do was to go and get his body—and we hoped to invite an argument with the killers.

I sent word to the Lutheran mission at Chimbu to watch the stream in case his body had been dumped into the river. Dwyer and I had discovered in 1930 that unwanted bodies were discarded in this fashion. On January 11 I received a note from the Lutheran mission on the drome, advising that the natives upriver had sent word down that a white man was lying wounded and to come and get him. Further intensive interrogation of Brother Eugene's boys could not shift them in their story of his death, and in any case there was nothing Tom or I could do until Dan and Jack arrived with our gear. We would go straight in and investigate the story about a wounded man.

Dan and Jack arrived at about nine in the morning on January 12, flooded rivers having delayed them. After a quick meal we were on our way again at ten thirty, climbing the limestone range at the back of the station. We dropped down into a stream coming in from the northwest and followed a track downstream toward the main river, keeping the limestone wall between us and the airstrip. We camped late, within a couple of hours' walk of the village where Brother Eugene had been attacked. We did not want to encounter an ambush at dusk and have to stand by all night. We would contact the natives early the next morning and would have all day to iron things out and bury Brother Eugene.

The locals avoided us and from a distance watched our progress toward the murder area. It was one of the few times when we were not the center of interest and given rowdy welcomes. We camped in isolation—no friendly bartering for food and pigs, no flirting girls. It was imperative that we resolve this unfortunate misunderstanding, or no white man could hope to have much influence in the future control and development of these people and these fabulous highland valleys.

We were settled in, with all watches posted and their night rotation arranged, when the bombshell fell. A sweaty local native, his skin shining from the pig grease which had melted and run over his body during his climb over the limestone range from the drome, arrived holding a long stick with a note in the cleft end of it. It was a note from the newly arrived Administration party on the drome, ordering us to return immediately to the drome and report to the district officer, Mr. Melrose, who had flown in to be in charge of the party.

The Administration had always been very fair with us, and I knew we were heading straight into trouble. As we were convinced Brother Eugene was dead, we had no justification, now that authority had arrived, to tangle with the killers. We would have liked to do just that, knowing both the murdered men as well as we did. We spent an uneventful night. The next morning we climbed back over the limestone wall and down to the drome, where we found the Administration party getting ready to investigate. I said, "We almost made it. Another hour and that native would have been too frightened to travel in the dark with your note." We were most disappointed that Melrose would not allow us to go in with them, but we were able to help by handing over fifty-eight of the Hagen natives we had with us to carry gear. Dan and I pushed on toward the Goroka Valley, where I would fly out from the Bena Bena strip and continue down into the Markham to recruit boys for Jim's mining operation on the Watut River.

We spent a pleasant few days traveling through friendly villages where many of the natives who had accompanied us on our first trips were now settled back into their still primitive way of life. Some of them were almost unrecognizable under the greasy, matted, wilted feathers, but all were pleased to see us. Some of the yaw-ravaged sufferers were brought along for Dan to treat, and many brought along children whom we had treated on an earlier visit and who were now entirely free from the painful scourge. The proud parents of one little bloke who had been ravaged by yaws and healed by Dan, brought along a small pig and asked Dan to buy it in exchange for the pleasure he had experienced by healing their son.

Lobo-na-gui stormed into the camp and immediately took charge. A constant procession of the boys who had tramped up and down the valleys and ranges with us were produced. Lobo introduced their families. Some of the by now well-groomed local lads being returned to their homes had to run the gauntlet of mud-plastered, pig grease-smeared parents. The customary fond public embraces left most of the mud and grease on the recipients.

Lobo assured us that he knew an easy track over the range to Bena Bena, and he led across the range rather than along the water course. We toiled up and down. The pack-carrying boys were quite sure that he was just showing us to his friends. When we arrived at a village on top of a steep range, we found that they were right. Lobo pointed to our old route down below, which we now had to climb down to reach. Lobo was well abused by the sweating line, but I feel sure that his reward from the villagers for arranging our visit was well worth it to him.

We reached the Bena Bena drome on January 18, after passing burned and devastated villages and gardens. Mahometofe village appeared to have won some of the wars; the villagers had extended their line of houses and enlarged their gardens. We heard tales of murder and suicide. Some of the villages appeared to have lost five or six of their men in battle. A mother and father had hanged themselves because their young son, who had run away after being lightly chastised, had been shot by several arrows from neighbors in the next village.

Dan mustered more than 100 locals for the grass-clearing job on the airstrip. By cutting the grass and tearing it out by the roots they cleared an area 550 by 40 yards before dark, ready for the plane.

A couple of mission boys sought refuge with us. They had recruited small boys from surrounding villages for instruction and had foolishly sent them out to hostile villages for food. Some of them were promptly killed in current feuds, and the rest left for the safety of their own villages. The mission boys were expecting reprisals from parents and preferred to stay with our boys until things quieted down.

The usual wait for the arrival of the plane gave us time to think about Brother Eugene. We wondered whether he had been killed outright, like Father Morscheuser, or were we only a couple of hours away from where he was wounded and waiting for help? The plane did not arrive until January 26. Les Ross, the pilot, shocked us with the news that Brother Eugene had been found alive four days after we were turned back and had died in the Salamaua hospital a few days earlier. He had eight arrow wounds and had been found stripped of all clothes and covering, lying in a native house. A couple of old men had brought him food and water and had kept the wounds open and draining with sharp slivers of stone. The news shocked Dan and me, as we had been so near to him, but all of us were sure that Brother Eugene's boys were telling the truth. We would have reached him the evening Melrose's note arrived and would have transported him to the strip the next day. I am quite sure the Administration party reached the same conclusion, and was dreadfully shocked to find him alive.

I flew down into Kaiapit in the Markham Valley to recruit labor, and Dan headed back to Hagen. He and his boys were sworn in as special constables by Jim Taylor, who was waiting at Chimbu to go back in and arrest the murderers of Father Morscheuser and Brother Eugene. Dan and Jim Taylor arrested more than fifty of them. Jim Taylor walked all of them more than 200 miles to Salamaua, a remarkable feat of law enforcement in a primitive country. They were held for some months, then brought back again to their villages. The Chimbu is now a well-controlled area. Traveling by plane, ship, and road transport, men from the Chimbu have worked in plantations and towns all over New Guinea and Papua.

I took my Markham recruits back to Jim on the Watut and, after finishing the business of New Territory New Guinea (our Melbourne prospecting company), flew back into Hagen and settled down to recovering the alluvial gold in the deep leads now buried under as much as fifty feet of volcanic ash and landslips on the Kuta Plateau above the valley.

Michael J. Leahy
Wabag Area
1934

CONCLUSIONS

The Highlands are destined to become the wealthiest and most politically influential part of Papua New Guinea. The perpetual spring climate, bounteous rainfall, and rich soil of the highland valleys make it possible with modern technology to produce cash crops and food sufficient to support a much larger population.

The awe-inspiring mountain ranges are scenic landscapes in perfection. The grass-covered summits and rocky peaks, towering more than 15,000 feet above sea level, stand out in isolation above the continually changing cloud patterns. Their folds and contours silhouetted by the early morning or afternoon sun sometimes are transformed by snowstorms into glittering beacons of white.

The most spectacular and fascinating element of this region is its people. Still living a Stone Age existence, these aboriginals have brought great perfection to their tools and weapons of stone, bone, and wood. Their beautifully carved spears and decoratively fabricated battle and ceremonial axes are works of art. Crudely but effectively bound to Man's first tool holder, this axe represents the initial step in the progression from a hand-held sharp rock to a higher technology.

Landscaped sing-sing grounds of colored shrubs and flowers border straight pathways under towering ornamental trees, and picturesque clumps of long feathery bamboos surround their park-like lawns. Trees planted in the center of gardens and surrounded by stone relic memorials to deceased warriors resemble giant potted plants. The perfection and initiative of these people in exploiting and arranging Nature's gifts are the measure of their artistic temperament.

They express their love of color and decoration in their personal adornment for sing-sings and even everyday wear. Perhaps Nature inspired some of this flamboyance by providing the highlanders with the bird of paradise, the world's most spectacular means of satisfying color-conscious humans. This bird, found in abundance and variety throughout the Highlands, ranges in color from gorgeous blue, yellow, and red to fantastic, iridescent, inbred mutations resulting from generations of existence in isolated islands of dense scrub and forest.

One cannot bridge the two- or three-thousand year cultural gap between these Highland people and ourselves after only a few years of contact, and it is inappropriate for us to inflict upon them the stresses and strains of our way of life. Black skins are the hallmark of the sun and an evolutionary history in the tropics. Technology and culture cannot be separated, and the difference between the people of the sun and those farther away from the equator is the difference between the bow and arrow and the hydrogen bomb.

Democracy or majority rule is a fallacy when applied to primitive people such as those in New Guinea. For many years to come, independence for them is only the sugar coating on the pill of callous abandonment, devastation, and domination by predatory adventurers from outside.

EDITOR'S AFTERWORD

Although Leahy devoted most of his time to his gold prospect at Kuta from the early part of 1935 until the start of World War II, his expedition experiences were neither forgotten by him nor ignored by others. In November of 1935 Mick forced the Royal Geographic Society in London to hold a hearing so that he could refute, as he did successfully, a statement by the territorial administrator that another individual had discovered the source of the Purari River and several mountains first seen by the Leahy team. This august body awarded Leahy its Murchison Grant and published his reports, most of which constitute this book. Collaborating with ghost writer Maurice Crane, Leahy published *The Land That Time Forgot* in 1937.

In the spring of 1940 Mick Leahy married Jeanette G. Best, the nineteen-year-old daughter of the manager of a sugar mill in Northern Queensland. Born on the main island of the Fiji group,

Jeanette was educated in Australia, where she met Mick in 1939. After a trip to the upper Watut River area in New Guinea to look over the prospects of being married to a man who intended to settle there, Jeanette accepted a life on the New Guinea frontier—where the nearest neighbor was an hour's walk away.

The Japanese attack on Pearl Harbor in December 1941, and the rapid and unexpected deployment of their forces throughout the southwest Pacific, forced the evacuation to Australia of European civilians in New Guinea. Given only a few hours' warning and limited to a few personal items, Jeanette carried her baby son Richard to the dirt airstrip where they and about forty other women and children were crowded into a tri-motor Junker airplane, normally used for hauling freight, and flown to Port Moresby on the southern part of the island. From there, they were lucky enough to be flown on to Cairns on the Queensland coast instead of making the trip on an overloaded ship. Within six weeks the Japanese army landed in New Guinea; until then, no one thought that they would get beyond Singapore.

Mick and a few of his "old boys" hiked into the Highlands where he remained until May of 1942. He refused to join the New Guinea Volunteer Rifles when offered only a corporal's rank; other miners and prospectors were made privates in the group. Using his knowledge of the backcountry to advantage during these months, Mick guided a group of European refugees from Madang, a coastal town on the Bismarck Sea, one hundred miles across country to Mt. Hagen, from which all were flown to Australia and safety.

Leahy offered his services to the Australian army, but he was told that there were plenty of New Guinea experts available already; besides, he was too old (at forty-one). With a family to support and desperate for employment, Mick finally was referred to the U.S. Army Engineers, who arranged for his assignment, as an Australian flight lieutenant, to the U.S. Fifth Air Force, by then a dominant element in the Pacific campaign.

In this capacity Leahy's knowledge of New Guinea was invaluable. During the Bena Bena campaign Mick located sites for airfields and water supplies to support the fight against the Japanese. His field maps provided the only data on the interior, marked simply "unknown" on Allied charts. Mick and some of his boys flew by glider into remote Telefomin in the Highlands to extend a small airstrip so that it could handle twin-engine DC-3 planes, an act that earned him the U.S. Medal of Freedom in 1948.

In this military capacity Mick Leahy became acquainted in 1943 with my father, a geologist and lieutenant colonel of engineers with the U.S. Fifth Air Force, who, too, was locating water supplies and sites for airfields. The two established a close relationship that lasted until their deaths in the late 1970s. Leahy and Jones were faithful correspondents after the war, visiting each other with their wives a number of times in the 1950s and 1960s.

After his discharge from military service in August 1945, Mick was denied official permission to return to New Guinea. Learning that one of his pre-war mining friends was to tow some barges from Australia to Finchaffen, north of Lae, Mick arranged to be a stow-away passenger. The trip across the Great Barrier Reef took six weeks because the lack of navigational devices forced the little convoy to stop at night. Mick remained at Lae, where Jeanette joined him in the summer of 1946.

In the spring of 1947 the couple settled at Zenag, some fifty miles south of Lae and not far from their pre-war home. Mick bought twenty surplus military trucks and a new, unassembled twenty- by forty-foot army barracks building. The former he used for commercial hauling in the region, and the latter became the Leahys' first permanent home and the one in which Jeanette still lives. Its size and configuration have changed a bit, but the ceilings and the interior walls are the same plywood salvaged from surplus U.S. army coffins after the war.

The fierce independence and determination that characterized Mick Leahy's exploration days extended through the rest of his life. He battled local and regional Administrative officials for what he considered his rights to favorable agricultural leases in the Highlands. Finally, after years of delay, he acquired farming properties at Zenag, not far from Edie Creek, the site of the gold discovery that had brought him to New Guinea in the first place.

Mick Leahy strongly opposed New Guinea's independence from Australia, which came in 1975, because he considered the natives incapable of allegiance to any principality except clan or tribe. Although various parts of the island had come under the influence of a number of European powers, particularly Germany and Britain, since its discovery in the early part of the sixteenth century, the large native population in the highlands remained unknown and uninfluenced by white men and their technology until the 1930s. The highlands were too remote, or too unimportant, to be affected even during the Japanese occupation. During one of the Leahys' visits to Alabama, my father asked Mick how many of his boys from the early days would stay with him in his family business after independence. Mick was quick to say, "Probably three—if it were to their advantage."

During the expedition years, Leahy was increasingly disgusted with what he considered to be the highlanders' indiscriminate savagery. He practiced forbearance but shot to kill. After a battle with the Kukakuka during the second trip (1930), Mick ceased to believe that nothing more lethal than a walking stick was needed to patrol or prospect. According to his admiring native retainers, "Masta" Mick never missed. The hostile reception of the Leahy team by some native groups resulted in the deaths of a number of highlanders, prompting protest to the League of Nations by the Antislavery and Aborigines Protection Society. Leahy was exonerated, but Italian diplomats cited his reprisals as justification for their action in Abyssinia.

Leahy became the leader of an enterprising clan of expatriates on the New Guinea frontier. It has been said that he closed the freebooting saga begun by the Spanish conquistador Cortez in the sixteenth century. In this capacity, Leahy would witness firsthand the emergence of the highland people into the twentieth century and their independence from external controls. The Leahy family enterprises prospered after Papua New Guinea's independence, although Mick's strong opposition to the proposed separation from Australian Administration was a matter of public record.

Mick Leahy died on March 7, 1979, and was buried with Catholic rites at Zenag. Ewunga Goiba, his loyal "shootboy" from the expedition days and the man after whom Mick named his most promising gold-bearing creek, hoped to join him soon.

Dan Leahy is the only white survivor of the expedition years. He lives at Goroka in the eastern highlands, where he raises coffee and tea. Mick Dwyer, Mick's partner on the first trip in 1930, went to

Australia at the start of World War II. He returned briefly to New Guinea in the 1950s before going back to Australia to farm in Queensland until his death in 1987. Patrol officer Jim Taylor, a Leahy companion on a number of forays into the interior and best man at Mick's wedding, retired as District Commissioner at Goroka in 1960 to become a coffee planter. Taylor died in 1987, leaving his widow and two daughters, one of whom recently was appointed ambassador to the United States from Papua New Guinea.

Ewunga Goiba and Tupia Osiro are the only survivors of Mick's "old line." Although native to the upper Waria River area near the eastern coast, they now live with their wives at Goroka, where Ewunga grew coffee for a time. Ewunga visits Jeanette several times each year and generally receives a pig and some kina (money) as gifts from one of his last links to the expedition years.

Along with Phillip, the fourth son and a veterinarian, Jeanette operates the family business at Zenag, which produces chickens, coffee, pork, and beef for markets throughout the region. Eldest son Richard, formerly a commercial crocodile hunter, operates a flying service out of Lae, providing transport for personnel, supplies, and equipment throughout that part of the world, especially to mining and mineral sites. Tim manages an import business, and Christopher is an attorney in Sydney. Meagan, the only daughter, is a pharmacist and married to a dentist in Sydney.

Other members of the large Leahy clan, Mick's nieces and nephews primarily, are engaged in various enterprises in New Guinea and Australia. Probably the most noted of these is the oligopoly of Collins and Leahy, pioneered by Mick's brother Jim and his sister Molly, and operated by their families today.

All members of the extended Leahy family are part of a New Guinea legacy that began in 1926 when Mick struck out for the goldfields at Edie Creek. One can only speculate how long the vast native populations of the highlands would have remained unknown had Mick not undertaken his forays in the early 1930s. It remains to be seen if the civilization imposed in part on these people by Europeans will be to their benefit in the long term. Maybe Mick's epitaph should be the comment he made to Jim Taylor while looking across the beautiful Goroka Valley: "Jim, good country, good climate, good kanakas (village natives), too good to find gold in." Ironically, at the time of this writing in 1989, Jeanette Leahy told me in a telephone conversation that a major gold discovery had just been made at Kare in the Southern Highlands, only a six-hour hike from the point at which Mick had turned back during a prospecting trip in 1948. The El Dorado Mick sought under such difficult circumstances was discovered by others. They, too, owe a debt to this enterprising pioneer.

D. E. J.

INDEX

Alexishaven, 235, 236

Alt, Mount, 102, 104, 105

Asaro River, 19, 54, 68–69, 73, 142, 156; at junction with Bena Bena River, 19, 65, 66; prospecting on, 51, 52

Banir River, 32

Bargai River, 220

Bena Bena airstrip, 68, 79, 142, 153, 155, 240

Bena Bena River, 19, 47, 51, 52, 54, 59–61, 64; at junction with Asaro River, 19, 65, 66; prospecting on, 98, 142

Bena Bena Valley, 47, 61, 139, 170

Bena Bena village, 75, 78, 131, 136–37, 142

Bismarck Range, 6–7, 16, 20, 169, 236; gold prospects in, 51, 102

Bismarck Sea, xiii, 246

Brisbane, Australia, 1, 2, 143

Buang River, 3
Bubu River, 171, 172
Bulolo River, 23–24, 32, 130;
    and Edie Creek gold shed,
    27–28, 30–31, 45, 142
Bulolo village, 44, 48

Cairns, Australia, 2, 246
Chimbu, 85, 162, 230, 232, 237,
    238, 241, 242
Chimbu River, 85, 158, 228, 237
Chuavi police post, 71, 80, 139

Diudar village, 175
Djambi Pass, 24
Doye, 207, 212
Drogarka village, 226
Drou River, 221
Dumpu airstrip, 22
Dunantina River, xii, 9, 16–18,
    51, 151, 153

Edie Creek, 49–51, 130; and
    Bulolo River gold shed,
    27–28, 30–31, 45, 142; gold
    rush at, 2–4, 6
Epunka village, 55, 149
Erap River, 50
Ewunga Creek, 130, 131,
    133–36

Fagonofe village, 151

Gai River, 123, 204, 207, 212
Gange River, 107, 119
Garaina village, 48, 143, 147
Garfatina River, 17, 18, 51, 149,
    152
Garfuku River, 19, 52, 69
Gavitula village, 153
Gibbitjebubu, 221

Gibinuit, 190
Goretufa Creek, 51, 60, 64, 65,
    76
Goroka Valley, xii, 9, 73, 80,
    100, 139, 147–48, 240, 248;
    airstrip at, 20; cannibalism in,
    170; people of the, 196–97
Gowil River, 177, 179, 200, 234
Gueabi, 169
Gumanche River, 94, 102
Gwaymil, 215

Hagen, Mount, xiii, 100, 112,
    113, 129, 203; camp at, 89,
    107, 162–63, 233–35, 237;
    climbing, 122–24, 213;
    description of, 94–95, 201;
    location of, 111; missionaries
    at, 117, 224
Henganofi police post, 55, 149
Herbert, Mount, 222
Huon Gulf, xiii

Ialibu, Mount, 129, 171, 187,
    191, 201, 216
Irambadi, Mount, 92, 230, 231
Irowat River, 30

Jimbunar, 138, 223, 226
Jimi River, 113, 118, 119

Kaiapit, 241
Kaigulen, 7, 16
Kailgu, 215, 220
Kainantu, 50, 61, 149, 151, 152,
    234
Kaindi, Mount, 3
Karmarmentina River, 17, 18,
    51, 149
Kartu village, 54
Keluwere, Mount, 95, 177, 181,

185, 216; climbing, 199–202; description of, 100, 113, 129; drome, 99
Kikori River, 115
Kimbe River, 227
Knoo village, 10
Koidendenoil, 221
Kokoda Trail, 16
Komparie village, 149
Komperere village, 17
Kormer River, 189
Korofagu village, 52, 60
Kundiawa, 85, 158
Kuruguru, 197, 214, 238
Kuta, xii, 190–91, 214, 224, 235, 245
Kuta Plateau, 215, 242

Lae, 23, 38–39, 45–51; air freight from, 134, 225
Lamani village, 171
Langemar River, 32, 34, 35, 41, 42
Lapumpa, 50, 51, 54, 55
Lehuna village, 7, 16
Leron River, 50
Liuba, 188

Mabagai River, 186, 187
Madang, 7, 34, 61, 246
Mahometofe village, 59, 66, 74, 142, 197, 240
Maralinin, 38, 41
Marifutiga River, 71, 80, 139, 157
Marin River, 165
Markham River, 7, 16, 22–23, 34, 41, 46–47
Markham Valley, 148, 237, 241
Marki River, 10–11, 70, 75, 228
Marli River, 71, 72, 80

Meeump River, 203, 204, 213
Memberambo River, 23
Merrie Creek, 3, 4
Millegar village, 216
Mingenda, 169, 197, 214, 222, 226, 227, 233, 238
Mingenda River, 137, 223
Mirani village, 85, 232
Mo River, 144
Mogai airstrip, 130, 168, 171, 198, 214
Moresby, Port, xiii, 16, 71, 84, 98, 143, 246
Morobe, xiii, 144, 234
Morobe goldfields, 44, 49
Munum Creek, 148
Muru village, 221

Nabilyer River, 128–29, 175, 189, 200, 214–15, 221–22, 234
Nabilyer Valley, 95, 190, 198
Nadzab, 46, 47
Nangamp, 162
Nargube village, 182
Nuyar Buram River, 188

Ogelbeng, 198, 234
Ougar, 234
Owen Stanley Range, xiii, 23, 24

Paldi River, 221
Palinger, 168
Porgubu, 185

Queensland, Australia, 1, 2, 142, 155, 245, 246, 249

Ramu River, xii, 7, 9, 16, 149, 169; on route to the, 20–22, 54–55

Roaring Creek, 24, 30
Rondeldai, 210, 211

Salamaua, xiii, 3, 4, 6, 47, 143, 144, 225
Samberigi River, 186
Samberigi Valley, 194
Seerupu village, 54
Sepik River, xii, 94, 100–101, 111, 115, 123, 200, 209–12, 234–35
Shaggy Ridge, 22
Sunubia Range, 9, 16–18
Surprise Creek, 24, 30

Taryoak, 210
Tauri River, 32
Toowoomba, Australia, 1, 142, 155
Townsville, Australia, 2
Tua River, 11
Tuman River, 164, 224

Vialalla River, 32
Vildai River, 215, 220

Wabag Valley, 100, 233
Wahgi River, 10, 75, 80, 94, 109, 159, 212, 225, 228; corpses in, xii, 61; prospecting on, 102, 125, 162
Wahgi Valley, 119, 122–23, 127, 131, 137, 214, 222–23, 225
Wankon village, 118
Wanton River, 149
Warababe village, 187
Waria River, 4, 144, 147, 159, 174
Waria Valley, 32, 172
Warit, 213
Water Bung Camp, 157
Watut River, 23, 32, 34, 40–42, 46
Wau, 23, 49–50
West Irian, 23
Wilhelm, Mount, 6, 61, 87, 105, 123, 138, 162, 222
Wobindamondai River, 212

Yalu, 147, 148
Yarlbu River, 187
Yen River, 107, 113, 119
Yuat River, 100, 202, 203

Zenag, 48, 247–49